Borland® C++Builder™ 3 For Dummies®

D1393051

Frequently Used Buttons

Component Buttons

A	Label
abI	Edit
OK	Button
✓OK	BitButton
	SpeedButton
	Memo
	Table
	DataSource

Action Buttons

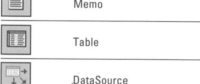

	Open Project
	Save All
	Open File
	Save File
	Add File to Project
Remove	Remove File from Project
	Select Unit from List
	Select Form from List
	Toggle between Form and Unit
	Create New Form
▶	Run Program
‖	Pause while Running Program
	Step over a Line while Debugging
	Step into a Function while Debugging

C++ Language Help

Basic Operators

Operator	In Action	Description
+	2 + 2	Add the two numbers
-	2 - 2	Subtract one number from the other
*	2 * 2	Multiply the two numbers
/	2 / 2	Divide the first number by the second
%	11 % 2	Provide the remainder after evenly dividing the two numbers

C++ Language Help

Advanced Operators

Operator	In Action	Description
++	i++	Increment the value of i
--	i--	Decrement the value of i
>>	i>>j	Bit right shift j bytes
<<	i<<j	Bit left shift j bytes

...For Dummies: #1 Computer Book Series for Beginners

Borland® C++Builder™ 3 For Dummies®

Cheat Sheet

C++ String Escape Character Sequences

Character Sequence	Effect
\f	New form or page
\n	New line
\t	Tab character
\b	Backspace
\0	Null character
\"	" character inside a string
\\	\ character

Debugger Keys

Key Combination	Action
F4	Execute program to current line
F5	Toggle breakpoint on current line
F7	Step into function at cursor
F8	Step over function at cursor
F9	Run program
Shift+F7	Trace to next source line
Ctrl+F5	Add watch dialog box
Ctrl+F7	Evaluate/modify dialog box

Editor Keys

Key Combination	Action
Ctrl+Shift+I	Indent blocked text
Ctrl+Shift+U	Cancel indent on blocked text
Ctrl+E	Start incremental editor search
Ctrl+K, N	Convert block to uppercase
Ctrl+K, O	Convert block to lowercase
Ctrl+K, R	Read a block from a file
Ctrl+K, W	Write a block to a file

Delphi IDE Keys

Key Combination	Action
F1	Help
F11	Toggle Form Designer/ Object Inspector
F12	Toggle Form Designer/ Code Editor
Ctrl+F6	Toggle unit code/ header files
Ctrl+F9	Make project

Surf's Up: Where to Go for Information on C++Builder 3

Borland Web Site	www.borland.com
Official Borland C++Builder Home Page	www.borland.com/bcppbuilder
"The Bits . . ."	www.cbuilder.dthomas.co.uk
UnOfficial C++Builder Home Page	www.nh.ultranet.com/~bsturk
The C++Builder Hobby Pages	http://home.pacbell.net/rmfci/bcbhp.htm
Author's C++Builder Page	http://ourworld.compuserve.com/homepages/ jpvokes/cbuilder.htm

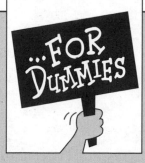

®

References for the Rest of Us!®

COMPUTER BOOK SERIES FROM IDG

Are you intimidated and confused by computers? Do you find that traditional manuals are overloaded with technical details you'll never use? Do your friends and family always call you to fix simple problems on their PCs? Then the *...For Dummies*® computer book series from IDG Books Worldwide is for you.

...For Dummies books are written for those frustrated computer users who know they aren't really dumb but find that PC hardware, software, and indeed the unique vocabulary of computing make them feel helpless. *...For Dummies* books use a lighthearted approach, a down-to-earth style, and even cartoons and humorous icons to diffuse computer novices' fears and build their confidence. Lighthearted but not lightweight, these books are a perfect survival guide for anyone forced to use a computer.

> *"I like my copy so much I told friends; now they bought copies."*
>
> **Irene C., Orwell, Ohio**

> *"Quick, concise, nontechnical, and humorous."*
>
> **Jay A., Elburn, Illinois**

> *"Thanks, I needed this book. Now I can sleep at night."*
>
> **Robin F., British Columbia, Canada**

Already, millions of satisfied readers agree. They have made *...For Dummies* books the #1 introductory level computer book series and have written asking for more. So, if you're looking for the most fun and easy way to learn about computers, look to *...For Dummies* books to give you a helping hand.

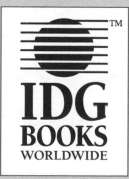

™

IDG BOOKS
WORLDWIDE

5/97

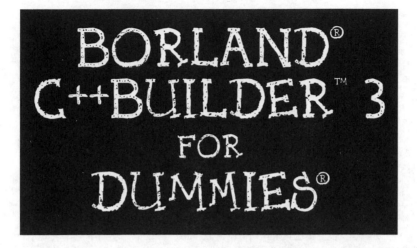

BORLAND® C++BUILDER™ 3 FOR DUMMIES®

by Jason Vokes

Foreword by Zack Urlocker

IDG BOOKS WORLDWIDE

IDG Books Worldwide, Inc.
An International Data Group Company

Foster City, CA ♦ Chicago, IL ♦ Indianapolis, IN ♦ New York, NY ♦ Southlake, TX

Borland® C++Builder™ 3 For Dummies®

Published by
IDG Books Worldwide, Inc.
An International Data Group Company
919 E. Hillsdale Blvd.
Suite 400
Foster City, CA 94404
www.idgbooks.com (IDG Books Worldwide Web site)
www.dummies.com (Dummies Press Web site)

Library of Congress Catalog Card No.: 98-85135

ISBN: 0-7645-0396-0

Printed in the United States of America

10 9 8 7 6 5 4 3 2 1

1O/SZ/QU/ZY/IN

Distributed in the United States by IDG Books Worldwide, Inc.

Distributed by Macmillan Canada for Canada; by Transworld Publishers Limited in the United Kingdom; by IDG Norge Books for Norway; by IDG Sweden Books for Sweden; by Woodslane Pty. Ltd. for Australia; by Woodslane Enterprises Ltd. for New Zealand; by Longman Singapore Publishers Ltd. for Singapore, Malaysia, Thailand, and Indonesia; by Simron Pty. Ltd. for South Africa; by Toppan Company Ltd. for Japan; by Distribuidora Cuspide for Argentina; by Livraria Cultura for Brazil; by Ediciencia S.A. for Ecuador; by Addison-Wesley Publishing Company for Korea; by Ediciones ZETA S.C.R. Ltda. for Peru; by WS Computer Publishing Corporation, Inc., for the Philippines; by Unalis Corporation for Taiwan; by Contemporanea de Ediciones for Venezuela; by Computer Book & Magazine Store for Puerto Rico; by Express Computer Distributors for the Caribbean and West Indies. Authorized Sales Agent: Anthony Rudkin Associates for the Middle East and North Africa.

For general information on IDG Books Worldwide's books in the U.S., please call our Consumer Customer Service department at 800-762-2974. For reseller information, including discounts and premium sales, please call our Reseller Customer Service department at 800-434-3422.

For information on where to purchase IDG Books Worldwide's books outside the U.S., please contact our International Sales department at 650-655-3200 or fax 650-655-3295.

For information on foreign language translations, please contact our Foreign & Subsidiary Rights department at 650-655-3021 or fax 650-655-3281.

For sales inquiries and special prices for bulk quantities, please contact our Sales department at 650-655-3200 or write to the address above.

For information on using IDG Books Worldwide's books in the classroom or for ordering examination copies, please contact our Educational Sales department at 800-434-2086 or fax 817-251-8174.

For press review copies, author interviews, or other publicity information, please contact our Public Relations department at 650-655-3000 or fax 650-655-3299.

For authorization to photocopy items for corporate, personal, or educational use, please contact Copyright Clearance Center, 222 Rosewood Drive, Danvers, MA 01923, or fax 978-750-4470.

is a trademark under exclusive license to IDG Books Worldwide, Inc., from International Data Group, Inc.

About the Author

Jason Vokes is an award-winning developer who worked for many years as a C++ and Delphi consultant before recently joining Borland as its UK Product Manager. Jason's commercial software development in C, C++, and Pascal goes back to his graduation from Portsmouth University in 1987. He freely admits to being a C++Builder "evangelist" and has been a crusader for Borland's highly successful Rapid Application Development product, Delphi, ever since its release. Jason has presented at the Borland Developer's Conference (UK) and regularly speaks around the UK about Borland development tools.

Jason lives in Portsmouth, Hampshire, UK, and, when he's not dreaming up new ways to use program development tools, can usually be found either on his PC or playing saxophone with his jazz band at local venues.

Feel free to drop Jason a line at `jpvokes@compuserve.com` or visit his home page at `ourworld.compuserve.com/homepages/jpvokes` — at your own risk.

ABOUT IDG BOOKS WORLDWIDE

Welcome to the world of IDG Books Worldwide.

IDG Books Worldwide, Inc., is a subsidiary of International Data Group, the world's largest publisher of computer-related information and the leading global provider of information services on information technology. IDG was founded more than 25 years ago and now employs more than 8,500 people worldwide. IDG publishes more than 275 computer publications in over 75 countries (see listing below). More than 60 million people read one or more IDG publications each month.

Launched in 1990, IDG Books Worldwide is today the #1 publisher of best-selling computer books in the United States. We are proud to have received eight awards from the Computer Press Association in recognition of editorial excellence and three from *Computer Currents'* First Annual Readers' Choice Awards. Our best-selling *...For Dummies*® series has more than 30 million copies in print with translations in 30 languages. IDG Books Worldwide, through a joint venture with IDG's Hi-Tech Beijing, became the first U.S. publisher to publish a computer book in the People's Republic of China. In record time, IDG Books Worldwide has become the first choice for millions of readers around the world who want to learn how to better manage their businesses.

Our mission is simple: Every one of our books is designed to bring extra value and skill-building instructions to the reader. Our books are written by experts who understand and care about our readers. The knowledge base of our editorial staff comes from years of experience in publishing, education, and journalism — experience we use to produce books for the '90s. In short, we care about books, so we attract the best people. We devote special attention to details such as audience, interior design, use of icons, and illustrations. And because we use an efficient process of authoring, editing, and desktop publishing our books electronically, we can spend more time ensuring superior content and spend less time on the technicalities of making books.

You can count on our commitment to deliver high-quality books at competitive prices on topics you want to read about. At IDG Books Worldwide, we continue in the IDG tradition of delivering quality for more than 25 years. You'll find no better book on a subject than one from IDG Books Worldwide.

John Kilcullen
CEO
IDG Books Worldwide, Inc.

Steven Berkowitz
President and Publisher
IDG Books Worldwide, Inc.

*Eighth Annual
Computer Press
Awards* ≥1992

*Ninth Annual
Computer Press
Awards* ≥1993

*Tenth Annual
Computer Press
Awards* ≥1994

*Eleventh Annual
Computer Press
Awards* ≥1995

IDG Books Worldwide, Inc., is a subsidiary of International Data Group, the world's largest publisher of computer-related information and the leading global provider of information services on information technology. International Data Group publishes over 275 computer publications in over 75 countries. Sixty million people read one or more International Data Group publications each month. International Data Group's publications include: **ARGENTINA:** Buyer's Guide, Computerworld Argentina, PC World Argentina; **AUSTRALIA:** Australian Macworld, Australian PC World, Australian Reseller News, Computerworld, IT Casebook, Network World, Publish, Webmaster; **AUSTRIA:** Computerwelt Osterreich, Networks Austria, PC Tip Austria; **BANGLADESH:** PC World Bangladesh; **BELARUS:** PC World Belarus; **BELGIUM:** Data News; **BRAZIL:** Annuário de Informática, Computerworld, Connections, Macworld, PC Player, PC World, Publish, Reseller News, Supergamepower; **BULGARIA:** Computerworld Bulgaria, Network World Bulgaria, PC & MacWorld Bulgaria; **CANADA:** CIO Canada, Client/Server World, ComputerWorld Canada, InfoWorld Canada, NetworkWorld Canada, WebWorld; **CHILE:** Computerworld Chile, PC World Chile; **COLOMBIA:** Computerworld Colombia, PC World Colombia; **COSTA RICA:** PC World Centro America; **THE CZECH AND SLOVAK REPUBLICS:** Computerworld Czechoslovakia, Macworld Czech Republic, PC World Czechoslovakia; **DENMARK:** Communications World Danmark, Computerworld Danmark, Macworld Danmark, PC World Danmark, Techworld Denmark; **DOMINICAN REPUBLIC:** PC World Republica Dominicana; **ECUADOR:** PC World Ecuador; **EGYPT:** Computerworld Middle East, PC World Middle East; **EL SALVADOR:** PC World Centro America; **FINLAND:** MikroPC, Tietoviikko, Tietoviikko; **FRANCE:** Distributique, Hebdo, Info PC, Le Monde Informatique, Macworld, Reseaux & Telecoms, WebMaster France; **GERMANY:** Computer Partner, Computerwoche, Computerwoche Extra, Computerwoche FOCUS, Global Online, Macwelt, PC Welt; **GREECE:** Amiga Computing, GamePro Greece, Multimedia World; **GUATEMALA:** PC World Centro America; **HONDURAS:** PC World Centro America; **HONG KONG:** Computerworld Hong Kong, PC World Hong Kong, Publish in Asia; **HUNGARY:** ABCD CD-ROM, Computerworld Szamitastechnika, Internetto online Magazine, PC World Hungary, PC-X Magazin Hungary; **ICELAND:** Tolvuheimur PC World Island; **INDIA:** Information Communications World, Information Systems Computerworld, PC World India, Publish in Asia; **INDONESIA:** InfoKomputer PC World, Komputek Computerworld, Publish in Asia; **IRELAND:** ComputerScope, PC Live!; **ISRAEL:** Macworld Israel, People & Computers/Computerworld; **ITALY:** Computerworld Italia, Macworld Italia, Networking Italia, PC World Italia; **JAPAN:** DTP World, Macworld Japan, Nikkei Personal Computing, OS/2 World Japan, SunWorld Japan, Windows NT World, Windows World Japan; **KENYA:** PC World East African; **KOREA:** Hi-Tech Information, Macworld Korea, PC World Korea; **MACEDONIA:** PC World Macedonia; **MALAYSIA:** Computerworld Malaysia, PC World Malaysia, Publish in Asia; **MALTA:** PC World Malta; **MEXICO:** Computerworld Mexico, PC World Mexico; **MYANMAR:** PC World Myanmar; **NETHERLANDS:** Computer! Totaal, LAN Internetworking Magazine, LAN World Buyers Guide, Macworld Netherlands, Net, WebWereld; **NEW ZEALAND:** Absolute Beginners Guide and Plain & Simple Series, Computer Buyer, Computer Industry Directory, Computerworld New Zealand, MTB, Network World, PC World New Zealand; **NICARAGUA:** PC World Centro America; **NORWAY:** Computerworld Norge, CW Rapport, Datamagasinet, Financial Rapport, Kursguide Norge, Macworld Norge, Multimediaworld Norge, PC World Ekspress Norge, PC World Nettverk, PC World Norge, PC World ProduktGuide Norge; **PAKISTAN:** Computerworld Pakistan; **PANAMA:** PC World Panama; **PEOPLE'S REPUBLIC OF CHINA:** China Computer Users, China Computerworld, China InfoWorld, China Telecom World Weekly, Computer & Communication, Electronic Design China, Electronics Today, Electronics Weekly, Game Software, PC World China, Popular Computer Week, Software Weekly, Software World, Telecom World; **PERU:** Computerworld Peru, PC World Profesional Peru, PC World SoHo Peru; **PHILIPPINES:** Click!, Computerworld Philippines, PC World Philippines, Publish in Asia; **POLAND:** Computerworld Poland, Computerworld Special Report Poland, Cyber, Macworld Poland, Networld Poland, PC World Komputer; **PORTUGAL:** Cerebro/PC World, Computerworld/Correio Informatico, Dealer World Portugal, Mac*In/PC*In Portugal, Multimedia World; **PUERTO RICO:** PC World Puerto Rico; **ROMANIA:** Computerworld Romania, PC World Romania, Telecom Romania; **RUSSIA:** Computerworld Russia, Mir PK, Publish, Seti; **SINGAPORE:** Computerworld Singapore, PC World Singapore, Publish in Asia; **SLOVENIA:** Monitor; **SOUTH AFRICA:** Computing SA, Network World SA, Software World SA; **SPAIN:** Communicaciones World España, Computerworld España, Dealer World España, PC World España, PC World España, PCaktiv, Windows World Sweden; **SWITZERLAND:** Corporate Computing Sweden, Internetworld Sweden, it.branschen, Macworld Sweden, MaxiData Sweden, MikroDatorn, Nätverk & Kommunikation, PC World Sweden, PCaktiv, Windows World Sweden; **SWITZERLAND:** Computerworld Schweiz, Macworld Schweiz, PCtip; **TAIWAN:** Computerworld Taiwan, Macworld Taiwan, NEW ViSiON/Publish, PC World Taiwan, Windows World Taiwan; **THAILAND:** Publish in Asia, Thai Computerworld; **TURKEY:** Computerworld Turkiye, Macworld Turkiye, Network World Turkiye, PC World Turkiye; **UKRAINE:** Computerworld Kiev, Multimedia World Ukraine, PC World Ukraine; **UNITED KINGDOM:** Acorn User UK, Amiga Action UK, Amiga Computing UK, Apple Talk UK, Computing, Macworld, Parents and Computers UK, PC Advisor, PC Home, PSX Pro, The WEB; **UNITED STATES:** Cable in the Classroom, CIO Magazine, Computerworld, DOS World, Federal Computer Week, GamePro Magazine, InfoWorld, I-Way, Macworld, Network World, PC Games, PC World, Publish, Video Event, THE WEB Magazine, and WebMaster; online webzines: JavaWorld, NetscapeWorld, and SunWorld Online; **URUGUAY:** InfoWorld Uruguay; **VENEZUELA:** Computerworld Venezuela, PC World Venezuela; and **VIETNAM:** PC World Vietnam.　3/24/97

Dedication

To my Dad, Ian — thanks for all the support, encouragement, and love. We all love you very much.

Author's Acknowledgments

I've spent many happy hours asking and answering numerous questions on developer forums, but it took just one e-mail message to get me into writing this book. A big thanks to Jill Pisoni, acquisitions editor at IDG Books Worldwide, Inc., for sending that message and for her encouragement in getting me to pursue this project.

Special thanks must go to project editors Nancy DelFavero and Melba Hopper, as well as all the other IDG editors and production people for all their hard work in making a ...*For Dummies* book out of my all-too-raw material.

Big congratulations must go to the development team in Scotts Valley, California, for making C++Builder 3 such a cracking good version! Thanks, too, must go to Zack Urlocker (now one of my ultimate bosses) for writing the Foreword to this book — keep the vision Zack!

Selina, thanks for your love, encouragement, support, and friendship and for putting up with my long absences — I love you very much. Thanks also to Ross and Karen for your encouragement and support. Big hugs to Deb and especially Chris. Hi, Naomi, Matthew, and Andrew!

Thanks to Mahmood Sheikh whose thorough technical reviewing has been invaluable. Professor Richard Welford — you're a dude for making me do this thing. Damien, what can I say! Allison and Dave, your special help deserves special thanks. Plus, all the *Dters,* especially Kev Bailey, who supported me while I was writing the first version of this book. I'm proud to have worked with you guys. Special mention to Colin Ridgewell (the RAD man). Another special mention to Paul Coombs (Mr. PC) for being the best person ever to bounce ideas off — Cheers, bloke!

Finally, *Big Mention* to the boys in the band (Skunk Funk) for putting up with my bum notes while I've had my mind on other things. It's not over 'til the next one!

Publisher's Acknowledgments

We're proud of this book; please register your comments through our IDG Books Worldwide Online Registration Form located at `http://my2cents.dummies.com`.

Some of the people who helped bring this book to market include the following:

Acquisitions, Development, and Editorial

Project Editor: Melba Hopper

Acquisitions Editor: Jill Pisoni

Technical Editor: Mahmood Sheikh

Media Development Technical Editor: Joell Smith

Permissions Editor: Heather H. Dismore

Associate Permissions Editor: Carmen Krikorian

Editorial Manager: Mary C. Corder

Media Development Manager: Joyce Pepple

Editorial Assistants: Paul Kuzmic, Donna Love

Production

Project Coordinator: Karen York

Layout and Graphics: Lou Boudreau, Linda M. Boyer, J. Tyler Connor, Angela F. Hunckler, Drew R. Moore, Brent Savage, Michael A. Sullivan

Proofreaders: Christine Berman, Kelli Botta, Rachel Garvey, Jennifer K. Overmyer, Rebecca Senninger, Janet M. Withers

Indexer: Ty Koontz

Special Help

Suzanne Thomas

General and Administrative

IDG Books Worldwide, Inc.: John Kilcullen, CEO; Steven Berkowitz, President and Publisher

IDG Books Technology Publishing: Brenda McLaughlin, Senior Vice President and Group Publisher

Dummies Technology Press and Dummies Editorial: Diane Graves Steele, Vice President and Associate Publisher; Mary Bednarek, Director of Acquisitions and Product Development; Kristin A. Cocks, Editorial Director

Dummies Trade Press: Kathleen A. Welton, Vice President and Publisher; Kevin Thornton, Acquisitions Manager

IDG Books Production for Dummies Press: Beth Jenkins Roberts, Production Director; Cindy L. Phipps, Manager of Project Coordination, Production Proofreading, and Indexing; Kathie S. Schutte, Supervisor of Page Layout; Shelley Lea, Supervisor of Graphics and Design; Debbie J. Gates, Production Systems Specialist; Robert Springer, Supervisor of Proofreading; Debbie Stailey, Special Projects Coordinator; Tony Augsburger, Supervisor of Reprints and Bluelines; Leslie Popplewell, Media Archive Coordinator

Dummies Packaging and Book Design: Patti Crane, Packaging Specialist; Kavish + Kavish, Cover Design

◆

The publisher would like to give special thanks to Patrick J. McGovern, without whom this book would not have been possible.

◆

Contents at a Glance

Cartoons at a Glance

By Rich Tennant

page 7

page 57

page 161

page 243

page 321

Fax: 978-546-7747 • E-mail: the5wave@tiac.net

Table of Contents

Foreword

· ·

Decisions, decisions. Here you are in your favorite local bookstore on a Saturday afternoon trying to choose between half a dozen different books on programming. After a while, they all kind of look alike don't they? There's a slew of books with "object-oriented" in the title, obscure titles on assembly language (what's that?), encyclopedic references to C++ libraries, and more. Before you give up and head over to the self-help section in search of "Book Buying For Dummies," let me tell you why Jason Vokes' book, *Borland C++Builder 3 For Dummies,* is just what you need.

Jason is one of the best regarded authorities on C++Builder. His work at Borland gives him an "insider" view on how to learn C++ and use all the features of C++Builder. Earlier this year, just prior to the commercial release of C++Builder 3, we held our annual worldwide system engineer and partner training session on all of our new products. Friday afternoon, we gathered in the "Borland Bistro" to celebrate an intense week with a few pints of local ale. Jason was holding court with a few folks and already working up his wish list for the *next* release of C++Builder. He's that kind of guy.

In this book, Jason cuts through the complications traditionally associated with learning C++. As a result, you get up to speed fast and can begin writing code in C++ with a minimum of fuss. As Jason makes C++ understandable, he isn't afraid to get you into some of the most powerful topics like using objects, designing advanced Windows user interfaces, building database applications, and the black art of debugging C++ programs. You get step-by-step guidance on what you need to know and what you can safely ignore. Plus, he's a funny, engaging guy with a wicked English sense of humor.

But the main reason Jason makes C++ programming so easy to learn is that he focuses on the latest version of C++Builder. C++Builder is the most advanced C++ compiler and development environment ever produced. C++Builder combines rapid application development (RAD) with the latest C++ compiler and language features to give you a powerful and productive environment to program in.

So, strap on your safety belt and prepare to enter into the exciting world of C++ programming with Jason Vokes as your guide.

Zack Urlocker
Vice President of Product Management, Borland International
Scotts Valley, California

Introduction

You're about to discover the easiest way ever to write Windows applications using the popular C++ programming language. With Borland C++Builder 3 (and the expert help in this book), you can create easy-to-use, great-looking Windows applications that will make your friends and coworkers envious (and your boss worried that you'll ask for a raise). C++Builder 3 takes the "brain strain" out of programming, which leaves you with more time to experiment with your own ideas.

About This Book

Books that force you to consume large portions of text before you get off the ground are fine if you want to test your grit and determination. But I suspect that you also have a life. Therefore, *Borland C++Builder 3 For Dummies* is designed to quickly turn you on to what you can do with this tool, and how you can do it.

C++Builder 3 offers you the means to develop applications rapidly with C++ programming, and *Borland C++Builder 3 For Dummies* offers you fast answers when you're developing C++ applications using C++Builder 3. Building on the first edition of this book, *Borland C++Builder 3 For Dummies* is revised to include all the essential new features that make C++Builder 3 such a great environment in which to construct your C++ Windows 95 and Windows NT programs.

What about You?

I would guess that you already use computers on a regular basis and are familiar with Windows and the most-popular Windows applications. You're probably quite self-reliant when it comes to installing software on your machine and would not shy away from setting up program shortcuts and macros that make your life easier. You're probably also at a point where you want to do more than just work with applications and want to begin developing some of your own. You'd like to test the waters of application development, see what makes things tick, and have more *control* over your computing environment.

If you're a "power user" type, I suspect that you've already experimented with configuring your system to suit your individual preferences. Because you're curious and creative, C++Builder 3 is an ideal development environment. You can start gradually by developing simple Windows applications using the speedy drag-and-drop capabilities available with C++Builder 3. As you gain experience and confidence, you can then increase your use of the C++ language to further tailor and control your applications.

C++ is a very powerful and highly respected commercial development language — the sky's the limit with this language, and C++Builder 3 fully supports it (if you use C++Builder 3, you are developing with C++). That doesn't mean to say that this book will make you an overnight C++Builder 3 expert, but there is nothing stopping you from becoming one once you get started.

Maybe you've been developing applications for some time, and you may even be an experienced commercial programmer. Or you may be writing programs in non-Windows systems and looking to switch to a visual Windows development method but still want to make the most of your experience.

Whatever route you have taken to arrive at the door of C++Builder 3, you are probably more interested in getting results than proving something just for the sake of proving it. That's why you chose this book — for the information you need to begin building Windows applications.

What's So Great about C++Builder 3?

C++ has a reputation for being a very powerful language, but with power comes responsibility. (In the case of the C++ language, it often means you're tending to the smallest developmental details yourself.) This requires a great deal of knowledge and experience when you are programming complex Windows applications. The fact is that C++ is a complex language with lots of rules and confusing terms; add to that the challenge of the user having to learn object-oriented programming technique, and it's enough to test the resolve of any would-be C++ developer.

Products such as Delphi (by Borland) and Visual Basic (by Microsoft) came along to irreversibly change the programming landscape. By using these tools, programmers could create applications much faster than before, and so they were freed from the hassle of having to perform many of the tedious and repetitive tasks, such as setting up project files (the development environment does it for you). Developers just pick out pieces they want to use, modify them accordingly (by just filling in the blanks in many cases), and Presto! — a running application is created.

C++Builder 3 essentially works along the same lines as Delphi and Visual
Basic. It's a rapid application development (RAD) tool that provides fast
drag-and-drop development capability to the C++ programming environment. (I dare you to try to impress strangers with that information at your
next cocktail party.) You get more power with less responsibility (unless you
like doing everything yourself).

C++Builder 3 enables you to produce 32-bit Windows 95 or Windows NT .exe
files (the program files that your computer can run directly). Because your
computer can use C++Builder 3 output directly (the executable files just
mentioned), your code runs many times faster than it would in an environment that requires you to run a program in order to run your program. I
could go on and on about other ways C++Builder 3 makes you a faster and
better programmer, but that would be spoiling the story.

How to Use This Book

There's nothing to stop you from reading this book in the bathtub (provided
you don't end up fishing it out of the water). You may even find this enjoy-
able bedtime or poolside reading. (I'm not about to tell you to put this book
down and work on your tan — after all, it's your vacation.) But remember
that *Borland C++Builder 3 For Dummies* is a "hands on" book for "hands on"
activities. So, if you do your reading away from work, be sure to make use of
what you've discovered as soon as you get back to your computer.

When you do place this book alongside your keyboard, you will, no doubt,
want to remove the CD from the back of this book and load the source code
from the examples onto your hard disk. Using the ready-made example
projects, you can rapidly acquire and extend the knowledge laid out for you
in this book.

Because you have ideas of your own from time to time that you want to try
out, but aren't sure of the best way to implement them, the subject matter is
presented in sections that are as self-contained as possible. This allows you
to dip into the book as needed.

As topics are introduced, you can try out your ideas. The examples used are
independent from one another, so you can hook your own code into them or
just try them out as they've been written.

How This Book Is Organized

You can use this book as a cover-to-cover guided tour of Borland C++Builder 3, or you can pick up this book as needed during those "Help me!" moments. I also include a number of specific examples that you may want to try out now and adapt later for your own work.

This book is separated into five parts for easier digestion:

Part I: Breaking Ground

Part I introduces you to C++Builder 3 — how it looks on-screen and how to start using it. I take you on a guided tour of this powerful product and tell you about its Integrated Development Environment (IDE). You're introduced to *forms* — the cornerstone of visually constructing Windows programs, and you can discover how to get forms into shape to build your own applications.

Part II: Components: Your Building Bricks and Mortar

This part introduces some power tools you can add to your developer's kit bag. C++Builder 3 provides you with a whole load of program development components (more than 130 with the Client/Server version!), and knowing how to use them really rocket-powers your application building. These components not only allow you to construct fully functioning user interfaces, but they also provide the means to access data and create attention-getting reports.

Part III: Wiring Your Building with More Components

Step-by-step examples enable you to find out how to build your own dialog boxes, file management programs, and other Windows interface applications. You also see how to construct report applications that you can connect to databases, and you even find example programs that show you how to add multimedia files to your applications.

Part IV: Advanced C++Builder 3 Development

Explore the C++ programming language and ways you can use C++ to add the finest details to your applications (underlying C++Builder is an industrial-strength C++ compiler that furnishes you with incredible programming power). You want to be sure that the applications you build are robust enough to stand up on their own out there in the real world. With that in mind, this part shows you how to fix any problems you find in your programs, as well as prevent problems from happening in the first place.

Part V: The Part of Tens

Developing applications is one of those things that will never become a spectator sport. Unlike football, you have to play the game before you can pretend to be an expert on the subject. You need to roll up your sleeves and get your hands dirty (especially if you haven't cleaned the crumbs out of your keyboard for a while). This section gives you some quick tips and ideas (ten in each chapter, give or take a couple) to make your application-building efforts that much better, easier, and stronger.

Icons in This Book

Directs you to the beginning of specific examples that show new concepts in action. (I created my own examples for you to follow. You may want to substitute the variables to suit your own purposes.)

Indicates that a C++Builder 3 project is on the CD-ROM at the back of this book.

Highlights items worth remembering (in fact, they may even bear repeating).

Accents some highly techno-nerd information you may want to skip (then, again, you may want to read it).

Points to advice that saves you time or helps you get the most out of C++Builder 3.

Alerts you to something to avoid or, at least, to handle with care!

Put on Your Hard Hat!

Get ready to power up your computer, fire up your tools, and enter the application construction zone with Borland C++Builder 3.

Part I
Breaking Ground

The 5th Wave — By Rich Tennant

"EXCUSE ME — IS ANYONE HERE NOT TALKING ABOUT RAPID APPLICATION DEVELOPMENT?"

In this part . . .

1n this first part of the book, you find the real get-you-started stuff, such as computer requirements and C++Builder 3 installation tips. You take a guided tour of the Integrated Development Environment (IDE), where the tools-of-the-trade, such as the C++Builder 3 Component Palette, Object Inspector, Form Designer, and Code Editor all reside happily in one intuitive workspace. You also see how to fire up a new project and start using the C++Builder 3 tools to get the most from your development time.

Speaking of time-saving features, this part introduces C++Builder 3's Object Repository of reusable, ready-made templates (where you can store your own templates or even whole projects for later reuse). Chapter 3 supplies essential information about forms — the foundations for your Windows programming (after all, without forms, you wouldn't have windows).

Chapter 1

The C++Builder 3 Floor Plan

● ●

In This Chapter

▶ Determining your PC and memory requirements

▶ Installing C++Builder 3

▶ Cruising the C++Builder 3 Integrated Development Environment

▶ Selecting your project options

● ●

*I*magine developing C++ programs so that they are as easy to use and as productive as the very latest desktop programs. Then imagine the elements of the environment so seamlessly integrated that you can skip between your visual development tools and your code writing without a lot of clumsy stopping and starting. That's exactly what you have with C++Builder 3, and in this chapter, you take a quick cruise through the C++Builder 3 environment, with which you can become intimately familiar in future chapters of this book.

If you read the Introduction, you already know that C++Builder 3 is designed to make you a faster and more proficient Windows programmer. You can create the elements of a user interface (the boxes, buttons, menus, and bars that make Windows so intuitive) or even a working database program, in a matter of minutes. You really do have all the tools you need to create a commercial-strength application.

Now that you're salivating with anticipation, you're probably wondering how to get started. A later section of this chapter covers just that, but first check out the three versions of C++Builder 3.

The Right C++Builder 3 Version for Your Construction Site

Borland offers three different versions of C++Builder 3 — including the "get up and go" basic version to the "all singing and dancing" versions for professional programmers. Which one of the following versions you plump for depends on the kind of programs that you are going to build, not to mention your budget.

- ✔ **C++Builder 3 Standard:** Provides everything you need to develop database applications. This version takes up about 90MB space on your hard disk.

- ✔ **C++Builder 3 Professional:** Gets you "under the hood" of C++Builder 3 with team development and some other beefy tools, plus library source code that you can learn from. This version provides some features you probably won't require immediately, but after you become more familiar with C++Builder 3, you will be glad you invested in this version. It takes up about 115MB space on your hard disk.

- ✔ **C++Builder 3 Client/Server Suite:** We're talking giant database capability here. This version is geared to professional developers who need to link to large corporate databases held on client/server architecture. Allow at least 150MB of hard disk space for this version.

What Are the PC Requirements?

To begin with, you need a PC with sufficient processing power and ample memory. It's a simple equation: The more muscular your PC, the more productive you are. C++Builder 3 is a fairly powerful product and, as such, makes significant demands on your machine.

To use C++Builder 3, you need at least a 486-based microprocessor, and preferably one based on a Pentium processor. You also need at least 16MB RAM, although Borland recommends at least 24MB or 32MB. Because C++Builder 3 develops programs that run on 32-bit PC operating systems, you must be running either Windows 95 or Windows NT. The amount of hard disk space you need depends on which version of C++Builder 3 you're using.

Installing C++Builder 3

If you haven't installed C++Builder 3 on your PC, you can remedy that right now. Slip the *Borland C++Builder 3 For Dummies* CD into your CD-ROM drive. You don't have to type a thing — the installation program kicks right in for you. After the installation process begins, you're led through the installation routine by a series of prompts, each of which ends with clicking the Next button.

As you run through the routine, you are asked to make selections regarding your program preferences. You can't go too far wrong if you select the default settings provided for you (but you do have to enter your personal information in order to register the product).

After running through a handful of screens, you're presented with the Install button. Click it, and C++Builder 3 is copied to your machine.

After the installation routine is complete, you're left with a new program group on your desktop. Double-click the Borland C++Builder 3 icon (shown at left) to run the C++Builder 3 program. (It looks like a skyscraper under construction.)

You can choose from three installation types — Full, Compact, or Custom. If you will be using C++Builder 3 regularly, you should opt for the Full installation. This option copies all of C++Builder 3 to your hard disk, including the full online help files.

If you're really hard up for disk space, you can go ahead and install the Custom version, but be prepared to have to keep the *Borland C++Builder 3 For Dummies* CD in your CD-ROM drive while you work with C++Builder 3. You can also expect the processing to be somewhat sluggish.

What Do You See? The Integrated Development Environment (IDE)

When you launch C++Builder 3, you notice straight-away that instead of seeing a single window as you would with many applications, C++Builder 3 presents you with a group of windows scattered around its main window. What you're seeing are elements of the C++Builder 3 Integrated Development Environment (IDE). Each part of the IDE's visual designers and code editors works seamlessly with the others — something you can really grow to appreciate. I cover each element of the IDE later in this section.

If you are running your screen at a resolution of 480 x 640, the multiple windows in the C++Builder 3 interface can create a bit of a squeeze. Ideally, you want to use a screen resolution of at least 800 x 600, or maybe higher. This resolution gives you room to arrange everything on your desktop and still have ample work space. But remember that when designing your forms, your end user may not be working with the same screen resolution that you are. You have to design forms to the end user's setting. The simplest way to do this is by making sure that your forms are never larger than 640 pixels in width and 480 pixels in height. (See Chapter 3 for information on sizing forms.)

The main menu and toolbar

See Figure 1-1, which obligingly points out where the main menu resides. Many of the options that you can access from the main menu are also available through the configurable panel of speed buttons on the toolbar (also shown in Figure 1-2). In general, toolbars provide a fast way of performing program operations simply by clicking your mouse.

Toolbar   Object Inspector   Main menu bar   Component Palette

Figure 1-1:
The
C++Builder 3
main
window
displays the
Integrated
Development
Environment
(IDE).

Code Editor   Form Designer

You can configure the toolbar (the area in the upper-left corner of the main window) by right-clicking the toolbar to activate its speed menu, and then choosing the Properties option from the speed menu. You then get the Toolbar Editor, shown in Figure 1-3.

As you can see from Figure 1-3, managing the Toolbar Editor is highly intuitive. To add buttons to the toolbar, just click a button's name and drag the button onto the toolbar. To remove buttons, just click a button on the toolbar and drag it anywhere off of the toolbar.

Speed menus are widely available within the C++Builder 3 IDE. Wherever you are, it's worthwhile to right-click to see what options are available.

Figure 1-2:
Many of the
C++Builder
3 main
menu
options
can be
accessed
through the
toolbar.

Open project
Save all files
Add file to project
Select unit from project list
Select form from project list
Run program
Pause while running
Step over line while debugging
Step into function while debugging
Create new form
Toggle between selected form/unit
Remove file from project
Save selected file
Open file

Figure 1-3:
The Toolbar
Editor
makes it
easy to
reconfigure
the speed
buttons.

The Component Palette

Expect to become "best buddies" with the Component Palette (refer to
Figure 1-1). It provides some of the real programming speed of C++Builder 3.
The Component Palette is somewhat like a catalog of ready-made reusable
parts that you can order as you need to build your applications (no need to

make them from scratch by cutting loads of code). What's really cool is that you never have to replace any parts that you use. You have an endless supply of each component or control on the palette, and each component is reusable for other applications.

The Component Palette is divided into tabbed pages, which neatly group components according to their functions. (In Figure 1-1, the QReport and OCX tabs are partially hidden off to the right side of the screen.)

Adding a component to a Form Designer (more about that later in this chapter) takes just a few steps: First, click the desired tab, click the button for the desired component, and then click the form to drop in a copy of the component. Presto — the component appears! (In the case of nonvisual components — for example, the Timer component from the System tab, which the user doesn't see at runtime — C++Builder 3 substitutes the component in the form with an icon that looks just like the component's button icon on the Component Palette.)

To select a component after you've dropped the component into a form, just click it. When you select a component, sizing handles surround the component to indicate that it's selected.

You will not find extensive coverage of the Component Palette in this book. (Actually, it would be exhausting to cover the Component Palette in its entirety — the C++Builder 3 environment supports dozens of components and countless component characteristics, such as properties and events.) However, this book does cover enough of what's available so that you can build robust applications; then you can explore further as you gain development expertise.

The Form Designer

When you launch C++Builder 3, the work space area automatically supplies you with a form window (refer to Figure 1-1 and the window titled Form1). This form is known as the C++Builder 3 Form Designer (or Form Editor if you prefer).

Each *form* represents an individual window (such as a dialog box) in your application. Within the Form Designer, you can add, delete, or reconfigure components as you create your application.

For a preview of how you can use forms in C++Builder 3, check out Figure 1-4. The figure shows a form with three ready-made components — a label, an edit box, and a button — dropped into the form.

Figure 1-4:
A sneak
preview
of form
development
— a form
with a label,
a box, and a
button.

The Object Inspector

The word *inspector* can fill people's hearts with dread. Fortunately, I am not referring to the Tax Man! This inspector allows you to view the characteristics, or *properties,* of components that you place on a form and change the values of those characteristics. The Object Inspector also lists the events associated with an object and the means to change the event you want to handle. When you select a component on a form, the Object Inspector automatically changes its contents to reflect the properties and events of that component. The Object Inspector could, as such, be called an "object editor" because it enables you to modify the properties of objects.

Properties

When you begin a project, the Object Inspector displays the properties of the main form (see Figure 1-5 for an example). The properties shown in the Properties tab page of the Object Inspector change according to the type of component selected in the Form Designer. The properties available for a particular component are shown in the Object Inspector as you move from component to component.

If at any time you can't see the Object Inspector, you can summon it by pressing F11.

Events

The Events tab page of the Object Inspector displays the events for each component (see Figure 1-6). When you select the Events tab by clicking it, you find that nearly every component has several events associated with it. These events are fired, or triggered, by either user actions or the Windows operating system itself. For example, the OnMouseDown event of a Label component is triggered when the user clicks that label component (see more about mouse events in Chapter 3).

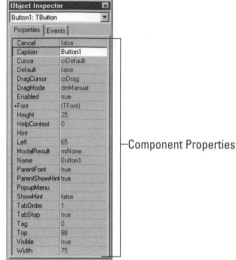

Component Properties

Figure 1-5:
The
C++Builder
3 Object
Inspector
displays the
properties
of a
component.

If you want something to happen when an event is triggered for a component, you have to enter some code for that particular component in the component's *event handler*. Using an event handler is like hooking your own functionality to empty clothing hangers. Just as you can leave your closet empty or fill it with designer outfits, you can use as many events or leave as many events blank as you want. But your application will not do much of anything if you choose not to use any events at all!

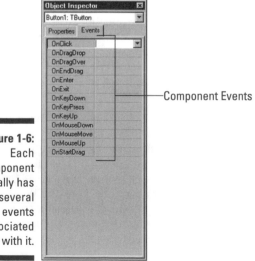

Component Events

Figure 1-6:
Each
component
usually has
several
events
associated
with it.

If events already exist on a form, you can hook in an existing event handler rather than create another one (if an existing one can perform the task you need). Event handlers are often shared between menu items and speed buttons, for example.

To add functionality to an event handler, first click the Events tab of the Object Inspector. Then double-click within the blank field in the right column that is next to the name of the event to be handled. C++Builder 3 automatically provides a name for this event (refer to Figure 1-6). After you do this, you invoke the Code Editor (covered in the next section).

The Code Editor

Lurking behind the Form Editor in Figure 1-1 is the Code Editor window. The Code Editor pops up when you name an event handler (refer to the previous section of this chapter). The Code Editor window contains the actual C++ code that drives your application. Figure 1-7 shows you how the event handler code is displayed after you double-click the empty field next to the event handler name in the Object Inspector. The line place your code here in Figure 1-7 is where you get in on the action by entering your event handler code.

Figure 1-7:
The Code Editor is where you enter code when you create your programs.

To generate the default event handler for a component, double-click the component in the form. The Code Editor displays the default event handler that the component most commonly needs to handle at runtime (for example, a button's default event is OnClick).

Certain components don't need to handle user events. For those components, double-clicking them in the form will not generate an event handler. Double-clicking certain other components, such as the Image component or either of the Menu components, opens a dialog box in which you can perform design-time property edits.

The Project Manager

A real C++Builder 3 project is seldom composed of just one file. A project is often an accumulation of many forms, and you'd be surprised by how quickly they can pile up. In order to manage these forms as they accumulate, you need the Project Manager. It can tell you at a glance the contents of a current project.

Choose View➪Project Manager to get the Project Manager dialog box that's shown in Figure 1-8. With C++Builder 3, the new advanced Project Manager provides you with a visual way to handle more than one project at once; projects are organized in project groups. The benefit of having project groups is that when several of your programs share common code files, you can recompile all of these programs at once (using the menu selection Project➪Build All Programs) without the bore of having to open and compile each of the projects in turn.

The Project Manager provides you with your projects and project modules organized in a tree view — much like the Windows Explorer. To view the details of an individual project, with your mouse, click the "+" to the left of the project name.

Figure 1-8:
Use the
Project
Manager to
get your
forms under
control.

If you have a file that you want to include in your project, click the Project New button to show the New Items dialog box. Then select the type of item that you want to add by double-clicking its icon. You then see the name of the item added to the list in the Project Manager dialog box.

For the flip side, click an item in the Project Manager tree view, and then click the Project Remove button. The item is deleted from the list.

Projecting Yourself with the Project Options Dialog Box

Nearly all your work in C++Builder 3 is done within a *project*. For example, your program file is made up of individual code files that you group within a project.

The end result of a project is a program's .exe (executable or "run") file. When a user runs the program, this single file performs the tasks that you build into the program.

You can access the details of a current project's configuration settings by choosing Project⇨Options from the main menu. This command opens the Project Options dialog box. The Project Options dialog box holds the settings for every project and can be accessed anytime during development. You may want to explore the eleven tabbed pages of the dialog box to see what options are available to you and what those options do. Just click any of the page tabs (see Figure 1-9). In general, the default settings are fine to start with.

Figure 1-9:
Access the details of the current project's configuration settings with the Project Options dialog box.

The Forms page

By default, forms in your project are included in the Auto-Create Forms list box. Autocreation means that C++Builder 3 takes care of creating a form within an application automatically, relieving you from the chore of having to create a form with code.

The Application page

The Application page contains four application settings. The text that you enter in the Title text box becomes the title of the application; it is displayed along with the Icon selection in the Windows taskbar when the application is minimized. The Help file setting lets you choose which help file to associate with your application, and the Target File Extension edit box allows you to change the extension of the program file produced — the default is the normal program extension, .exe.

The Compiler page

The Compiler page is where you set the options you're using for the compiler in a particular project (see Figure 1-10). Most of the time you want to select the Full debug options. They enable you to step through a program's code line by line to view the contents of variables and generally poke around the internals of your program to fix any problems while the program is actually running.

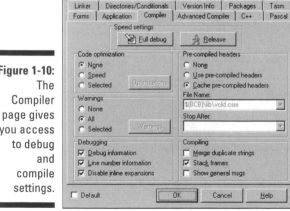

Figure 1-10:
The
Compiler
page gives
you access
to debug
and
compile
settings.

Be prepared for a shock when you see the size of a program with debug settings on. Even a project that does absolutely nothing can be hundreds of kilobytes.

Refrain from using the Release option until after you kill all the bugs that you're aware of in your program. After you sufficiently test your code and before you turn your program loose on the outside world, use the Release option for the last compilation.

Selecting the Pre-compiled headers option saves you a great deal of time, although it does use up some extra disk space. The C++ compiler has many things on its mind as it runs through checking, compiling, and linking a program. One of the tasks the compiler must perform is including references to other code units that you borrow to include in your program. This process of code collection means that there's more code to be compiled than you may expect when you build your application. Pre-compiled headers save time because they're built only once and then stored, ready to be slotted into another program.

When in doubt, just click the Full debug or Release buttons, and you end up with an adequate set of compiler options.

The Pascal page

C++Builder 3 has an older sibling called Delphi. Delphi is also a Rapid Application Development (RAD — as in radical!), but it uses Pascal as its underlying language. You may have even used Delphi. Borland cleverly built C++Builder 3 so well that you can seamlessly include Delphi forms and code in your applications. In your own programs, you can use parts of those cool Delphi forms that your friends have written (as long as you ask the friends first, of course!).

The Linker page

Linking is the stage that follows compiling as your code goes through the processing "mill." The Linker pulls all the compiled files (.obj files) into one machine-readable executable (.exe) file. Unless you're a bit of a programming guru, not many of the settings on the Linker tab (shown in Figure 1-11) are going to change your life. (The Include debug information check box is set or not set according to the Full debug or Release buttons in the C++ page.)

Figure 1-11:
The Linker page pulls all your compiled files into one executable file.

The Version info page

C++Builder 3 provides a version management page and even enables you to enter details of your company and your program within your project. You activate the version information by clicking the check box at the top of the Version info page. (Include version information in your project.) You can increment version numbers yourself or let C++Builder take care of incrementing version numbers for you by setting the Auto-increment build number check box.

The version information for your program appears on the Version page of the Windows Properties dialog box for the project's .exe file. To access this dialog box, open the .exe file (by right-clicking the file in Windows Explorer), and then from the speed menu that appears, select the Properties option.

The Packages page

C++Builder 3 has a really neat way of managing its components. Each component is grouped with other similar components, and these component groups are called *Packages*. You can use the Packages page to set up the Component Palette for your project and which runtime package modules you want to use with your program's .exe file. At this stage, I recommend that you leave this page at the default setting.

The Advanced Compiler, C++, Directories/ Conditional, and Tasm pages

You really don't need to touch the settings under the Advanced Compiler, Directories/Conditionals, and Tasm pages. At this early stage in your C++Builder 3 programming career, you have more fundamental stuff to handle than the settings on these pages. For now, leave these pages for the techno-nerds. Just take it easy, and let C++Builder 3 take care of these settings.

Note: C++Builder 3 is centered around what's called a component-based architecture. Beginning with Chapter 4, this book provides you with the detailed knowledge that you need to make full use of the components that come with C++Builder 3 and those that you may want to install to rocket-power your programming. The Packages page enables you to (guess what?) manage the component groups, called Packages.

That's it for your introductory tour around the various parts of the C++Builder 3 environment that team up to create the most awesome C++ RAD tool ever created. The following chapters show you how to use this tool to quickly build professional-looking Windows programs.

Chapter 2

Laying the Foundation of a C++Builder 3 Program

· ·

In This Chapter

▶ Creating a brand new application — from scratch

▶ Developing faster with Object Repository templates

▶ Examining how and where your work is saved

▶ Getting to know file formats

▶ Cleaning out unneeded files

· ·

Maybe you've been skipping around this book to see what kind of juicy applications you can whip up with C++Builder 3, or maybe you plan on taking this book page by page to absorb every morsel of information. Either way, if you keep on reading this chapter, you can find out how to create a working Windows 95 or Windows NT program in less time than it takes to set the dining room table (unless you're one of those people who customarily dines over the kitchen sink, in which case, you can build an application faster than you can microwave leftovers).

Before C++ and object-oriented programming came along, you had C — a popular structured programming language and one of the first languages that let developers implement Windows applications. C did not provide object classes from which you could derive other classes to speed your programming. (I'm showing my age, but if you remember the days of C, so are you.)

Borland C++Builder 3, although powerful, has no extensive drag-and-drop user interface to make development really simple — loads of code-writing grunt work is still required to create even a basic program. (Some folks may argue that C++Builder 3 has more of a pluck-and-place interface — nevertheless, C++Builder 3 does much of the code-creation work for you.)

Form + Component + Properties = Program

You probably want to get going on creating a program of your own using C++Builder 3. You can use the following steps to build a simple example program designed to display an on-screen message:

1. **Select <u>F</u>ile⇨New Application from the main menu to get a blank form in a new application.**

2. **Click the Standard page of the Component Palette, move your mouse slowly over the palette icons until you see the text "Label" under your cursor, and then click the Label component button.**

3. **Move the mouse pointer to the blank Form Designer, and click somewhere in the center of the form to drop in a new Label component.**

4. **Using the Object Inspector, change the contents of the** Caption **property from** Label1 **by clicking the property value and entering** Hello Universe! **(including the exclamation point).**

   The programming part's done. Next, you compile, link, and run the program. That process sounds far more complicated than it really is, and you can do it in any one of the three ways listed in Step 5.

5. **Choose <u>R</u>un⇨<u>R</u>un, or press the F9 key, or click the Run speed button (solid arrow icon) in the C++Builder 3 Speed Bar to run the program.**

   Allow C++Builder 3 a few seconds to do what's necessary to produce the .exe (executable) file and run your application. The program should look like the one in Figure 2-1.

Figure 2-1:
Your first
program
could look
like this —
and all
done with
no code
required!

Throughout the rest of this book, you will be running a program simply by pressing F9. But if you like the menu or button methods, you may want to keep in mind the other options listed in Step 5.

Your first C++Builder 3 program is a success. How many lines of code did you have to write to get this basic program going? None. Yes, that's right, *none!*

Save Energy — Use Ready-Made Objects from the Object Repository

C++Builder 3 provides far more than just a blank form on which to build your applications. A number of template objects are stashed in the C++Builder 3 Object Repository; these templates are like stencils for parts of programs — and even whole projects!

The Object Repository stores predefined forms, dialog boxes, and even other applications that you can incorporate into your own programs. You can also store your own applications in the repository. Any new application can copy, inherit, or reference an existing structure from the repository — and that includes forms, dialog boxes, reports, menus, or whole C++Builder 3 projects. This reuse of common program pieces helps to ensure consistency across applications.

To view the templates that are available in the Object Repository, choose File⇨New to get the New Items dialog box. In this dialog box are five pages of templates (objects, that is) that you can add to your applications. These five pages are how you reuse many of the items in the Object Repository. (An exception to this is menu items. Refer to Chapter 7 for more on storing and retrieving menus in the Object Repository.)

- ✔ **New:** This page allows you to choose from creating a new form, an application, a code unit, a component, or a data module.

- ✔ **ActiveX:** When you want to hot up a Web page, you might look into trying some of the icons on this page.

- ✔ **Project1:** When you have a project open, this page displays the title of the current project on the tab (in this case, `Project1`) and contains an icon for each of the forms in your current project. The icons on this page allow you to adapt existing project forms very quickly.

- ✔ **Forms:** For creating standard forms from prebuilt form templates.

- ✔ **Dialogs:** For choosing from a number of basic form-type components that you commonly need to include in an application. (Figure 2-2 shows the Dialogs tab page selected within the Object Repository window.)

- ✔ **Projects:** A sample of whole project structures are provided for you on this page. Later in this chapter, you find out how to add your own project shells icons on this page.

✔ **Projects:** For accessing complete projects.

✔ **Data Modules:** For choosing from a number of data modules.

✔ **Business:** This page contains the BusinessInsight component wizards for charts, reports, and other goodies. Try these when you want easy and professional ways of presenting data to your users.

Don't worry too much at the moment about what's available on the New page of the New Items dialog box; it's the other pages that give you access to the Object Repository tidbits.

Figure 2-2:
The Dialogs page of the New Items dialog box contains time-saving application form templates.

Click the Forms tab to get the Forms page, which provides not only templates for forms, but also some generic reports. (See Chapter 11 for more on reports.) You can include any of these dialog boxes or forms in an application you're currently building simply by double-clicking the template that you want to use. Because only one application project can be open at a time, the template is automatically added to the current project.

At the bottom of each page in the New Items dialog box are three radio buttons — Copy, Inherit, and Use — which are used to select form, dialog box, and data module options. These three options (refer to Figure 2-2) each have a different effect on how the form that you add to an application is implemented.

✔ If you select the *Copy option,* all the code for the object that you copy is added to your project, and you can modify the copy to suit your purposes without affecting the original object or any other applications that may also use the object that was copied.

✔ If you select the *Inherit option,* you retain a link between the form that you added to your application and the original repository form (or any other type of original object). Then any modifications made to the original form will automatically be made to your application form. The reverse is not true, however. Any modifications you make to an inherited form won't affect the original object.

Remember that if you inherit from the template for your application and the template is changed, you need to recompile each application that uses an inherited version of the template in order to update the application. When you use the Inherit option, you can't remove any of the original objects (text boxes, buttons, and so on); that would be like selling the family silver. The form must retain the components that it inherits from the parent. You can change the decor of the form only by increasing the number of components placed in it.

✔ If you select the *Use option,* you are opening the actual template object. Any changes that you make inside your application are made to the object in the repository and will be reflected in *all* other projects that use that template. This option creates a permanent change to the original object and should be used only when you want those changes to be reflected in any other form that inherits from it. Proceed with extreme caution if you are including template forms in your applications with the Use option; otherwise, you can really muck up your other applications.

Grabbing a form from the Object Repository

Getting your hands on objects held in the Object Repository is a simple task. For example, you can use the following steps to add an About Box form from the Object Repository to a sample application:

1. **Select File⇨New from the main menu to get the New Items dialog box.**

2. **Click the Forms tab of the New Items dialog box, click the About Box icon in the dialog box that appears, and then click the Inherit button in the next dialog box.**

3. **Click OK, and you get an About Box form ready to tailor to suit your application.**

Adding a form to the Object Repository

You can expand the contents of the Object Repository by adding any of your own forms, applications, dialog boxes, or even entire projects. Then you can reuse an object whenever you need it without having to re-create anything, which saves you valuable time.

To add a form to the Object Repository, use the following steps:

1. **Right-click the mouse anywhere in the form that you want to add to the repository.**

   The form's speed menu appears.

2. **Choose the Add to Repository option to display the Add To Repository dialog box, which is shown in Figure 2-3.**

Figure 2-3:
Add your
own forms
to the
Object
Repository
in just a few
steps.

Add To Repository	
Forms:	Title:
Form1	Order Form
OKBottomDlg	Description:
OKHelpBottomDlg	Useful start form for all order processing
	Page: Author:
	Forms I Didit
	Select an icon to represent this object
	Browse...
	OK Cancel Help

3. **Enter details about the form that you are adding into the Add To Repository dialog box.**

   You are provided with text boxes to enter the Title that you want the form to have, a brief Description, and the name of the object's Author.

4. **Select which page of the repository you want the form to be added to from the Page drop-down list.**

5. **Click OK, and you're done.**

If you want to add an entire project to the repository, choose Project⇨ Add To Repository from the C++Builder 3 main menu.

You can also create your own repository pages to help organize your additions to the repository. Choose Tools⇨Repository from the main menu, and you see the Object Repository dialog box, which is shown in Figure 2-4.

Figure 2-4:
You can
add, delete,
or rename
pages in the
Object
Repository
dialog box.

The Object Repository dialog box is used for managing repository pages, and the New Items dialog box is used for accessing the repository objects. Is this confusing enough?

To add your own page to the Object Repository, follow these steps:

1. **Click the Add Page button on the Object Repository dialog box to show the Add Page dialog box.**

2. **Type the name of the new page that you want to create, and then click OK.**

You can also use the Object Repository dialog box to reorder the repository pages by using the up and down arrow buttons, or use it to edit the details held on individual repository items by selecting from the Objects list and then clicking either the Edit Object or Delete Object button.

The Object Repository is actually held in a subfolder of the Cbuilder installation folder called Objrepos. The source code for all the forms and dialog boxes is copied to this folder. All projects that are included in the repository are included as subfolders of Objrepos. It all adds up to this: You don't have to copy forms and projects manually from folder to folder.

The Object Repository is an amazingly powerful tool in the fight against the "zero-code-reuse" syndrome. When you write a form that may be useful in another application, you don't have to re-create it — just stash it in the Object Repository, and then go get it when you need it!

C++Builder 3 File Formats

When you write an application with C++Builder 3, your insight into solving the problem at hand is what counts the most, so you need to preserve the files that represent all your hard work. When you back up your work (you're conscientious enough, or just plain lazy enough, to avoid having to redo everything if a file is lost—right?), you want to know which files you need to keep permanently and which files you can discard when you're done with a project.

This section is divided into two parts. The first part covers source files that you want to guard with your life; the second part covers files essential to a particular project but that you can discard later if disk space is at a premium.

Project source files

A distinction exists between the files that you create yourself (even with the help of C++Builder 3) and those that C++Builder 3 uses in its role as the facilitator for your programming ideas. The files that you, the programmer, create are called *source files*. Source files contain the details of your form layouts and event-handling code. They're the critically important files to a project because they're the ones you labored over. Back up your source files to floppy disk and be extremely careful not to lose these files because you can use them to re-create an application without having to redo all that work from scratch.

The default filenames that C++Builder 3 gives to your source files are listed here. (You can change these default names as you want during the course of building an application.) Any file that has one of the following file extensions (indicating it's a source file) is vital to your C++Builder 3 project.

- **Project1.bpr:** This is the project options file. Each project will have its own .bpr file. A Project file is stored in a text format, and you can take a peek (editing it is not recommended!) by choosing <u>V</u>iew⇨Project <u>M</u>akefile. This file contains instructions to C++Builder 3 on how to construct the .exe program file for a project.

- **Project1.cpp:** This is the main source code unit for a C++Builder 3 project. The first part of this filename is the same as the first part of the filename of the project makefile; only their extensions are different. (The .cpp extension stands for C Plus Plus, in case you're wondering.) This file contains the code that starts the application; from here, the application launches into action. If you want to view this file for the project, choose <u>V</u>iew⇨Project Source from the main menu. You don't want to make many changes in this file to start with (later, maybe).

✔ **Unit1.cpp:** When you're working in the Code Editor window (see Chapter 1 for information about the Code Editor), the window opens with this type of .cpp file by default. This file contains the code that drives your forms, as well as all the event handlers for the components that you place in those forms. You should be extremely careful to protect these files (unless you find re-creating code particularly thrilling).

✔ **Unit1.h:** Form files come in pairs. For every .cpp file, C++Builder 3 automatically creates a corresponding .h (header) file. The header file contains the declaration of the form; it tells C++Builder 3 what components have been placed on the form and what events have been handled. If you were to drop a few buttons and labels onto a form (using steps described in later chapters of this book), you would have a way to see what changes have been made to this file. Go to the Code Editor and right-click the unit1.cpp file to bring up the speed menu; then choose the Open Source/Header File option to open this file or press Ctrl+F6. C++Builder 3 keeps the names and types of all components contained within a form.

All .cpp files need a corresponding header file in order to work. When it comes time to back up or move a form from one folder to another, the .h file must go with it.

✔ **Unit1.dfm:** The .h and .cpp files hold a form's declarations and definitions, but another important source file also holds information about forms. The .dfm file holds the details of the form's properties (size, color, text, and so on), as well as details on each of the components placed on the form. The file also stores all property values that you have changed from their starting values.

The .dfm extension indicates that this file holds the data for the form in a binary format (computer-readable zeros and ones). You can't read this file as is, but you can convert it to view its contents. Just click the form, right-click it to bring up the speed menu, and choose the View as Text option to see all of the form's vital statistics. Figure 2-5 shows the inner workings of the example form shown earlier in Figure 2-1 displayed in all their coded glory.

Another file extension that you may see from time to time is a .bpg file extension (for example, ProjectGroup1.bpg). Files that end with .bpg contain the information referring to a C++Builder 3 project group. Project group files are created by C++Builder 3 when you have more than one project within Project Manager at any one time.

Figure 2-5:
The inside
story on
Figure 2-1
as seen
through the
Unit1.dfm
file.

Inside the figure window:

```
object Form1: TForm1
  Left = -9
  Top = 484
  Width = 179
  Height = 132
  Caption = 'Form1'
  Font.Charset = DEFAULT_CHARSET
  Font.Color = clWindowText
  Font.Height = -11
  Font.Name = 'MS Sans Serif'
  Font.Style = []
  PixelsPerInch = 96
  TextHeight = 13
  object Label1: TLabel
    Left = 48
    Top = 40
    Width = 75
    Height = 13
    Caption = 'Hello Universe !'
  end
end
```

Good housekeeping files

Nobody likes housework — except maybe the truly weird. But after a while, the mess gets to you, and you eventually have to clean it up or find a new place to live.

What does housekeeping have to do with C++Builder 3? You need to know which files you should hang onto and which you should throw out after they've done their job. The files described in this section are important for enabling C++Builder 3 to construct the .exe file for your project and for enabling the compiler to build the .exe file as quickly as it can. But they're not critically important to a project, and in some cases, they use up hard disk space unnecessarily.

- ✔ **unit1.obj:** Producing a computer-readable program file requires a two-stage process. The first stage involves compiling source files into binary .obj (object) files; the second stage is linking the compiled files into the program's .exe file. (Every source file in your application has an .obj file, no matter how small the source file is.)

    The object files are recompiled every time you choose Project➪Build All from the main menu. If you choose Project➪Make instead, only those object files that are older than their corresponding source files are rebuilt (for example, if you have changed some source code using the Code Editor since the source file was last compiled). That's why a "make" takes much less time to complete than a "build."

✔ **Project1.exe or Project1.dll:** These files are what the whole process of compiling and linking is all about. The .exe and .dll (Dynamic Link Library) files consist of machine-readable code that is produced by compiling and linking your work. A project produces only one or the other of these file types — the .exe file is a program file that you can run and the .dll file is a code library that can be called from either a program or from other .dll libraries.

✔ **Project1.res:** These files are used to store the resources that Windows applications need to do their job. Resources in this case mean icons, bitmaps, and all those things that make Windows applications look so good.

✔ **Project1.tds:** You'll soon notice these files as they can get to be quite large. These files are created by C++Builder 3, and they contain compiler debugging symbol information. For the sake of space on your hard disk, you should feel free to remove these files when you move on to another project.

✔ **Project1.dsk:** These files contain desktop setup information — such as which windows are open in C++Builder 3 for a project, the size of the open windows, where windows are located on-screen, as well as any debugging that you may have set up. If you opt to store the desktop settings for your project, when you boot up your machine the next time you use it and then open the project, you can carry on straight from where you left off; everything will be just where you left it.

You can save desktop settings by choosing Environment Options from Tools in the main menu to get the Environment Options dialog box. Then click the Desktop check box in the AutoSave options group on the Preference page. This file is a nice one to have and could be a bit inconvenient to lose, but it's hardly the *raison d'être* of the project.

✔ **Project1.il?:** (The ? stands for any letter after il, for example, ilc, ilf, ild, and so on.) The .il? extension indicates a file used for *incremental linking*. C++Builder 3 uses very fast compiler technology, but it can be made even faster the second time that you compile a project. C++Builder 3 stores a load of preprocessed data in the program code. This half-compiled file data is then used for all subsequent compilations and makes compiling lightning-fast from then on, but it does temporarily cost you some hard disk space (however, it's well worth it).

✔ **~??, ~ma, ~cp, or backup files:** When you save a file in C++Builder 3, the current version is renamed and its file extension changes. For example, .cpp files become ~cp files, .dfm files become ~df files, and so on with other file extensions. The creation of these files is actually a safety feature. This file renaming allows you to go back to the last version of a file using the Windows Explorer if you happen to mess up the current copy of a source file.

So that's what .il? stands for!

Threading together all the different source files that constitute an application can be a big task for C++Builder 3, and after it performs this task the first time, it doesn't want to have to repeat it. So, for the first compile of an application, a sort of "halfway house" of information is created in the form of *incremental linking* files. These files really save on compiling time later during project development.

Incremental linking (.il?) files can grow to be quite large, and after you save more than a handful of C++Builder 3 projects, you can end up with many megabytes of incremental linker files on your hard disk. The .il? files are invaluable for the project you're currently working on, but when you move on to another project, you should delete the .il? files to free up your disk space.

When you do remove these files, you have to wait a bit longer the first time you recompile the new project, but after that, the C++Builder 3 compile times get cookin' again.

By knowing which files are created as your project progresses, you can pick out and discard the ones that eat up space on your hard disk, and you can also save yourself a lot of disk-shuffling when backing up your project. Make sure to back up C++Builder 3 project source files — those with the file extensions .mak, .cpp, .h, and .dfm. The others you can keep or delete, depending on how much time and disk space you have to spare.

Chapter 3

Forming a Working Relationship with Forms

In This Chapter

▶ Transforming your forms — using properties to change appearance and behavior

▶ Forms within forms — it's all a matter of style

▶ Working with subproperties

▶ The main events — getting forms to react to mouse and keyboard events

*I*n the first two chapters of this book, you can tour the C++Builder 3 development environment and sit in on the creation of a C++Builder 3 program. Stepping into the spotlight in this chapter is the *Form* object. Form components are a big deal in C++Builder 3 because almost everything that you develop is based on a form or contained within a form. I think you'll agree that this makes them pretty important players on the C++Builder 3 ball park.

The term *form* refers to any application window that you create during your program development. With the C++Builder 3 visual programming environment, you use the actual program forms to create your applications. You accomplish this in the Form Designer, which is basically an application form in design mode. Figure 3-1 shows a simple form in design mode with several components already in place. (If you are not too familiar with the C++Builder 3 desktop features, you may want to run through the previous chapters of this book.)

Developing with Form Properties

Like any object in the real world, a Form object has characteristics that allow you to distinguish it from other types of objects. These characteristics are called the *properties* of the form. A property holds information about an object such as its size, color, name, and other distinguishing features. You can change these properties using the Object Inspector, which by default parks itself on the left side of the C++Builder 3 workspace window.

Figure 3-1:
Here's a
simple form,
shown in
design
mode, with
a few
components
dropped
into place.

I start this section with an example of a character-entry property, which determines the characteristics of a form when you enter text into the Object Inspector. You can use the steps in the following example to change the Caption property of a form:

1. **Choose File⇨New Application from the main menu to get a blank form in a new program.**

2. **Select the form by clicking it, and then click the Object Inspector.**

   If you don't have the Object Inspector showing, press F11.

3. **In the Object Inspector, click the field in the right column next to the line that reads Caption.**

   For the first form of a C++ Builder 3 project, the default value for the Caption property of each form is Form1.

4. **Remove the current contents of the Caption property by deleting it, and then enter a caption of your own.**

   I typed Hello Universe ! into the Caption property of the form shown earlier.

You have now successfully changed the contents of the Caption property using the Object Inspector (see Figure 3-2).

The Hint property

The Hint property is a simple text property used to hold a short "help" message for users; you can type whatever text you like in the property's value field using the Object Inspector. As long as the form's ShowHint property has been set to true (also using the Object Inspector), the text that you enter into this property appears near the mouse pointer whenever the user slowly passes the mouse pointer over the form.

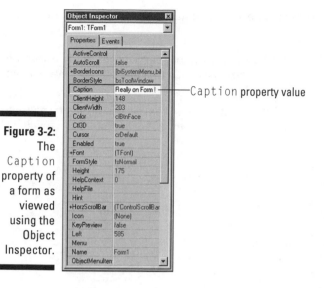

Caption property value

Figure 3-2:
The
Caption
property of
a form as
viewed
using the
Object
Inspector.

Height and Width properties

When you resize a form by clicking a form's edges and dragging with your mouse, certain numeric-type properties change value in the Object Inspector. Try resizing a selected form and watch as the values in the Height and Width properties on the Object Inspector change accordingly. You can also resize a form by entering numbers directly into the properties on the Object Inspector; some properties, such as Left and Top, even allow you to enter negative values.

The ClientHeight and ClientWidth property values refer to the amount of space that you actually have to work with on a form. The working space on a form is called the *client area* and is essentially the size of the form minus its title bar, status bar, and scroll bars.

The Visible property

Some properties offer you a choice of values, but you can choose only one value at a time. Other properties, such as the Visible property, offer only true or false values. (For example, when the Visible property is set to true using the Object Inspector, the user can see the form when the program runs; when the property is set to false, the user can't see the form.)

To select a value when the property has multiple values, you can do either of the following:

✔ Click the drop-down list button for the property in the right column of the Object Inspector (see Figure 3-3) and then make your choice from the list.

✔ Double-click the field in the right column next to the property name in the Object Inspector to cycle through the available alternative values.

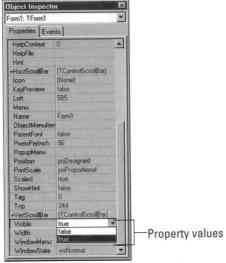

Figure 3-3: You can select from among Form component properties and set their values in the Object Inspector.

Property values

Set type properties

One way to distinguish *set type* properties is by the plus sign (+) next to the property name on the Object Inspector. (Other properties also have a plus sign in front of them, such as `enum` types, properties that can be selected through dialog boxes, or properties that are actually other objects.) Clicking the plus sign expands the property within the Object Inspector to display a list of options that you can select (by setting the option to `true`) from as many or as few of these settings as you require.

You can find multiple items in a set of subitems (where a component has several characteristics grouped together under one property), and you can select as many subitems as you want from a set. You expand the list of available options by double-clicking the set type property name.

Whenever you select an option from a sublist and set its value to `true`, the option appears in brackets and highlighted in the field next to the property itself. For example, with the `BorderIcons` set type property, if `biSystemmenu` and `biMinimize` are set to `true` in the Object Inspector, those options appear in the `BorderIcons` value field as shown in Figure 3-4.

Property selection sublist

—Values set to true

Figure 3-4:
Border
Icons is a
set type
property
that
expands in
the Object
Inspector to
show a
sublist of
settings.

The properties of a component can actually be other objects. For example, a Form component has a Font property, and Font itself is an object with its own subproperties. When you look at objects within components, you come across other property categories. The Font property, for example, is made up of other properties, such as Color, Height, and Name (see Figure 3-5).

Font subproperties

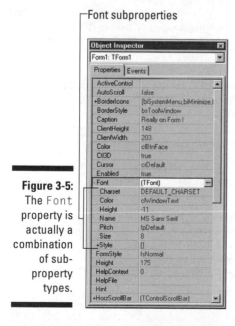

Figure 3-5:
The Font
property is
actually a
combination
of sub-
property
types.

Another way that you can set the values for properties that have more than one type of subproperty is by using a property editor. If a property is complex, when you click in the value field next to the property on the Object Inspector, an ellipsis button appears. Clicking the ellipsis button displays a property editor dialog box, which functions as a friendly user interface for what would otherwise be a complicated procedure. The property editor for the Font property is shown in Figure 3-6.

Figure 3-6: Editing complex properties is made easy using the Font property editor.

The BorderIcons property

After you have a feel for how you can manipulate properties, you can begin to customize your forms. The BorderIcons property is a set type property that allows you to specify which icons appear in the title bar of a form. (The *title bar* is the dark horizontal strip at the top of each window that contains the name of the program and sometimes the name of the file you're currently working in.)

The following table lists the value choices within the BorderIcons property and the effect those values have when selecting true from the property drop-down list in the Object Inspector:

BorderIcons Subproperty	What Happens When It's Set to true
biSystemMenu	The currently selected form offers a control menu, which you can access by right-clicking anywhere on the title bar.
biMinimize	The title bar of the currently selected form contains a minimize button, which when clicked reduces the form to an icon in the Windows 95 taskbar.

biMaximize	The title bar of the currently selected form includes a maximize button, which when clicked resizes the form to fill the application window.
biHelp	Places a "?" button on the form. When the user clicks the button, the mouse pointer changes to a question mark and then the user can view context-sensitive help and definitions by clicking form components.

Figure 3-7 shows what the title bar of a form looks like with the biMaximize and biMinimize options set to false in the Object Inspector. A close button (showing an X) is visible, but the maximize and minimize buttons are missing (refer to Figure 3-1 for a comparison).

If you turn off all the options within the BorderIcons property, you have to provide the user a way of closing the form either through a button or pop-up menu. If you don't, your users are going to get stuck with a form they can't get rid of!

Figure 3-7:
This title bar without its minimize and maximize buttons.

Take The Max !

If you end up with a window that you can't close, choose Run⇔Program Reset from the C++Builder 3 main menu to get rid of the guest that won't leave!

The BorderStyle property

The six BorderStyle property settings (bsDialog, bsNone, bsSingle, bsSizeable, bsSizeToolWin, and bsToolWin) in the Object Inspector are divided between those that allow a form to be resized and those that don't.

When a form has the BorderStyle property settings in the following bulleted list, the mouse pointer doesn't change when you move the mouse over the edges of the form (which means, of course, that you can't resize it).

Here are three points that cool developers might bear in mind when thinking of changing the BorderStyle property of a form:

✔ The bsNone setting results in the user not being able to move or resize a form. If you set BorderStyle to bsNone, you need to provide the user some way of closing the form because no title bar is shown.

✔ The bsDialog and bsSingle settings provide a standard dialog box border. Either of these BorderStyle settings results in a slightly thinner border than you get with the resizable border settings. That's because the nonresizing borders aren't meant to be selected or dragged.

✔ The bsToolWindow setting is used for utility or tool-type forms, such as property editors, in which you just want to provide some options and perform some actions. The border of this form is thinner than forms you may have seen so far, and no icon is in the upper-left corner with which you can access the default system menu (see Figure 3-8).

Figure 3-8:
With the
bsTool
Window
option in the
Border
Style
property,
the form
has subtle
differences.

Most of the time, you won't have a problem with allowing the user to resize forms, such as a dialog box window. In that case, you can use one of the following settings in the Object Inspector:

✔ **The bsSizeable setting:** A default value that provides a resizable border

✔ **The bsSizeToolWin setting:** A cross between bsSizeable and bsToolWindow

How these options translate to actual measurements depends on the type of font that you select for your form text — which means they vary. But I can give you some basic guidelines: The bsTool setting is not used in applications, but rather for programming utilities that are added into C++Builder 3

components; the bsNone setting is used for *splash screens* (the initial bitmap or other graphic that appears to tell the user that Windows is loading your application); the bsSizeable setting works for most normal application forms; and the BsDialog setting is used for anything that returns a *modal result* (such as a dialog box in an application in which an option is selected before anything else is done).

The Color property

Color can dramatically change the appearance of a form. You can use the Object Inspector to set the Color property in any one of several ways:

- ✔ Enter the text definition of a color (clBlue, clGreen are examples) directly into the property if you're already familiar with the color names and what they produce. (Techno-whizzes may prefer to enter the color in a numerical format.)

- ✔ Select from the extensive color assortment in the Color property's drop-down list.

- ✔ Double-click the Color property field in the Object Inspector to display the Color dialog box (shown in Figure 3-9). Then you can go nuts mixing your own custom colors.

You won't see the right part of the Color dialog box when you open it until after you click the Define Custom Colors button (grayed out in Figure 3-9). When you experiment with the color mixer, you soon discover that you can concoct some amazingly vibrant (and some truly horrible) colors for your forms.

Figure 3-9:
Choose
from basic
colors or
mix some of
your own to
add color to
your form.

The FormStyle property and MDI forms

The FormStyle property gives you four options to choose from. The default setting is fsNormal, which you can leave as the setting for most forms used in your applications. If you want to keep a form under your user's nose the whole time that the form is active, set the FormStyle property to fsStayOnTop, and that is exactly what the form does — it always appears on top of every other form on the screen and other forms can't cover it, no matter what the user tries to do.

Two related options — fsMDIForm and fsMDIChild — within the FormStyle property allow you to create applications using a main form that acts as a container for other application forms. You may have already used applications in which one form "contains" several other forms, a technique commonly used in word-processing and spreadsheet programs. This type of form treatment, called a *Multiple Document Interface* (MDI), is easy to create. In fact, you can use the following steps to create a MDI application right now:

1. **Choose File⇨New Application from the main menu to provide a blank form in a new program.**

2. **Using the Object Inspector, set the** Caption **property of the new form to** MDI Parent Form **and the** FormStyle **property to** fsMDIForm.

3. **Add a second form to the project by choosing File⇨New Form.**

   Another form appears.

4. **Change the** Caption **property of the new form to** MDI Child Form **and the** FormStyle **property to** fsMDIChild **using the Object Inspector.**

   That's all you need to do to create a simple MDI application.

5. **Press F9 to compile, link, and run the application.**

When you run the example MDI application, you see that the *child form* becomes a permanent part of the *parent form* and moves in tandem with the parent form. The child form can still be moved, or closed or opened, but only within the boundaries of the parent form. Scroll bars appear to allow users to view the whole child window if the parent form is resized so that part of the child form is no longer visible. Figure 3-10 shows two child windows, with the one on the left minimized.

Figure 3-10: MDI applications feature child forms that operate only within the confines of a parent form.

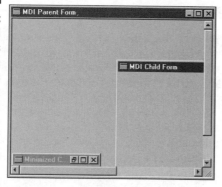

The Icon property

By default, the Icon property of a form is the Borland C++Builder 3 logo (a skyscraper image), but you can pick out another icon to display. To load a new icon onto a form, click the ellipsis button within the Icon property on the Object Inspector. A dialog box titled Picture Editor (shown in Figure 3-11) appears. Click the Load button to browse the icon files that you have on disk and select an icon file (icons have an .ico extension).

Figure 3-11: You can select a new form icon from the Picture Editor.

You can choose from some sample .ico files in the Program Files\Common Files\Borland Shared Files\Images\Icons folder for C++Builder 3.

Try experimenting with the Image Editor to create icons of your own. You can open the Image Editor by choosing Tools➪Image Editor from the main menu.

The Position property

A form's Position property determines where a form is first displayed on the computer screen when the user activates the form. If you select the default setting (poDesigned) for the Position property, wherever you leave the form on-screen at design time is where the form appears when the program is run.

One of my favorite settings for this property is poScreenCenter. When you use this setting, the form remains at the same size that you designed, but the form appears in the exact center of the screen's desktop (the user can always relocate the form by clicking into its title bar and dragging).

The poDefault setting gives control back to Windows in terms of where the form is placed and sized. If you run more than one copy, or *instance,* of your form at the same time, every new copy appears down and to the right of the preceding one. When you use the poDefaultPosOnly setting, the positioning of the form is left up to Windows; Windows does, however, use your design size. When you use the poDefaultSizeOnly setting, the form is sized for you, but placed where you left it at design time.

The WindowState property

WindowState is another property that determines how your form makes its entrance "onstage." This property has three settings: wsNormal, wsMaximized, and wsMinimized. You want to use the wsNormal setting most of the time because the form is displayed the way you designed it. Setting WindowState to wsMaximized fills the entire screen with the form, no matter how you positioned the form at design time. The wsMinimized setting reduces the form to a small caption and icon bar when the form is loaded. No matter how the form is initially loaded onto the screen, you can still move and resize the form as desired.

Making Events Happen

Way back, programmers used to be able to decide the exact order in which end users performed tasks — as well as decide just how many tasks users could perform at a time. With the advent of Windows, end users have been liberated somewhat from the tyranny of programmers. Now users can open multiple programs simultaneously, merrily jumping from program to program, copying data from one to the other as they go. Users can even load a program at dawn and leave it unused until dusk if they want.

When you are developing in Windows, you don't know what's going to be thrown at you until it occurs. Therefore, you have to respond to occurrences that are triggered by either the system or the user. These occurrences are known as *events,* and the actual function that is called when an event is triggered is an *event handler.* (Example applications created in future chapters of this book make extensive use of event handlers.)

A wide variety of events can happen to and around a form. As is true of nearly all objects within C++Builder 3, forms have "hooks" on which you can "hang" your code. As a program executes, it cruises by these hooks, even if the hooks are empty. When the program encounters a hook that has some of your code attached to it, the program knows that at that point, it must perform the set of instructions you wrote. (Your instructions are coded in C++.) This list of instructions is executed only if the program happens to pass that way while running (that's up to the end user). But, if and when the program does encounter a hook, the program needs to know how to react to your instructions.

In C++Builder 3, the code that handles events in your applications (and the "hooks" that they hang on) can be seen by clicking the Events tab of the Object Inspector (see Figure 3-12) and then double-clicking any of the fields in the right column of the Events page. C++Builder 3 then moves over to the Code Editor, where a basic functional skeleton of code awaits you.

Figure 3-12:
You gain access to a form's events (and the Code Editor) through the Events page of the Object Inspector.

Clicking with mouse events

The OnClick event occurs whenever the user clicks a blank area of a form using the main mouse button (in most cases, that means the left and not the right button). The following steps demonstrate how the OnClick event operates:

1. **Choose File⇨New Application from the main menu to create a new form in a new application.**

2. **Click the Event tab on the Object Inspector, and then double-click the blank field to the right of the word OnClick in the Object Inspector.**

   The Code Editor is invoked.

   C++Builder 3 then creates a framework function called FormClick and places the cursor exactly where you can start typing your list of instructions. Now you're ready to write your first line of C++ code for this example.

3. **Enter the following line into the Code Editor (as shown in Figure 3-13):**

   ```
   ShowMessage("I've been clicked !") ;
   ```

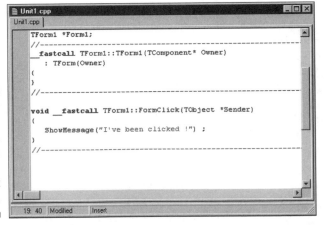

Figure 3-13:
The Code Editor is where you enter a form's event handlers.

4. **To see what this line of code does, press the F9 key or choose Run⇨Run to run the program.**

   C++Builder 3 automatically compiles and links your program before running it.

5. **Click the background of the form.**

   The program and its OnClick event then delivers the I've been clicked! message shown in Figure 3-14.

Figure 3-14:
A mouse
event made
this
message
appear.

You can see that C++Builder 3 provides a framework to which you just add the instructions for what you want to happen.

The `OnDblClick` event handler is triggered when the user double-clicks a blank area of a form. For example, follow the preceding steps for the `OnClick` event, but this time double-click the blank `OnDblClick` event handler in Step 2. Place the same message in the event handler function. (You need to prevent the `OnClick` event handler from being called by clicking the `OnClick` event handler name in the Object Inspector and then using the Delete key to remove the reference to the function from the Object Inspector event name.)

You're in trouble if you include both an `OnClick` and `OnDblClick` event on a form: The double-click event never gets called because the first of the two mouse clicks always sends the program to the `OnClick` event first.

Like many event handlers, the names of `OnMouseDown`, `OnMouseUp`, and `OnMouseMove` provide clues as to when they're triggered. The `OnMouseDown` event is fired when the mouse button is depressed. The `OnMouseUp` event is fired when the mouse button is released. The `OnMouseMove` event is called whenever the user drags the mouse pointer over a form. You, as a developer, have more control over these functions than you do with the `OnClick` event handler functions because the program can determine which mouse button was clicked and whether any keys (such as the Shift key) are being pressed by the user at the same time. You can accomplish this by using an argument that's passed into the event handler function. (See Chapter 16 for more on arguments.)

To experiment with mouse events some more, follow these example program steps:

1. **Choose File⇨New Application to get a new form.**

2. **Press F11 to move over to the Object Inspector.**

3. **Click the Events tab of the Object Inspector, and then double-click the empty field next to the `OnMouseDown` event handler name.**

You're now in the Code Editor, where you enter the following line shown in bold:

```
void __fastcall TForm1::FormMouseDown(TObject
        *Sender, TMouseButton Button,
        TShiftState Shift, int X, int Y)
  {
    Caption = "I'm Feeling Down !" ;
  }
```

4. **To make this example a bit more interesting, click the Events tab of the Object Inspector, and then double-click the blank name field for the** OnMouseUp **event handler.**

   This puts you in the Code Editor, where you're ready to type the following line of code:

```
Caption = "";
```

C++Builder 3 is *case-sensitive,* so be sure to use uppercase and lowercase letters exactly as required by the code, or your code may not work correctly (or at all).

5. **Click the Events tab of the Object Inspector, and then double-click the blank** OnMouseMove **event handler name. After you're in the Code Editor, enter the following line of code:**

```
MessageBeep(0) ;
```

6. **Press F9 to run your program.**

   As you move the mouse over the form, you hear a series of beeps. Keep your eye on the title bar of the form as you press and release the mouse buttons. The message that you placed in the OnMouseDown event handler in Step 4 appears in a dialog box when either the right or left mouse button is clicked; the OnClick event works only when the left mouse button is clicked.

I list the entire FormMouseDown event handler function in Step 4 of this section so you can see that C++Builder 3 is trying to tell you something — the TMouseButton button is being clicked. The OnMouseDown event handler can manage up to three mouse buttons, but PC mice normally have only two buttons. One of the arguments (TShiftState Shift) tells you about any keys that the user is holding down. The coordinates indicating the mouse's positions on the form (*x* pixels across and *y* pixels down) are also provided.

Entering key events

In Windows applications, a *key event* is triggered every time a user presses or releases a key. The OnKeyPress, OnKeyDown, and OnKeyUp key events are similar to their equivalent mouse events, which you can see in the following example program steps:

1. **Choose File⇨New Application to create a blank form in a new program.**

2. **Press F11 to display the Object Inspector.**

3. **Click the Events tab on the Object Inspector, and then double-click the empty OnKeyPress event handler name.**

   You end up in the Code Editor, where you enter the following code:

   ```
   if ((Key >= '0') && (Key <= '9'))
     MessageBeep(0) ;
   ```

   The two previous lines translate to the following instructions: If the keyboard key pressed is greater than or equal to 0 *and* the keyboard key pressed is less than or equal to 9, the computer makes a beeping noise.

4. **Press F9 to run the program.**

   Try pressing some keys on the keyboard. You hear a beep only when you press a number key.

Having no events associated with some keys is useful for preventing certain key combinations from having any effect on a program.

Form events, courtesy of Windows

Not all events are instigated by users; some are triggered by the Windows operating system itself. Those events are known as *system events,* which are listed in the following table:

Event	Occurs	Use It To
OnActivate	When the form becomes active	Bring the form up-to-date
OnClose	Before the form is closed or destroyed when the application closes	Close or free the application or resources that were used during the running of the form

(continued)

Event	Occurs	Use It To
OnCloseQuery	When an attempt is made to close a form	Check that data is saved and files are closed; or to prevent the close
OnCreate	When the form is constructed	Place initialization code
OnDeactivate	When the form stops being active	Store any temporary variables (generally, the reverse of OnActivate)
OnDestroy	At the last opportunity to hook in code before the form is removed from the computer's memory	Free any memory used in the form
OnPaint	When the form needs to be repainted; when another application window is moved over the form	Draw graphics and repaint text to the form's background area
OnResize	When the form's size changes	Move or resize any components in the form

To see how the OnResize system event works, for example, follow along with these steps to make a program that always keeps its component in the center of the form:

1. **Choose File⇨New Application to create a new form in a new program.**

2. **In the Standard page of the Component Palette, click the Label component button, and then click anywhere in the center of the form.**

    C++Builder 3 places a new Label component into the form.

3. **Using the Object Inspector, click the Caption property of the Label component and delete the text Label1.**

    Replace it with the text **My Label**.

4. **Click the background of the form to load its details into the Object Inspector.**

5. **Click the Events tab of the Object Inspector, and then double-click the blank field next to the** OnResize **event handler name.**

6. **You're in the Code Editor, ready to enter the following code:**

```
Label1->Left = (ClientWidth/2) - (Label1->Width/2) ;
Label1->Top = (ClientHeight/2) - (Label1->Height/2) ;
```

7. **Press F9 to run the application.**

   You should see a form like the one shown in Figure 3-15.

Figure 3-15:
Make your
components
locate
themselves
by using
OnResize
events.

If you resize the form by clicking its lower-right corner and then dragging, you see that the label you placed on the form in Step 2 always automatically locates itself in the center of the form, thanks to the OnResize event handler.

Part II

Components: Your Building Bricks and Mortar

The 5th Wave   By Rich Tennant

WITH OBJECT-ORIENTED PROGRAMMING, I UNDERSTAND THE "ENCAPSULATION" AND "INHERITANCE" PART PRETTY WELL. IT'S THAT DARN "CLUTTERMORPHISM" THAT STUMPS ME.

In this part . . .

You can get a first-hand look "under the hood" of
C++Builder 3 and what makes visual programming so
downright cool — ready-to-use program components
that you can add to a project with just a few mouse clicks.
Tap into C++Builder 3's Visual Component Library (VCL)
using the Component Palette, and you find edit boxes, list
boxes, buttons, main menus, and many other programming vitals that simplify your program development. In
fact, components make programming in C++Builder 3 not
just easy, but fun too!

You can build applications right from the start by following the step-by-step examples provided throughout these
chapters. Just drop components into a form and then
tailor the components to your individual needs by setting
their properties and defining events. Your programs will
do exactly what *you* want them to (in this case, power
trips are definitely allowed).

Chapter 4

The Object of Building: C++Builder 3 Component Basics

*S*top for a second and take a look around you. What do you see? A desk, a chair, a computer screen plastered with stick-on notes, yesterday morning's cup of coffee? We're surrounded by countless *objects,* and our perception of the world is influenced by our understanding of these objects and how they work.

Objects are described in terms of their distinct characteristics — size, color, composition, and so forth. Descriptions such as "John's big red van" or "Mary's fiberglass surfboard" are basic ways to identify objects. In this chapter, you see how developing programs in C++Builder 3 is an extension of how we understand the real world and the objects in it.

Using *objects* to achieve a particular end result is exactly what you're doing in C++Builder 3. Just like real-world objects, C++Builder 3 objects have certain characteristics. For example, a Windows button can have a text caption (which means it's identified with a label of sorts) and can support certain operations that distinguish it from the other bits and stuff on your computer screen.

In object-oriented programming, an *object* consists of data and *routines, functions or methods* to process data, and each object is just one of many objects that make up a program that has real-world applications.

So What Do Objects Have to Do with Components?

The applications you construct with C++Builder 3 are designed to solve real-life problems. To problem-solve effectively, you need a way of creating "models" of the objects in the world. The more realistically you can represent the real world within your applications, the more relevant your applications are to the task at hand and the more readily the applications can adapt to changes that you need to make to them as real-world situations change. C++Builder 3 provides a way of representing real-life objects through the use of *components*.

Components enable you to determine both the characteristics of objects (by using the *properties* that are available) and the operating capabilities of objects (by using function *methods* and *events*). For example, you can change a Form object's color characteristic by changing the value held in its Color property. Or, by entering your own instructions into the Form's OnMouseMove event, for example, you can change how the form behaves when an end user moves a mouse across it. (You can find information about properties throughout the rest of this book.)

I just threw a few terms at you that you may already know from your programming background, but here's a refresher anyway. A *property* is a single characteristic of an object or component and holds data specific to only that characteristic. A *method* is any function that defines an action that an object can perform. An *event* is an application occurrence for which you can define code that will be run every time that application occurrence arises. Events can be triggered either by Windows or as a result of the user interacting with the program.

Exploring the Component Palette

The Component Palette (the top window in C++Builder 3, which is shown in Figure 4-1) is like one of those spring-loaded display racks you find in a retail store. When you remove an item (the top component), the next one takes its place. The difference is that when you take a component from the palette, you don't have to replace it. You can just go on forever taking the items that you require without replenishing the stock.

Figure 4-1:
Here, the
C++Builder 3
Component
Palette
shows the
Standard
page set of
components.

Before going into the details about each of the parts in the never-ending supply of components, briefly check out the various kinds of components available to you and how to use them.

The Component Palette is divided into several groups according to their functions. You can access each group of components by clicking each of the tabs directly above the Component Palette bar (refer to Figure 4-1). Here's a rundown of the purpose of each tab:

- ✔ **Standard:** This tab contains the parts that make up the bread-and-butter Windows applications. Nearly all Windows applications make some use of the components this tab provides, including components for displaying and editing text, as well as buttons, scroll bars, and menus.

- ✔ **Additional:** The Additional tab, far from being an afterthought as its name suggests, contains some of the coolest gear in the Component Palette — such as the bitmap and speed buttons, grid components, and a shape component.

- ✔ **Win32:** These components allow you to access the Windows 95-type user-interface controls. The most prominent are the TreeView component (you know it from Windows Explorer), Page Control (for creating tabs of your own), Track bar (for creating sliding-bar values), Status bar, and the Rich Text editing component. For C++Builder 3, Animate, DateTimePicker, Coolbar, and Toolbar were added to ensure that you can provide up-to-date application interfaces for your users.

- ✔ **System:** You can get your applications talking to one another by using DDE (Dynamic Data Exchange) and OLE (Object Linking and Embedding). Do you need a wake-up call, or do you want to schedule tasks? That's no problem if you use the Timer component that lives here.

- ✔ **Internet:** This tab gives C++Builder 3 its Internet savvy and is referred to as the Internet Toolkit.

✔ **Data Access and Data Controls:** You gain access to data from your applications by using the components that reside in these two data tabs. The Data Access tab allows you to hook into data tables and queries. The Data Control tab enables you to automatically link the user interface to these tables.

✔ **Decision Cube:** Easy and impressive business graphics are the aims of these components, but you'll need to be using the Client/Server version of C++Builder 3 to have them available. To see how these components operate, load up the sample application by using File➪New to get the New Items dialog and then double-clicking your mouse on the Decision Cube Sample icon on the Business page.

✔ **QReport:** C++Builder 3 offers its own built-in form-based reports. The QReport (or Quick Report) tab provides components that take the headache out of generating user reports. By dropping these components into a simple form and then setting properties in the usual way, you can rapidly get even complicated reports up to speed and looking good. This tab also includes a preview facility.

✔ **Dialogs:** Ready-made dialog box components can really speed application development by providing boxes for opening and saving files, for selecting fonts, colors, and printers, and much more. Dialog boxes can really boost productivity and enhance program standardization.

✔ **Win 3.1:** Many of the controls on the Win 3.1 tab have equivalents in the Win32 tab, but the controls on the Win 3.1 tab can be useful for giving a 3.1 feel to your applications. This tab includes an outliner as well as page controls, notepad component, and individual controls for selecting files, folders, or drives.

✔ **Samples:** This component provides a mixed bag of useful components including a gauge, color grid, and handy calendar.

✔ **ActiveX:** This tab contains an ActiveX spell checker, as well as several impressive graphing components.

Note: In Figure 4-1, the Win 3.1, Samples, and ActiveX component palette tabs are covered. You can access these tabs by using the directional arrow buttons on the right-hand side.

This book is not designed to give you an exhaustive tour of the entire C++Builder 3 Component Palette. Coverage that extensive would take several books of this size. In the following chapters, you find out how to build applications using many but not all of the components on the palette. Nevertheless, you get a good taste of how you can use this tool to create your own fully functioning programs.

You can view a list of all components, regardless of which pages they reside on, by selecting View⇨Component List from the main menu.

Using Components

You may have discovered in previous chapters of this book that introducing components into your program requires just a few simple steps. If you can use Windows, you can start to program in C++Builder 3.

Selecting and deselecting components

To select a component from the Component Palette, do the following:

1. **Click the desired palette page tab (such as Standard, Win32, and the rest).**
2. **Click the speed button that displays the component's icon.**

   You can select only one speed button at a time, and the button for the selected component remains depressed until it is deselected.

At this point, you can click into the form you're working on, and the component is dropped in. (This process is repeated many times in the following chapters.)

To *deselect* a component, either select another component or click the arrow button (shown in this margin) to the left of the Component Palette tabs. This action puts the original component in "neutral gear."

If you're not sure which button on the Component Palette tabs controls your component, pass your mouse pointer over each icon until an on-screen message appears identifying the button.

If you have components placed on a form, you can *select* them by clicking them. The selected components display small squares in each corner, or sometimes halfway up each side. Figure 4-2 shows some selected components.

You can always select a group of components by clicking and holding down the left mouse button just outside the group and then dragging with your mouse until each component is selected. When you release the left mouse button, components that are within the dotted rectangular area created by dragging the mouse are selected. Figure 4-2 shows the rectangle that appears when you group select or deselect.

Group select/deselect indicator square

Figure 4-2:
Gray
squares
appear at
the corners
of selected
components.

Placing components

After you select a component in the palette, you can place it on a form by moving the mouse pointer to the desired location on the form and then clicking the left mouse button. A copy of the component appears at the spot where you click.

You can also select components directly from the Component List dialog box, which you can display by choosing View⇨Component List. This dialog box shows all the components in the Component Palette in alphabetical order, rather than sorted by component-group tabs. Use the Add to form button to place a copy of the selected component into the form.

Locking into components on Component Palette

When you first construct a form, you often need to repeatedly place several components of the same type on the form. You can avoid having to reselect the component from the Component Palette each time.

Assume, for example, that you want to place seven EditBox components on a form. Hold down the Shift key, and click an Edit box component in the Component Palette. The Edit box button is highlighted, indicating that it's selected. Now move to the form, and click the mouse seven times in different locations. You get a copy of the component for every click without having to ferry back to the Component Palette to pick up another one each time.

When you're done, don't forget to change the mouse pointer to its normal state by clicking the mouse pointer button on the palette.

Choosing visual or nonvisual components

You can place two types of components onto forms: those that you can see at runtime and those that you can't see at *runtime*. (Runtime is when your program is actually running, as opposed to the view you get of your forms while designing them in C++Builder 3.) *Visual components,* such as edit boxes, labels, and gauges, are visible to the user. Other components, such as timers and tables, disappear at runtime; you get to see those elements only at design time, and the user works with them only indirectly. They're known as *nonvisual components*.

Place nonvisual components in an orderly fashion in an unused area of the form (so that you don't have to move them out of your way every five minutes). You can actually set the form during design time to be larger than you need for the final program and then set the Height and Width properties as part of the OnCreate method for the form.

Figure 4-3 shows a form with three nonvisual components placed off the Panel to the right side of the form. Now you know what nonvisual components "look like" at design time — they resemble their respective icons from the Component Palette button bar.

Figure 4-3: A form showing three visual components on the left and three nonvisual ones on the right.

Resizing components

You want to make the most of the space that is available on a form, and part of that task is moving and sizing the components that you place on the form.

To move a component, select it by clicking it and then dragging it around the form anywhere you like. Another way to move a selected component is to hold down the Ctrl key and then press the arrow keys to move the component up, down, left, or right.

You also have a choice in the way that you resize a component. Select the component or components that you want to resize and then use one of these two methods:

- Place the mouse pointer on any one of the handles (those black squares) on the component's border; the pointer changes to indicate the direction you can drag to resize. Then hold down the mouse button and drag to adjust the component as required. Figure 4-4 displays sizing handles on a Button component.

- You can also resize components by using the arrow keys. Hold down the Shift key, and press the arrow keys to adjust the bottom and right sides of the component as required.

Figure 4-4: Click and drag the squares surrounding a component to size it as needed.

Moving and resizing collective components

You can move or resize any number of components in one fell swoop by group selecting them and then using the Shift and Ctrl keys in conjunction with the arrow keys.

You can resize only visible components. Nonvisible ones spring back to their original size when you release the mouse button.

When you need to create several components of matching size, use the Size dialog box, shown in Figure 4-5. With the components that you want to resize selected, just right-click anywhere on the form to bring up the speed menu, and then choose the Size option to display the Size dialog box.

Copying or moving components between forms

You can copy or move any number of components between forms. This procedure uses the Windows Clipboard in the same way that you may have used it with other tools. Try this:

1. **Create two new blank forms by twice selecting File⇨New Application from the C++Builder 3 main menu.**

2. **Place a few components in one of these forms.**

   Use the steps in the sections, "Selecting and deselecting components" and "Placing components," earlier in this chapter. You can use components of any type.

3. **Select as many of these components as you like by holding down the Shift key and clicking the ones that you want to choose.**

4. **After you select some components, choose Edit⇨Copy from the main menu, or press Ctrl+C.**

5. **Click the form that is still blank.**

6. **Choose Edit⇨Paste from the main menu, or press Ctrl+V.**

   An exact match of the components is placed in the second form.

Check out the Edit⇨Select All command, or press Ctrl+A, which picks up all the components at the same time without you having to click all over the place. Then you can deselect individual components as needed, which may be a method that's faster for you.

If you have several components of the same type to replace or change on a form, choose Search⇨Replace while viewing the form as text.

Table 4-1 offers some helpful tips for working with components.

Table 4-1	Component User's Quick Reference
Operation	*How To*
Select	Click the desired component, or click and drag around a group of components, or hold down the Shift key and click the component that you want to multiple-select.
Place	Move the mouse to a location on a form and click.
Deselect	Click the Neutral button (the arrow button on the Component Palette) to deselect the Component Palette. Click the form itself to deselect a component on a form.
Move	Select a component and then drag; *or* select a component, hold down the Ctrl key, and use the arrow keys.
Size	Select a component and then click one of the sizing handles and drag; *or* select the components, hold down the Shift key, and use the arrow keys.
Copy	Select components by clicking them, and then choose Edit⇨Copy; *or* press Ctrl+C.
Cut	Select components by clicking them, and then choose Edit⇨Cut; *or* press Ctrl+X.
Paste	Place components in the Clipboard, and then press Ctrl+V on a form.

Aligning: View alignment from the main menu

Your applications should look as smart as possible. Part of achieving that professional look is lining up your components neatly in the form.

You can spend a long time setting the Left and Top properties of components or using the Ctrl and arrow keys to make sure that all the components line up, or you can choose some quicker methods.

In Figure 4-6, four buttons that are in serious need of alignment have been dumped onto an empty form. You can align these components by choosing View⇨Alignment Palette for the Align palette (see Figure 4-7). By clicking a button in the palette, you can right-align, left-align, center vertically or horizontally, or evenly space and align groups of selected components on a form.

Figure 4-6:
Four
buttons in
need of
alignment.

Figure 4-7:
The Align
Palette
offers
options for
aligning
selected
components.

Another tool in the battle against crooked controls is the Alignment dialog box, shown in Figure 4-8. You can gain access to this alignment selector by clicking the controls that you want to straighten out and then right-clicking anywhere on the form to bring up the speed menu and choosing the Align option from this menu.

Figure 4-8:
The
Alignment
dialog box
offers
methods of
aligning
your
controls.

Working with Standard Components

This section introduces you to some components you're sure to rely on heavily. Because at least one component on the Standard page of the Component Palette appears in virtually every application you create, these components are a good place to start for basic application development.

The Label component

The *Label* component is an unassuming little fellow represented by the "A" button. You can use the Label component to identify other components on a form or to display text that you don't want the user to change.

Use the Alignment property (it's shown in the Object Inspector Properties page when the Label component is selected) to state how you want your text to be placed inside the Label component — either left-justified, right-justified, or centered.

If a Label component sizes itself around the text when you enter the text into the Caption property in the Object Inspector, that means the AutoSize property is set to true. To make the Label component stick to one size, set AutoSize to false in the Object Inspector. This setting enables you to set a fixed size for the Label component. You may want to use this setting when you plan on changing the caption while running the program or when you're using several labels.

You can use the Label component as a link to another component on the form by using the FocusControl property and by following these example steps:

1. **Place a Label component on a form by clicking the Label component button and clicking anywhere on the form.**

2. **With the Label component selected, click the down-arrow button inside the** FocusControl **property value field in the Object Inspector.**

   You then see a list of the other controls on the form that are not Label components.

3. **Select one of those controls from the list.**

4. **Enter text into the** Caption **property of the Label component, and prefix any one letter with an ampersand (&).**

   That character becomes a shortcut "hot key" to menu items when used with the Alt key.

Now, when you run your program and press Alt plus the underlined character, the cursor moves to the component that you specified in the FocusControl drop-down list.

Use the Color property to set the background color of the Label component. If you need to, you can even remove the background by setting the Transparent property to true. This leaves you with just the text floating over whatever background you choose to place (see Figure 4-9).

Color property options⌐

Figure 4-9:
Use the
Color
property to
set the
background
color of a
label.

If you need labels that take up more than one line, set the WordWrap property to true. You can adjust the Caption property and even see how your Label component is going to look at design time. The centered text example in Figure 4-10 shows this arrangement.

Figure 4-10:
The two-
line
"Centered
Text" was
achieved
with the
WordWrap
property.

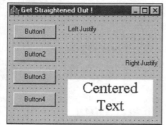

The EditBox component

Your program users need some sort of method to enter text-based data (or what nontechies like to call "words"). The *EditBox* component provides a way they can do this.

To place EditBox components onto your forms, follow these steps:

1. **Select the EditBox component button from the Standard page of the Component Palette.**

2. **Click on the form wherever you want the EditBox to appear.**

   As with the Label component described in the previous section, after you select the Edit component on the form (by clicking it), its properties are shown in the Properties tab on the Object Inspector.

EditBox properties

The EditBox component has a single-line edit control, the contents of which are stored in the Text property. The property is initially set to the name of the component when you first place it on the form. The Text property can accept many more characters than you would expect a user to enter in one line, and in many cases you may want to use the MaxLength property from the Object Inspector to restrict the number of characters that users can enter.

Use the AutoSelect property with caution when it is set to true because all the text entered in an EditBox component is highlighted to be overwritten as the user moves to the EditBox. If you press a key by mistake when all the text is highlighted, you lose the current text. To be honest, all is not lost if you do make this error because you can use a combination of Alt and Backspace (or Ctrl+Z) to retrieve the overwritten text.

The user can enter information into the Edit component in a couple of ways:

✔ The CharCase property can be used to indicate that you want all input converted to either lowercase or uppercase characters; the default setting of ecNormal allows for mixed-case entry.

✔ If the user needs to enter confidential information, you can hide the user's typed entry behind the single character of your choice by setting the PasswordChar property. Figure 4-11 shows this setting in action.

Using the EditBox control to validate user entry

The EditBox component events allow you to impose data-entry validation rules on a user entering text in the EditBox component. (These events can be accessed from the Events page on the Object Inspector after you've selected an EditBox component.) Combinations of the OnChange event, which is triggered every time the user makes a change in the EditBox, and the OnKeyPress event can be invaluable in preventing the user from entering rogue or garbage data.

Figure 4-11:
The
PasswordChar
property at
work,
disguising
the user's
password
entry.

The following steps show you how you could set up an EditBox that accepts only numeric keys to allow entry of a number no larger than 9,999:

1. **Choose File⇨New Application from the main menu.**

2. **Drop an EditBox component onto the form by clicking the EditBox button and then clicking in the form.**

3. **In the Events page of the Object Inspector, double-click the blank** OnKeyPress **event name field, and enter the following code:**

```
if ((Key < '0') || (Key > '9'))
  {
  MessageBeep(0) ;
  Key = '\0' ;
  }
```

This code means that if the integer entered is less than 0 or greater than 9, the computer beeps and sets the integer to a blank character. This setting ensures that the user can enter only positive numeric values in the EditBox.

4. **Set the** MaxLength **property to 4.**

This action sets the maximum value of the number that the user enters at 9999.

5. **Compile, link, and run this program by pressing F9, or by clicking the C++Builder 3 Run button (the one with the green arrow on it), or by choosing Run⇨Run.**

Play with this application a little to see how it controls what you enter.

The OnEnter and OnExit events are triggered as the user enters and leaves a field. These events can be used to validate the text as a whole rather than by one character at a time.

Be aware that if you change the Text property within the OnChange event, the event handler triggers itself again. You may create a cyclical call that results in your having to reset your machine!

The Panel component

The *Panel* component can be used as a background component in order to group components within forms. Panels are also useful for understanding some of the more complex components that have a great deal of behavior in common with Panels.

You can place a Panel onto your form by selecting the Panel button from the Component Palette and then clicking your form wherever you require a panel. With the Panel selected, you can access the properties and events for the Panel component by using the Object Inspector.

The Caption property of a Panel is always initially loaded with the name of the Panel. Even though a caption may not be required for many panel applications, Panel components always have a Caption property, so don't forget to clear out the Caption property if you are not going to use it.

One of the most significant properties of Panels is the Align property, which allows you to insert panels onto a form that tailor themselves to fit the available space and remain where you set them even when the user resizes the form. Figure 4-12 shows an example of this property.

Figure 4-12: Panel alignment options.

To produce the example form in Figure 4-12, follow these steps:

1. **Select File⇨New Form from the main menu.**

2. **Click the Panel button on the Standard page of the Component Palette.**

3. **Using Steps 1 and 2, drop six Panels in the free space of the form.**

4. **Set the Align properties for each Panel as indicated earlier in Figure 4-8.**

I also indicate the order in which I placed each Panel on the form.

After you place the Panels on the form, resize the form by clicking the lower-right corner of the form and dragging; then pull the form around the C++Builder 3 workspace to see how the panels react. When the form is resized, the Panel components align themselves automatically.

By using the Align property, you can lock Panel components into place on a form. In addition, if you select a Panel and then place another Panel within it, you can experiment with aligning panels within other panels.

Don't confuse the Alignment property with the Align property. The Alignment property provides the same function for the Panel component as it does for the Label component — it tells C++Builder 3 how you want the *text* of a Caption property aligned within the panel: left, centered, or right.

In the example that follows, a pair of properties — BevelInner and BevelOuter — are used on a panel. Why surround one component with two bevel borders? By using a combination of these two properties, each of which has three options — alLower, alNone, and alRaised — you can create up to nine "3-D" panel effects, which are shown in Figure 4-13.

The two letters in the middle of each panel in Figure 4-13 indicate the settings of each of the properties: alNone/alNone is in the upper-left corner, alLower/alRaised is in the center, and alRaised/alRaised is in the bottom-right corner.

Figure 4-13: An assortment of "3-D" panel effects, courtesy of the Bevel properties.

The Memo component

The *Memo* component has similarities to the Edit component with one major advantage — the Memo component can hold multiple lines of text.

You can select the Memo component using the Memo button on the Standard page. After you place a Memo component onto a form, you can gain access to its properties and events in the Object Inspector.

The Memo component also shares one functionality with the Panel component — the Align property. This property allows you to set aside an area of the form for note entry. Once again, don't confuse Align with the Alignment property, which is set to alLeft by default.

The Lines property enables multiple lines of text to be held within a Memo component. This property can hold a list of strings (a *string* being a sequence of characters).

Follow these steps to preload some lines of text for your user:

1. **Click the** Lines **property field in the Object Inspector.**

2. **Click the ellipsis button in the** TStrings **field to display the String list editor shown in Figure 4-14.**

   A couple lines of text that I entered for this example appear in the Lines property.

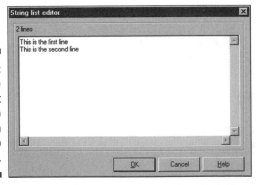

Figure 4-14: Use the String list editor to enter text in a Memo component.

Several properties add versatility to the Memo component:

✔ By using the ScrollBars property, you can turn the vertical and horizontal scroll bars on and off. This property has four settings: ssNone, ssHorizontal, ssVertical, and ssBoth. These settings provide either vertical or horizontal scroll bars, both vertical or horizontal scroll bars, or no scroll bars at all alongside the Memo.

✔ The properties WantReturns and WantTabs determine whether the Enter and Tab commands that a user enters in a Memo are held as part of the text or are sent out to the form. If you set WantReturns to false, the Enter key does not drop the text to the next line in the Memo, but instead sends it out to the form. The same applies to the WantTabs property: If it's set to false, a Tab entry sends the focus to the next control instead of placing a tab in the text of the Memo.

✔ If the WordWrap property is set to true, the user doesn't have to be concerned with overrunning a line. The user can keep typing away, and the component takes care of moving to the next line as the user reaches the right side of the Memo.

You can use the following set of steps to put the Memo component to work by creating a dedicated code file editor:

1. **Choose File⇨New Application from the main menu.**

2. **Click the Memo button on the Standard page of the Component Palette, and then click the form to drop in a component.**

3. **Click the background of the form, and then click the Events tab on the Object Inspector.**

4. **Double-click the blank field next to the OnCreate event handler to get into the Code Editor.**

5. **Enter the following lines in the Code Editor:**

```
Memo1->Lines->LoadFromFile("unit1.cpp") ;
Memo1->Lines->SaveToFile("unit1.bak") ;
```

6. **Double-click the blank field next to the OnCloseQuery event handler, and then enter the following line of code in the Code Editor:**

```
Memo1->Lines->SaveToFile("unit1.cpp") ;
```

7. **Set the Align property of the Memo component to alClient from the Object Inspector.**

8. **Run the program by pressing F9.**

You should see the same code that you just entered displayed in the Memo component in the program. The program reads in the contents of the unit1.cpp file and then starts using the LoadFromFile method. The program then makes a backup version of the file called unit1.bak. When you close the program, changes made to the file are automatically saved by using the SaveToFile method.

If you save your work in a directory other than the C++Builder 3 default directory, you may receive an error message telling you the program can't find the unit1.cpp file.

The ListBox component

The *ListBox* component can prevent users from making text-entry mistakes by limiting choices to those that are already valid. A ListBox can contain up to 32,000 items that users can choose from. (Of course, if you include anywhere near that many items, you'll be very unpopular with your end users — for making them scroll up and down the list so much.)

To start, take a look at the ListBox component:

1. **Click the ListBox button, and then click the form to drop the ListBox into position.**

2. **Click the ListBox to display its properties and events in the Object Inspector.**

The Items property bears a resemblance to the Lines property of the Memo component described in the previous section of this chapter. You can enter a list of data into the ListBox component at design time by using the following steps:

1. **Click the ellipsis button on the Items property in the Object Inspector to open the String list editor.**

2. **Enter the lines of text that you want the ListBox to hold.**

3. **Click OK on the String list editor to save your changes.**

If you set the IntegralHeight property to true, only items that can be shown vertically in their entirety in the ListBox are shown at all.

If you are writing a program that picks tracks to play from a CD, for example, you can allow the user to select more than one item at a time by using a combination of the ExtendedSelect and MultiSelect properties. The following table summarizes how these properties affect the behavior of the ListBox component.

MultiSelect Setting	*ExtendedSelect Setting*	*Effect*
true	true	Holding down the Ctrl key while clicking allows user to select noncontiguous items in a list; holding down the Shift key while clicking allows user to select a range of items.

MultiSelect Setting	ExtendedSelect Setting	Effect
true	false	User can select multiple options without using the Ctrl or Shift key, but can no longer select a range of options.
false	N/A	Only individual items can be selected.

You can create a ListBox that contains more than one column, as shown in Figure 4-15, by increasing the Column property number (by default, the Column property is set to 0). You may not use this option very often, but it's there if you happen to need it.

When your program is in use, the OnClick event is triggered every time you select an item from the ListBox list, either by pressing the arrow keys or by clicking a ListBox item with the mouse. In this event, you determine what you want the program to do when the user makes selections.

The following steps provide an example program that makes use of the OnClick event:

1. **Choose File⇨New Application from the main menu.**

2. **Click the ListBox component button, and then click the position on the form where you want to drop in a ListBox.**

3. **Click the ellipsis button in the Items property field to show the String list editor, and then enter ten lines of text.**

4. **Click OK.**

5. **Click the Label button on the Standard page of the Component Palette, and then click the form.**

6. **Click the ListBox component on the form, then click the Events tab on the Object Inspector, and then double-click the empty field next to the `OnClick` event handler.**

You're now in the Code Editor, where you enter the following line:

```
Label1->Caption =
    ListBox1->Items->Strings[ListBox1->ItemIndex] ;
```

7. **Run the program by pressing F9.**

As you click items in the ListBox, the Label's caption changes with your choices (see Figure 4-16).

Figure 4-16:
The ListBox
`OnClick`
event
enables you
to create
label
captions
that change
with the
user's list
selection.

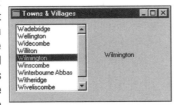

The ComboBox component

The *ComboBox* component combines the features of an EditBox and a ListBox. ComboBoxes can offer your users a selection box that doesn't take up as much room on your form as a full ListBox does. Three types of ComboBox components are available: Simple, DropDown, and DropDownList:

- ✔ The Simple type of ComboBox isn't capable of showing drop-down menus (see Figure 4-17). It functions much like an Edit control attached to the top of a ListBox. The user can choose from the list or enter text in the edit box.

- ✔ The DropDown components offer a far more compact alternative to the Simple type of ComboBox. The user can't see the list of choices until clicking the down-arrow button on the right side of the EditBox. The user still has the option of entering text in the edit box.

- ✔ Typing new entries is not a user option for the DropDownList ComboBox; users can select from the list, but can't enter text of their own.

Figure 4-17:
Simple
ComboBoxes
scroll rather
than drop
down.

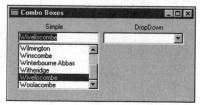

The ComboBox shares many properties with the EditBox and ListBox components. One of them is the DropDownCount property, which allows you to determine how many choices are displayed when the drop-down list appears. If the Items property contains fewer items than the DropDownCount property does, the ComboBox is clever enough to use up only the room that is needed to show the available items. When you've crammed more than DropDownCount items into a ComboBox, the ScrollBar component automatically arrives on the scene, offering assistance with navigating to the choices that aren't visible.

The OnDropDown event is triggered when the user opens the ComboBox. The OnDropDown event gives you the opportunity to update the values in the Items property or to make other components visible in your form when the user clicks the down-arrow button on the ComboBox.

To add a ComboBox to a form, click the ComboBox component button, and click the form where you want your ComboBox component to appear. If you then select the ComboBox on the form, you have access to its properties and events through the Object Inspector.

By using the following set of steps, you'll get a program that adds items to the ComboBox Items list while the program is running:

1. **Choose File➪New Application from the main menu.**

2. **Click the EditBox component button, and then click the form.**

3. **Click the ComboBox button, and then click the form.**

    The Style property of the ComboBox is set to csDropDown by default.

4. **Click the Events tab on the Object Inspector, and then double-click the empty field next to the onDropDown event handler and enter the following in the Code Editor:**

```
ComboBox1->Items->Add(Edit1->Text) ;
```

5. **Press F9 to compile, link, and run your application.**

6. **With the application running, enter any word of your choice in the EditBox, and then click the down-arrow button in the ComboBox.**

    The new word is added to the ComboBox list of items.

You now have complete control over the selections that a user sees at runtime. As a bit of an extension to this example, you could perform the following steps to enable the user to clear out the ComboBox list while the program is running:

1. **Close the program by clicking the program window's Close button.**

2. **Select the ComboBox, and click the Events tab on the Object Inspector.**

3. **Double-click the empty** `OnDblClick` **event handler field to get into the Code Editor, where you enter the following line:**

```
ComboBox1->Items->Clear();
```

4. **Press F9 to run the program again.**

Get Your Windows Moving with the ScrollBar Component

Scroll bars are used most often in partnership with other controls, but it's difficult to imagine how many Windows programs could work without a scroll bar. (The *ScrollBar* component resides on the Standard page of the Component Palette.)

Click the ScrollBar button on the Standard page of the Component Palette, and then click a form anywhere you want to place the ScrollBar component. With the ScrollBar selected on the form, you have access to its properties and events.

- ✔ The `Kind` property allows you to set scroll bars to run vertically. (ScrollBar components run horizontally by default.)

- ✔ The `Max` and `Min` properties hold the value of the scroll bar button's position relative to the scroll bar's two end positions; all positions in between each end are automatically graded relative to the `Max` and `Min` values.

- ✔ The `Position` property holds the current value for the scroll bar that controls how other components are scrolled.

- ✔ The `LargeChange` property sets the distance that the scroll bar moves when the user clicks either side of the scroll bar button.

- ✔ The `SmallChange` property adjusts the distance the `Position` property moves when the user clicks one of the end-arrow buttons.

You can use the following steps to create an example program using a ScrollBar Component:

1. **Create a new application by choosing File⇨New Application from the main menu.**

2. **Click the ScrollBar button on the Standard page of the Component Palette, and then click the form.**

3. **With the ScrollBar component selected, set the following values for the ScrollBar properties:**

Property	Value
LargeChange	32
Max	255
SmallChange	16

4. **Press Ctrl+C to place a copy of the ScrollBar component in the Clipboard, and then press Ctrl+V twice.**

   This step places two more copies of the ScrollBar on the form.

5. **Arrange the ScrollBar components on the form as shown in Figure 4-18.**

Figure 4-18: Another use for scroll bars — in a color hue selector.

6. **Click the Panel button on the Standard page of the Component Palette, and then click alongside the ScrollBars on the form.**

7. **Remove the name from the Panel's Caption property.**

   You won't need it for this example.

8. **Select all three ScrollBar components by pressing Shift and clicking each one.**

9. **In the Events tab on the Object Inspector, double-click the empty field next to the OnChange event handler.**

10. You're in the Code Editor, where you enter the following lines:

```
Panel1->Color = RGB( ScrollBar1->Position,
    ScrollBar2->Position,
    ScrollBar3->Position ) ;
```

This single event handler is cleverly triggered for a change in position of any of the scroll bar buttons. For example, in Figure 4-18, each bar represents the amount of red, green, and blue that goes into making up the color that the solid panel on the right displays.

11. Run your application by pressing F9, or by clicking the Run speed button, or by selecting Run⇨Run from the main menu.

Experiment with your new color selector application by sliding the scroll bars back and forth. Don't forget to examine the LargeChange and SmallChange properties in the Object Inspector to see the degree to which they change.

You can also place a Label component next to each scroll bar and enter the relative position of each scroll bar button in the Label's Caption property. Do this by entering the following code after the Panel color assignment entered in Step 10 in the OnChange event handler:

```
Label1->Caption = IntToStr(ScrollBar1->Position) ;
Label2->Caption = IntToStr(ScrollBar2->Position) ;
Label3->Caption = IntToStr(ScrollBar3->Position) ;
```

The result is what you see in Figure 4-19 — the improved version of the previous example. This one keeps track of the numerical value of each setting as you move through the color spectrum, and it illustrates the power of integrating components.

Figure 4-19:
ScrollBars
working
with other
components
for
precision
control.

Chapter 5

Button It Up! Adding Buttons and Boxes to Forms

• •

In This Chapter

▶ Selecting button properties

▶ Adding graphics to a button

▶ Using check boxes

▶ Using radio buttons and radio groups

• •

*Y*ou don't have to go very far in a Windows application before you're required to click a button of one kind or another. Buttons are part of what a graphical user interface environment (GUI, to you acronym fans) is all about.

Buttons can be used to lead users through complicated situations by allowing them to react in the most primitive of ways: by punching something! Buttons are used for many Windows application tasks, including opening and closing dialog boxes and changing program settings such as fonts or colors.

No doubt, you're already using buttons extensively; now you can start controlling how they work in your own applications.

Adding a Button to a Form

The "plain vanilla" standard Windows button resides on the Standard page of the Component Palette. To place a button on a form, just follow these steps:

1. **Click the Button component button on the Standard page of the Component Palette.**

2. **Move the mouse pointer to the location on the form where you want to place the Button, and then click.**

   A Button component appears on your form.

Specifying Button Properties

As with all other C++Builder 3 components you find on the Component Palette, Button components have characteristics (such as color and size) that you set by using the Object Inspector. To load the properties of a Button component into the Object Inspector, simply select the component on the form by clicking it.

Setting Button text

The Caption property is an essential part of a button application. This property displays the button text that the user sees and indicates to the user the likely outcome of clicking a button.

By placing an ampersand (&) before any letter in the text of the Caption property of a Button component, you can use that letter as a menu *hot key*. This means that instead of clicking the Button with the mouse, you can press the Button's hot key in combination with the Alt key to essentially "click" the button. Here's an example of how you can do this:

1. **Select File⇨New Application from the main menu.**

2. **Press and hold the Shift key, and then click the Button component button on the Standard page of the Component Palette.**

   This "locks" the mouse pointer to the selected component for placing it on the form more than once.

3. **Place the mouse pointer within your new form, and click three times, each time in a different location on the form.**

   Move the pointer down slightly after each click so that the three new Button components don't overlap each other.

4. **To deselect the Button component button, click the Pointer button on the far-left side of the Component Palette button bar.**

5. **Click one of the Button components, and using the Object Inspector, enter the text string &abc into the Button component's Caption property.**

6. **Repeat Step 5 for the other two Button components using the text strings** a&bc **and** ab&c.

7. **Select all the Button components by holding down the Shift key and clicking each.**

8. **Click the Events tab on the Object Inspector, and then double-click the empty field next to the** OnClick **event handler.**

   This transports you to the Code Editor, where you type the following line:

   ```
   ShowMessage("Hi there!") ;
   ```

   Each of the buttons will display the text "Hi there!" when clicked by the program user.

9. **Compile, link, and run the program by pressing F9.**

   Each of the letters (a, b, and c) that was preceded by an ampersand is underlined, as shown in Figure 5-1.

Figure 5-1:
Here are three buttons all equipped with "hot keys" in their captions.

After you create the buttons in this example, press the Alt key and then a, b, and c in turn to see the buttons selected (pushed in). Don't forget that you can still click the buttons with the mouse, if you so choose.

As you place components onto a form, you can quickly align them (including buttons) by selecting all of the components and then using the Alignment Palette dialog box found under View⇨Alignment.

How properties affect a Button's behavior

Properties can affect the way that a Button component reacts. For example, if you set the Cancel property of a Button component to true using the Object Inspector, when the user presses the Esc key or clicks the button, the OnClick event (which is automatically created for you when you set the Cancel property to true) for that Button component is triggered.

Hello? Buttons to program!

Here's a Button component property that comes in handy if you are creating a dialog box in which your user performs a specific task and then, after that task is completed, closes the dialog box. The property is called ModalResult, and you find it by using the Object Inspector. This property enables a value to be returned by the buttons in a dialog box to the main form of your program.

The default value for the ModalResult property of a Button is mrNone (which pretty much does nothing). If you change this value to something else using the drop-down list in the Object Inspector, when the user clicks the Button, the ModalResult property of the Button is returned to the main form.

For example, if you provide a dialog box for the user to make an immediate decision, place two buttons in the dialog box — one with the ModalResult set to mrYes and the other to mrNo. When the user presses either of these buttons in the dialog box, the dialog box is closed, and the mrYes or mrNo result is returned accordingly.

If the Default property of the Button component is set to true using the Object Inspector, when the user presses the Enter key, the Button's OnClick event is triggered (see the following section, "Specifying a Button event").

By setting the Default property to true for one of the Buttons on a form, the user is free to move around all the buttons on the form by pressing the Tab key. A dotted line is shown around the caption text indicating which button is selected when the user presses Enter. (Refer to the top button in Figure 5-1.) The Button with this dotted outline is called the *focus button*.

Specifying a Button event

Button components must be capable of reacting to relevant actions (or *events* in programming-speak) going on within your program. You can define what happens as these Button events occur via the Events tab on the Object Inspector. The most critical event for a button is the OnClick event. This event tells the button what to do when the user clicks the mouse or presses a key combination that "selects" the button.

You can also play some tricks with Button events. Try this example for fun:

1. **Choose File⇨New Application to open a new form.**

2. **Click the Button component button on the Standard page of the Component Palette, and then click anywhere on the new form.**

3. **With the Button component still selected on the form, click the Events tab on the Object Inspector, and then double-click the empty field next to the** OnMouseDown **event handler.**

You're then in the Code Editor, where you enter the following line:

```
Button1->Caption = "I feel Down" ;
```

4. **Double-click the** OnMouseUp **event handler name in the Events page of the Object Inspector.**

Enter the following line in the Code Editor:

```
Button1->Caption = "I'm Up" ;
```

5. **Press F9 to run this example program.**

You can see that the caption of the Button component changes as you press and release the mouse button.

The previous example hints at two things: First, you can perform a task while a button is down and then stop the task once the button is released. Second, you can change the action of a button at runtime. Is this dangerous and confusing? That depends on how you change the action of the button.

Why place more buttons onto a form than you really need when you can save space on a form (and save yourself some work) by having one button do two things? (As long as the button isn't doing the two things at the same time, though!) This comes in handy for a program in which the user toggles (switches back and forth) between modes of operation — for example, from read-only to edit. The buttons in Figure 5-2 allow the user to set a program into edit mode by clicking the Edit button and then save any changes by clicking the Save button.

Figure 5-2:
With this
form, the
user can
easily
toggle
between
the two
buttons.

You can save some space in the form in Figure 5-2 by alternating the Caption property of a single Button between Edit and Save. In this example, the code in the OnClick event would look like this:

```
if (Button1->Caption == "&Edit" )
  {
  Button1->Caption = "&Save" ;
  // Do other code here

  }
else
  {
  Button1->Caption = "&Edit" ;
  // Do other code here

  }
```

This single-button approach produces a win-win situation — you don't have to worry about which button the user may press next, and the user is left in no doubt about the appropriate action to take because only one action is offered at a time.

Getting the Picture: Adding a Graphic to a Button

In this section, I demonstrate how to improve on the appearance of the rather bland Edit and Save buttons shown earlier in Figure 5-2. Wouldn't they look more interesting with a graphic or two?

Don't worry; you don't have to draw pictures for the buttons. You've got 162 graphics to choose from in the files found in the Program Files\Common Files\ Borland Shared Files\Images\Buttons folder. (You can find bitmap images there to suit most of your needs.) The graphics that I placed in the buttons to create Figure 5-3 are Edit.bmp and FileSave.bmp — the ones best suited to this purpose.

Figure 5-3:
Edit and Save: Two buttons made a bitmap better.

BitButton is a component that acts as a standard button, but allows you to embed bitmap pictures as well as text in a button. You can find the BitButton component button on the Additional page of the Component Palette.

You can put pictures into your BitButtons by using the somewhat strangely named `Glyph` property on the Object Inspector. Try using the steps in the following example:

1. **Click the BitButton component button on the Additional page of Component Palette.**

2. **Click a form in the location that you want to place the BitButton component.**

3. **With the new BitButton still selected on the form, select the `Glyph` property on the Object Inspector.**

   An ellipsis (. . .) button appears.

4. **Click the ellipsis button on the `Glyph` property to get the Picture Editor, shown in Figure 5-4.**

Figure 5-4:
The Picture Editor enables you to select a bitmap image for a BitButton.

5. **To select a bitmap graphic, click the Load button in the Picture Editor box to bring up a Load Picture dialog box. (If you are not in the directory called Common files\Borland Shared files\Images\Buttons, go to that directory and load the glyph.)**

6. **Locate the file that you want to use in the BitButton component by using the Load Picture dialog box, and then click the Open button.**

   This returns you to the Picture Editor, except that now your picture is visible in the center of the framed area of the Picture Editor.

7. **Click OK to close the Picture Editor.**

   The graphic that you selected is now displayed on the button.

> # Me and my shadow Glyph
>
> You may wonder why back in Figure 5-4 the graphic in the center of the Picture Editor box appears to be two images in one — the left half an icon with recognizable images, and the right half a mere shadow of the other side.
>
> This happens because the graphics that are shown on a button change according to the state of the button. The NumGlyphs property states how many images are within a Glyph (the default is two). One of the images is the complete one, which is shown to the user when the button is clickable. The second one is normally much dimmer (often grayed) and is shown to the user when the button has been disabled (the Enable property has been set to false). When the button is dimmed, it can't be clicked. And you thought you were seeing things!

By selecting one of the four Layout property options available to you in the drop-down list in the Object Inspector, you can determine exactly how the Caption and the Glyph should be placed in relation to each other on the button. The four layout choices are: blGlyphRight, blGlyphLeft, blGlyphTop, and blGlyphBottom. The result of all four choices is shown in Figure 5-5.

Figure 5-5:
Here, you can see the four Glyph Layout choices in action.

You can also modify the default of four pixels of space between button text and button image by using the Spacing property in the Object Inspector. If you set this value to -1, the picture and the text are evenly spaced on the button.

A useful property included in the BitButton is the Kind property — again, you gain access to this property using the Object Inspector. The Kind property offers 11 different settings, the results of which are shown in Figure 5-6. Setting this property not only chooses your Caption and Glyph properties (in other words, you have text and a picture already made for you), but also sets the ModalResult property of the button (see "How properties affect a Button's behavior" earlier in this chapter for details on the ModalResult property). Talk about a helping hand!

Figure 5-6:
The `Kind`
property
gives you 11
different
`Glyp` and
`Caption`
combin-
ations to
choose
from.

Working with SpeedButtons

SpeedButton components provide users with an alternative way of executing a task that can otherwise be accessed as a selection on a menu bar. The SpeedButton component provides a special type of button that usually displays a graphic. Because SpeedButtons also often appear in groups, they have special properties, such as `GroupIndex` and `AllowAllUp`, that enable you to manage clusters of SpeedButtons.

Many Windows applications make extensive use of speed buttons, usually by organizing SpeedButtons on a Panel component (refer to Chapter 4 for details on Panel components).

A cluster of speed buttons is shown in Figure 5-7.

Figure 5-7:
Does this
group of
SpeedButtons
look
familiar?

You can group SpeedButton components by using the `GroupIndex` property in the Object Inspector. SpeedButtons with their `GroupIndex` property set to the same value cooperate with each other so that only one button in a group can be depressed at any one time. When one of the SpeedButtons is clicked, any other depressed SpeedButton in the group pops up.

Using the Object Inspector, set the SpeedButton Down property for a group of SpeedButtons that you want to appear depressed (or selected) when the form is first shown in the program. You can also take control of SpeedButtons by setting the Down property from within your code by using this line:

```
SpeedButton1->Down = true ;
```

Note: This setting does not trigger the button's OnClick event. If it did, the program would perform the action that has been associated with the OnClick event. By setting the Down property in code, you're just changing the button's appearance.

You can set the AllowAllUp property to true if you want the user to be able to deselect all the buttons at once. If one of your program options must be in use at all times, don't use this property.

If a SpeedButton component has no text caption and just relies on a graphic to convey the SpeedButton's purpose, use the Hint property in the Object Inspector to enter some text to give the user a clue as to the button's function. Then, when the user passes the mouse pointer over a button, a label pops up identifying the button's purpose.

Give the SpeedButton component a test drive. Just follow the steps in this example:

1. **Select File⇨New Application for a new form.**

2. **Hold down the Shift key while you click the SpeedButton component button in the Component Palette on the Additional page.**

   This locks the component selection on the SpeedButton component.

3. **Click four times in line anywhere on the new form.**

   Four SpeedButton components are placed.

4. **Click the Pointer button on the Component Palette to "unlock" the component selection.**

5. **Use the Object Inspector to change the Caption properties for each SpeedButton.**

   Enter the < and > characters as shown in Figure 5-8 for the Caption properties. The resulting buttons resemble those you'd see on a VCR or CD player.

6. **Use the Object Inspector to enter a value of 1 into the GroupIndex property for each SpeedButton on the form.**

   Now each of the SpeedButtons on the form belongs to Group 1. Setting the GroupIndex property for each of the SpeedButtons to the same value gives them the look and behavior of a set of push buttons.

Figure 5-8:
Directional
arrows
were added
to these
SpeedButton
components
by using the
`Caption`
property.

7. **Click the SpeedButton at the far left in the row of four SpeedButtons, and using the Object Inspector, set the `Down` property for the SpeedButton to `true`.**

   If you follow the steps in this example, you end up with a set of buttons similar to those in Figure 5-9. You can see that the far-left button has the *focus;* that is, it looks selected.

Figure 5-9:
By using
SpeedButton
properties,
you can
give a
button
focus.

8. **Press F9 to run the program.**

   When you click an unselected button, the button in the depressed position automatically pops up.

Checking Out Check Boxes

At times, you may want your users to check off a list of items, or you may want to offer a list of settings that can be clicked to either on or off, true or false, or done or incomplete.

 CheckBox components, selected via the CheckBox button on the Standard page of the Component Palette, give you this ability. (Even though check boxes are not truly buttons, they have so much in common with button components that this chapter is the best place to cover them.)

You can place a check box on either side of a caption in a dialog box. In Figure 5-10, I put one check box to the right of the top caption and the rest of the check boxes to the left of the captions. (Use the `Alignment` property on the Object Inspector to make this kind of choice.)

Figure 5-10: What a to-do! Here's a check list with checked, unchecked, and grayed-out boxes.

If you use the Object Inspector to set the `AllowGrayed` property to `true`, the CheckBox component has three states: `cbChecked`, `cbUnchecked`, or `cbGrayed`. You can access these options via the `State` property on the Object Inspector. As you can see from Figure 5-10, a check box can be both checked and grayed out. Does this mean that I am not sure whether I have walked the dog? No, in this case, it means that I'm halfway around the park with the mutt. The task is neither completely done nor undone. If I didn't care how far I got with the dog, I would omit this halfway notation and set the state to the default value of `false`.

At the end of the day, I can check through the list I created in this example by using the `Checked` property to see which jobs are completed. You could do this in your own code by using the following:

```
if (CheckBox1->Checked == true)
  ShowMessage("Check Box1 is Checked !!") ;
```

Tuning in to RadioButtons

Radio buttons take their name from the old-fashioned car radio buttons that popped out as others in the set of buttons were pushed in. Like speed buttons, radio buttons normally come in groups. *RadioButton* components are used when you are looking to provide a set of choices to the user in which only one choice can be selected at a time. (Such as, how do like your coffee — black or au lait?)

You can select a RadioButton component by clicking the RadioButton component button on the Standard page of the Component Palette. After the RadioButton is selected, click a form to drop in the component. C++Builder 3 automatically groups radio buttons for you on a form or panel (and you don't have to limit yourself to just one set of buttons if you want more).

As with the CheckBox component described in the previous section of this chapter, use the Alignment property (on the Object Inspector) to choose which side of the RadioButton you want the Caption property text placed — either left or right. Examine the Checked property on the Object Inspector to see whether the RadioButton component is selected.

Follow these steps to include a RadioButton component in an example program:

1. **Select File⇨New Application for a new form.**

2. **Hold down the Shift key while you click the RadioButton component button on the Standard page of the Component Palette.**

3. **Click five times to form a column of five RadioButton components on your new form.**

4. **Use the Object Inspector to change the** Caption **property of each RadioButton to correspond to the five lines of text shown later in Figure 5-11.**

5. **Click the BitButton component button on the Additional page of the Component Palette.**

    This selects the BitButton component.

6. **Click the bottom center of your form to place a new button.**

7. **Using the Object Inspector, select** bkOK **from the drop-down list in the** Kind **property for the BitButton component.**

8. **Press F9 to run the program.**

The next steps in this example program create a *radio group,* so that your buttons can work as a team. The *RadioGroup* component offers a way of adding radio buttons while providing an integrated heading for the group at the same time.

Select the RadioGroup component using the RadioGroup button on the Standard tab of the Component Palette. Next, click on a form to drop in the RadioGroup component.

You can add RadioButtons to a RadioGroup by doing the following:

1. **Click the** Items **property on the Object Inspector.**

2. **Click the ellipsis button on the** Items **property to display the String list editor.**

    Each line of text that you add to the String list editor becomes a caption for a radio button in the RadioGroup component shown in Figure 5-11.

Figure 5-11:
Integrated group of radio buttons, courtesy of the RadioGroup component's Items property.

If you want to split a RadioGroup button into several columns, use the Columns property in the Object Inspector.

You can either set or read a selected radio button by using the ItemIndex property. If ItemIndex is set to -1, the user hasn't touched the button. The ItemIndex value for the first button in a RadioGroup component starts, in good old computer style, at 0 for the first selection. If you want to determine whether the first radio button was set in a RadioGroup component, you can use the following code:

```
if (RadioGroup1->ItemIndex == 0)
  ShowMessage("Radio Button 1 has been set !") ;
```

Chapter 6

Developing with the Additional Components

In This Chapter

▶ Limiting user input with EditMasks

▶ Displaying a graphic on a form with the Image component

▶ Shaping up to real effect with the Shape component

▶ Scrolling, scrolling, scrolling with ScrollBox components

▶ Getting a line on Grid components

The components that reside on the Additional page of the Component Palette may seem to be a mixed bag of items (which indeed they are). In this chapter, you can find example programs built with StringGrids and DrawGrids, plus Shape, Bevel, MaskEdit, Image, and ScrollBox components.

The examples in this chapter are also included as ready-made C++Builder 3 projects on the CD that's in the back of this book. So, if you want to instantly start testing the features covered in this chapter, you might want to delve into the delights on your *Borland C++Builder 3 For Dummies* CD. For instructions on how to install the CD source code, please refer to the Appendix.

So what do the Additional controls have in common? They're all standard components that Borland enhanced for added capabilities. (For example, the MaskEdit component is basically an Edit component with an input filter attached to it.)

Unveiling the MaskEdit Component

The term *mask,* in computer-speak, is a digital "overlay" of sorts that can be used to prevent a user from entering invalid data into a data field. Or, put another way, a mask is a mechanism that can help to validate data input.

The *MaskEdit* component allows you to construct patterns of code that restrict the type of characters that a user can enter into a MaskEdit text box.

To see how the MaskEdit component works, you first place a component on a form, as follows:

1. **Choose File⇨New Application from the C++Builder 3 main menu to get a new form in a new application.**

2. **Click the MaskEdit button on the Additional page of the Component Palette.**

3. **Click on the form where you want the MaskEdit control to appear.**

Entering EditMask property values

Understanding the MaskEdit component has a lot to do with understanding its `EditMask` property from the Object Inspector. Assume that a program requires a user to enter an account code that consists of exactly four letters, followed by four numbers. After placing a MaskEdit component on a form, you could do the following:

1. **Double-click the empty field next to the `EditMask` property in the Object Inspector, or click the ellipsis button (. . .) in the empty field.**

   This action invokes the Input Mask Editor dialog box (the property editor) shown in Figure 6-1.

— Option to save formatting characters

Mask characters loaded into `EditMask` property

Ready-made sample masks

Figure 6-1:
Here's the
Input Mask
Editor
dialog
box — the
property
editor
for the
`EditMask`
property.

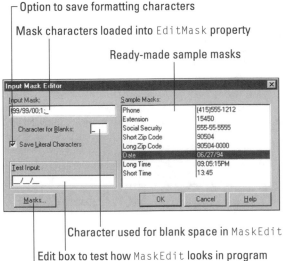

Character used for blank space in `MaskEdit`

Edit box to test how `MaskEdit` looks in program

Click to see sample foreign `EditMasks`

2. Enter the following value in the Input Mask field of the dialog box:

```
LLLL0000
```

The four Ls placed in the EditMask property restrict users to entering
only text characters in the first four positions and the four 0s (zeroes)
restrict a user to entering only numbers for the last four characters.
This means users could successfully enter ABCD1234, but not 12ABCD34
(in fact, users wouldn't be permitted to get past entering the first
character).

Table 6-1 summarizes the basic character code you can enter in the
EditMask property of a MaskEdit component. This code determines which
characters a user can enter into an edit box and in what position those
characters will appear.

Table 6-1	Character Code Used for EditMask Property
Mask Character	**Description**
A	Permits letter or number characters (for example, A–Z, a–z, 0–9 character ranges are permitted).
L	Permits letter characters only (for example, A–Z, a–z character ranges are valid).
0	Permits numeric characters only.
#	Permits numeric characters (including numbers with a plus or minus sign).
_ (underscore)	Inserts a character space in the MaskEdit text.
>	Converts all characters to uppercase until a < character is found.
<	Converts all characters to lowercase until a > character is found.
!	When entered as the first character in a mask, removes leading spaces (that is, character spaces) from strings loaded into the MaskEdit's Text property (for example, the four space characters at the beginning of the acbd1234 string would be removed).

Examining the property editor

You don't have to string a bunch of mask characters together inside the `EditMask` property before you can get a useful MaskEdit component. C++Builder 3 provides some ready-made masks for you. But in order to use them, you need to cruise around the Input Mask Editor a bit more. In case you didn't use the steps from the previous section, do the following:

1. **Choose File⇨New Form from the main menu.**

2. **Click the MaskEdit button on the Additional page of the Component Palette, and then click the mouse anywhere on form.**

3. **With the MaskEdit component still selected on the form, click the `EditMask` property in the Object Inspector, and then click the ellipsis button (. . .) for the property.**

These steps produce the Input Mask Editor dialog box.

In the example shown earlier in Figure 6-1, the Date mask is highlighted by clicking it. The Date mask's string of coded characters is then loaded into the Input Mask edit box in the upper-left corner of the window. The Mask entry is divided into three sections, or *fields,* separated by semicolons:

✔ The first field shows the mask characters.

✔ The second field (in this example, the number 1) indicates that you want to retain the formatting characters. For example, if you place a zero in the second field in this example, the slash (/) characters are not stored in the `Text` property for the MaskEdit.

✔ The underscore character in the third field represents characters not yet entered into the MaskEdit component by the user at runtime (an indication to users that they need to enter something here).

The following is a sample mask string that provides a MaskEdit component formatted for displaying a date:

```
!99/99/00;1;_
```

If you managed to resist the temptation to try out the Masks button in the lower-left corner of the Input Mask Editor (refer to Figure 6-1), go ahead and click it now. You will see an example of the international appeal of C++Builder 3 — the Open Mask File dialog box, shown in Figure 6-2. Mask files are available for 13 countries. When you choose one of these files, you see the appropriate time zone, postal rates, currency, and more information specific to that country.

Figure 6-2:
The Open
Mask File
dialog box
is where
you can find
masks for
different
countries.

Previewing how a mask looks in use

You can find out how a mask is going to look and react at design time by
using the Masked Text Editor. After you choose the Date mask, and with the
MaskEdit component selected, click the Text property in the Object Inspector. You'll see that an ellipsis button (. . .) has been added, which when
clicked opens the Masked Text Editor (see Figure 6-3). If you don't have a
mask entered into the EditMask property of this MaskEdit component, you
won't see much going on in there. If the date mask is chosen, it enables you
to test how the MaskEdit is going to look and act for real.

Figure 6-3:
Use the
Masked
Text Editor
to see how
the mask
looks at
design time.

In Figure 6-3, a Date mask from the Input Mask Editor (refer to Figure 6-1)
was selected and a date entered into the Input Text edit box (in short
format) for 20 March 1998. The contents of the MaskEdit component's
EditMask property are also shown in this dialog box, so you know what
your Input Text entry is being checked against.

TIP

Into the next millennium

Date entry is a hot issue right now, but ensuring that the applications you write in C++Builder 3 can clearly and easily handle dates after the year 2000 needn't take much effort. The EditMask component can easily help. Earlier in Figure 6.1, the Input Mask field showed the mask !99/99/00;1;_. Although this mask string is great for handling dates where the year needs to show only two characters, to bridge a change in century, change the mask string to !99/99/0000;1;_. With four zeroes now in the date mask, the user is required to enter a four-digit year, which neatly zaps the dubious date dilemma in a clear, simple, and easy way.

Putting the MaskEdit to work in a program

The following steps use the MaskEdit component to create an example age-checking program:

1. **Choose File⇨New Application for a new form.**

2. **Click the Label button on the Standard page of the Component Palette, and then click the form to drop a Label component onto the form.**

3. **Click the Button component button on the Standard page of the Component Palette, and drop a Button component onto the form.**

4. **Click the Panel button on the Standard page of the Component Palette, and then drop a Panel component onto the form.**

5. **Click the MaskEdit button on the Additional page of the Component Palette, and then drop a MaskEdit component onto the form.**

6. **Click the Label component, and press F11 to bring up the Object Inspector.**

7. **Click the** Caption **property in the Object Inspector and type** Please Enter Date of Birth.

8. **Click and drag the Label component to position it alongside the MaskEdit component.**

9. **Select the MaskEdit component, select the** EditMask **property in the Object Inspector, and then click the ellipsis button (. . .) to get the Input Mask Editor.**

TIP

See how the mask looks before you put it on!

Type any six digits in the `Text` property of the MaskEdit component using the Object Inspector, and then click the ellipsis button (. . .). Did C++Builder 3 display an `Invalid input value` message? If so, you entered text that was not in the format that the MaskEdit requires according to its `EditMask` property. If you choose a Date mask, as shown in Figure 6-1, the MaskEdit accepts entries in a date format only. The standard U.S. date format, for example, is MM-DD-YY, so 31 January 1998 must be entered as 01/31/98.

You can check how the edit line is going to look and react at design time by using the Masked Text Editor (refer to Figure 6-3). Don't forget to also use the Masked Text Editor first to check out any masks that you create yourself.

10. **Choose the Date mask from the list, and click OK to close the Input Mask Editor.**

11. **Click the Panel component, and then select the `alBottom` option from the `Align` property's drop-down list on the Object Inspector.**

    The Panel moves down to the bottom of the form.

12. **Size the Panel component by clicking and dragging out its top edge so that it can show a single line of text in its `Caption` property.**

13. **Click the background of the form.**

    The form's details are loaded into the Object Inspector.

14. **Click the Events page of the Object Inspector, and then double-click the blank `OnCreate` event for the form.**

    You're in the Code Editor, where you enter the following line of code in the event handler:

    ```
    MaskEdit1->Text = DateToStr(Now()) ;
    ```

    This code loads today's date into the date field as the program begins.

15. **Click the Button component button on the form, and then enter the text How Old Am I? into its `Caption` property in the Object Inspector.**

16. **Click the Events tab in the Object Inspector, and then double-click the empty field of the `OnClick` event handler to get into the Code Editor, where you enter the following:**

```
unsigned short nYear, nMonth, nDay ;
if (Now() < StrToDate(MaskEdit1->Text))
  {
  ShowMessage("Hey, you're not born yet ?") ;
  }
else
  {
  DecodeDate(Now() - StrToDate(MaskEdit1->Text),
    nYear, nMonth, nDay) ;
  Panel1->Caption = "You are " + IntToStr(nYear%100)
    + " years" ;
  }
```

This code is designed to figure out the difference between today's date and the date that you entered, and it places the number of years between them in the caption of the panel. (This nifty application comes in handy if the end user happens to be an insurance agent or financial planner.)

17. **Run the application by pressing F9, and enter some dates into the MaskEdit that was just built.**

    Don't forget to click the "How Old Am I?" button to perform the calculation that you placed in the OnClick event handler, the result of which is placed in the caption of the Panel.

Figure 6-4 shows the age-calculator application created using these steps.

When you run the example program and enter an invalid date, you may see a message that says something like Project Project1.exe raised exception class EConvertError. This is not actually an error. C++Builder 3 is checking your program and notifying you of an exception (see Chapter 18 for more on exceptions). Try running the program from outside C++Builder 3, or you can turn off the Exception Handling Mechanism by choosing Project⇨ Options and then deselecting the Enable Exceptions setting on the C++ tab page. Then you won't be bothered with this message.

Figure 6-4:
This is an age calculator program built with the MaskEdit and other components.

Working Out with the Shape Component

The *Shape* component on its own won't shake the earth from its axis (fortunately), but when fused with other components (plus a modicum of imagination and a smidgen of coding), it can end up being the life of the party.

 You can get a Shape component going by clicking the Shape button from the Additional page and then clicking a form at the location where you want the Shape component to be placed. With the component selected, you can check out its properties in the Object Inspector.

The Shape property

The Shape property determines how a component will be configured on a form. You select the shape that you want by clicking the Shape component placed on the form and then choosing from the Shape property drop-down list on the Object Inspector. You have a choice of the six shapes that are shown in the All Shapes, All Sizes box in Figure 6-5.

Figure 6-5:
The shapes
of things to
come:
Shape
property
assortment.

Height and Width properties

You can also adjust the size of a component. Just select the component and modify the Height and Width properties in the Object Inspector, or click and drag the edges of the Shape component to resize it as needed.

Pen and Brush properties

You determine the way that a shape is drawn by using the Pen and Brush properties in the Object Inspector. By setting the Pen property, you can control the way that the outline of the shape is defined. The Brush property fills the area contained by the shape.

The Pen property contains three subproperties:

✔ Width determines the thickness of the shape's outline.

✔ Color sets the tint of the outline.

✔ Style provides a range of fixed settings including psClear for no outline around the shape and psSolid for an unbroken outline. These options can be selected by using the drop-down list that appears in the Style property on Object Inspector.

The Brush property has only two subproperties: Color and Style. You can access these by double-clicking Brush in the Object Inspector. By using the Style property, you can fill in or clear the contents of the shape, and you can choose whether you want the shape to be filled with diagonal, horizontal, or vertical lines.

Creating a sample program

To create a Shape program of your own, you can use the following steps:

1. **Choose File⇨New Application to get a blank form in a new program.**

2. **Click the Panel button on the Standard page of the Component Palette, and then click the form to place the Panel component.**

3. **Set the Width property of the Panel to 40 and the Height property to 90 by dragging out the edges of the form.**

4. **Remove the Caption property text in the Object Inspector, and select clBlack from the Color subproperty drop-down list of the Brush property.**

5. **Place three Shape components in a vertical column on the panel by clicking the Shape button and then clicking the Panel component.**

   Click and drag each shape so that they each take up one-third of the panel.

6. **Set the Shape properties of the three components to** stCircle **by using the Object Inspector.**

You now have three circles stacked one on top of the other.

7. **Also in the Object Inspector, set the** Color **subproperties in both the** Brush **and** Pen **properties to** clRed, **set the** Name **to** Red **for the top circle, set the middle circle to** clYellow **and** Amber, **and set the bottom circle to** clGreen **and** Green.

8. **Click the Button component button on the Standard page of the Component Palette, and click the form to place a component.**

Repeat this step twice to drop in three buttons.

9. **Arrange the Button components on the form one above the other, next to the three Shape components by clicking and dragging the Button components.**

10. **Select the top Button component and enter** Ready **into the** Caption **property using the Object Inspector; do the same for the middle and bottom buttons, except enter** Steady **on one and** Go **on the other.**

11. **Double-click the top button to get into the Code Editor, and enter the following code:**

```
Red->Visible = true ;
Amber->Visible = false ;
Green->Visible = false ;
```

12. **Double-click the middle button, and enter the following code:**

```
if (Green->Visible!= true)
   Red->Visible = true ;
Amber->Visible = true ;
Green->Visible = false ;
```

13. **Double-click the bottom button, and enter the following code:**

```
Red->Visible = false ;
Amber->Visible = false ;
Green->Visible = true ;
```

The end result should look like Figure 6-6.

14. **Press the F9 key to run the program.**

To try out your new program, click the buttons to run the OnClick event handlers you've just written.

Figure 6-6:
Follow the steps for the Shape events exercise, and you can be your own traffic cop.

Getting the Picture with the Image Component

Whenever you want to display a graphic image on a form, you can do so by using the *Image* component.

To give the Image component a trial run, just follow these steps:

1. **Select the Image component by clicking the Image button on the Additional page of the Component Palette, and then click the form wherever you want the Image control to appear.**

2. **With the Image component selected, click the** Picture **property on the Object Inspector.**

3. **Click the ellipsis button (. . .) of the** Picture **property to invoke the Picture Editor dialog box.**

4. **Click the Load button to invoke the Load Picture dialog box.**

5. **Find and select the picture file that you want to use in the Image component, and then click the Open button.**

   The Load Picture dialog box closes, and the picture is shown in the Picture Editor.

6. **Click OK to close the Picture Editor, and load the Image into your picture.**

   You don't have to compile and run your application to view the image on the form.

If you set the Stretch property of an Image component to true using the Object Inspector, the image is proportioned to the size that you set for the Image component on the form. If the image is too large for the Image component and the Stretch property is set to false, the image is cropped so you see only part of it.

Mouse events, such as clicking and dragging, are the only events an Image component responds to; keyboard events just won't work with an Image component. (For more on mouse events, see Chapter 2.)

When you include an Image component in your program, C++Builder 3 also includes the image data as part of your program, which means you could end up with a very large .exe (executable) file. And, as you know, a very large .exe file takes a long time to load.

Making Your Forms Scroll

What happens when a user resizes an application and makes a form so small that he or she can't see all the components on the form? Not to worry — C++Builder 3 forms can display scroll bars automatically to allow users to scroll to see the entire form's contents. Try this example to see how it works:

1. **Choose File⇨New Application to begin a new form.**

2. **Click the Panel button on the Standard page of the Component Palette, and drop the component onto the form by clicking the form.**

3. **Use the Object Inspector to set the** Align **property of the Panel to** alTop.

4. **Click the SpeedButton button on the Additional page of the Component Palette, and then click the Panel component on the form.**

   Repeat this step three times to place a row of speed buttons within the Panel.

5. **Click the Button component button on the Standard page of the Component Palette, and then click in the lower-right corner of the form.**

6. **Select the form, and move the mouse pointer to the lower-right corner of the form until the pointer changes to a double arrow, and then click and drag to downsize the form until the Button component can't be seen.**

   When the button is no longer visible, scroll bars are shown above the panel with the speed buttons.

7. **Select the Button component in the lower-right corner of the form, and then choose Edit⇨Cut from the main menu.**

   The button moves into the Clipboard.

8. **Click the ScrollBox button on the Additional page of the Component Palette, and then click the form.**

9. **Set the ScrollBox component's `Align` property to `alClient` in the Object Inspector.**

   The ScrollBox component expands to fill the form.

10. **With the ScrollBox selected, choose Edit⇨Paste to place the Button component into the ScrollBox component.**

You won't see any difference in the form's appearance after placing the ScrollBox until you resize the form by clicking one of the form's edges and dragging. Now, when the user shrinks the form, scroll bars are contained within the panel, and the speed bar can be seen.

Using Bevels Instead of Panels

At times you may want to create separate areas on a form, but you may not want all the features of a Panel component. The component you want for simply creating defined areas within a form (without any other gadgets) is the *Bevel*.

The Bevel component does give you the 3-D look of a Panel component, but the Bevel component can't act as a container for other components. In fact, a Bevel is one of the few components that has no events whatsoever, so if you select a Bevel and click the Events tab on the Object Inspector, you won't find any entries.

This section describes the properties that you can set for a Bevel component whenever you need to create separate form areas, but don't need all the functionality of a Panel component.

Figure 6-7 (the box I call "Speak of the Bevel") shows various sample Bevel settings that you can select by using combinations of the Bevel Component's `Shape` and `Style` properties. The `Style` property can be set to either `bsRaised` or `bsLowered`, making it appear grooved or bumpy. The `Shape` property provides boxes, frames, or just a single line along one edge of the Bevel.

Try these steps to create a sample bevel effect using the Bevel component and its `Shape` property:

1. **Select File⇨New Application to create a new form.**

2. **Click the Bevel button on the Additional page of the Component Palette, and then click anywhere on the form to place a Bevel component.**

Shape - bsFrame
Style - bsRaised

Shape - bsBox   **Shape** - bsLeftLine
Style - bsRaised   **Style** - bsRaised

Figure 6-7:
Here are
some Bevel
components
and their
equivalent
settings.   **Shape** - bsBox   **Shape** - bsFrame
             Style - bsLowered   **Style** - bsLowered

3. With the Bevel component selected, set the Bevel's Align **property to** alTop **using the Object Inspector.**

4. Set the Bevel's Shape **property to** bsBottomLine.

You should end up with a horizontal groove dividing your form.

Drawing a Grid

The grid components, *DrawGrid* and *StringGrid,* that you find on the Additional page are somewhat like extended ListBox components (which are described in Chapter 3), but instead of housing just one column of information, they enable you to have almost as many columns as you want, which makes them useful for presenting multiple items of information of the same type.

 To place a DrawGrid component on a form, select the DrawGrid component by clicking the DrawGrid button on the Additional page of the Component Palette. Then click a form where you want the DrawGrid control to appear.

Column and row properties

To determine how many rows and columns you want in a grid (after you place a DrawGrid component onto your form), you need to set the ColCount property and RowCount property in the Object Inspector (you probably want more than the default five rows and five columns).

You can set fixed rows and columns by using the FixedCols and FixedRows properties. You can use these properties to create headers that remain in place as the other cells in the DrawGrid are scrolled in and out of view. Fixed cells can be distinguished easily by you and the program user because they have their own color-setting property — FixedColor — and they run along the top and down the left side of the DrawGrid.

To control the height and width of the cells, use the DefaultRowHeight and DefaultColWidth property setting from within the Object Inspector.

DrawGrid events

The code that you place in the OnDrawCell event handler is accessed within your program for every cell in the grid, so it gets called many times in the course of using the program. (Try to keep the code that you place in the OnDrawCell event handler to a minimum. You can really slow down drawing the grid if you include code that does not directly relate to the DrawGrid design.)

The following steps contain a fair amount of code, but result in a DrawGrid application that'll have others asking, "How did you get it to do *that?*"

1. **Choose File⇨New Application to get a blank form.**

2. **Click the DrawGrid button on the Additional page of the Component Palette, and then click anywhere on the form.**

3. **With the DrawGrid selected and using the Object Inspector, set the following properties to the values shown here:**

Property	Value
ColCount	3
DefaultColWidth	30
FixedCols	0
FixedRows	0
Font.Type	MS Sans Serif
Font.Style	Bold
Font.Size	14
Height	78
RowCount	3
ScrollBars	ssNone
Width	96

4. **With the DrawGrid component selected, click the Events tab on the Object Inspector, and double-click the empty OnDrawCell event-handler name field to get into the Code Editor.**

5. Enter the following in the Code Editor:

```
if (nGridArray[Col][Row] == 1)
  DrawGrid1->Canvas->TextRect(
      Rect,Rect.Left+7,Rect.Top+2, "X") ;
if (nGridArray[Col][Row] == 2)
  DrawGrid1->Canvas->TextRect(
      Rect, Rect.Left+7, Rect.Top+2, "O") ;
```

6. Double-click the empty onMouseDown **event handler name field, and enter the following in the Code Editor:**

```
int Col=0, Row=0 ;

DrawGrid1->MouseToCell(X, Y, Col, Row) ;

if (Counter%2)
  nGridArray[Col][Row] = 1 ;
else
  nGridArray[Col][Row] = 2 ;

Counter++ ;

if (Counter == 9)
    {
    for (int i=0 ; i < 3; i++)
      for (int j=0 ; j < 3; j++)
        nGridArray[i][j] - 0 ;

    DrawGrid1->Invalidate() ;
    Counter = 0 ;
    }
for (int i=0 ; i < 3; i++)
    for (int j=0 ; j < 3; j++)
      nGridArray[i][j] = 0 ;
```

7. Select the form by clicking its background.

The details of the form are loaded into the Object Inspector.

8. Click the Events tab of the Object Inspector, and then double-click the blank OnCreate **event field, and enter the following lines in the Code Editor:**

```
for (int i=0 ; i < 3; i++)
  for (int j=0 ; j < 3; j++)
    nGridArray[i][j] = 0 ;
Counter = 0 ;
```

Next, you add a couple of items to the form — a counter (to keep track of turns in the game) and an array of numbers to hold the game scoring. (Now you have an idea what this application is about.)

9. **Right-click anywhere in the Code Editor to bring up its speed menu, and choose the Open Source/Header File option.**

   The code header opens up the header file for this form. This is where the "blueprint" for the form is held.

10. **Use the down-arrow key to move the cursor to the line that says** `private` **in the header file now displayed in the Code Editor.**

11. **Enter the following line shown in bold into the header file:**

    (C++Builder 3 provides the other lines of code as part of creating the form for you.)

```
private:     // User declarations
  int nGridArray[3][3] ;
  int Counter ;
public:      // User declarations
```

12. **Press the F9 key to play a lively game of tic-tac-toe (see Figure 6-8).**

    Plus, when the board is full, it automatically starts a new game for you!

Figure 6-8:
With some event-handling code, you can create your own tic-tac-toe game.

StringGrids: More powerful than DrawGrids

When you place a *StringGrid* component on a form, you've introduced a grid monster. The StringGrid is the most powerful of the grids and probably is the one you're going to use most often. StringGrids share many of the properties of DrawGrids, but take organizing information in ordered cells one stage further.

Two properties differentiate the StringGrid from the DrawGrid — the Cells property, which refers to strings by referencing them by the Row and Column in which they appear in the StringGrid, and the Objects property, which can hold information as a reference. The reference can point to just about anything on the computer screen!

The following steps show you how to use the StringGrid component to construct an application that combines text and graphics in an orderly fashion:

1. **Choose File⇨New Application to get a new form.**

2. **Click the Panel button on the Standard page of the Component Palette, and then click anywhere on the form to place a Panel component.**

3. **Using the Object Inspector, set the component's Align property to alLeft, and remove the default text Panel1 from the Caption property of the Panel component.**

4. **With the Panel still selected on the form, click the Button component button on the Standard page of the Component Palette, and then click in the middle of the Panel to drop in a button.**

5. **Use the Object Inspector to enter the word Load into the Button's Caption property.**

6. **Click the Win 3.1 tab on the Component Palette, select the DirectoryListBox component button, and then click anywhere in the Panel to place a DirectoryListBox component.**

7. **Click the StringGrid button on the Additional page of the Component Palette, and then click anywhere in the background of the form to place a StringGrid component.**

8. **Using the Object Inspector, set the Align property of the StringGrid to alClient.**

9. **With the StringGrid selected on the form, use the Object Inspector to set the properties to the values shown in the following table.**

Property	Value
ColCount	10
DefaultColWidth	80
DefaultRowHeight	40
FixedCols	0
FixedRows	0
RowCount	10

10. **With the StringGrid still selected on the form, click the Events tab of the Object Inspector, and then double-click the empty name field of the** `OnDrawCell` **event.**

11. **You are now in the Code Editor, where you can enter the following code:**

```
if (StringGrid1->Objects[Col][Row]!= 0 )
  {
  StringGrid1->Canvas->Draw(Rect.Left + 10,
    Rect.Top + 20,
      (Graphics::TGraphic*)
        StringGrid1->Objects[Col][Row]);
  }
```

12. **Click the button that you placed on the Panel in Step 4, and double-click the empty** `OnClick` **event handler field in the Events page of the Object Inspector.**

13. **You end up back in the Code Editor, where you enter the following:**

```
int Col, Row ;
ffblk fbFileData ;
TPicture *picThis ;

String strPath =
  DirectoryListBox1->Directory + "\\";
String strWildCard = "*.bmp" ;
String strTemp = strPath + strWildCard ;

findfirst(strTemp.c_str(), &fbFileData, 0) ;

strTemp = strPath ;
strTemp += fbFileData.ff_name ;

for (Row=0; Row < 16; Row++)
  {
  for (Col=0; Col < 16 ; Col++)
    {
    StringGrid1->Cells[Col][Row] =
      fbFileData.ff_name ;

    picThis = new TPicture ;
    picThis->LoadFromFile(strTemp) ;
```

```
    StringGrid1->Objects[Col][Row] =
        (TObject*)picThis->Graphic ;

    findnext(&fbFileData);
    strTemp = strPath ;
strTemp += fbFileData.ff_name ;
    }  // for col
        }       // for row
```

14. Move to the top of this file in the Code Editor by pressing Ctrl+Home.

15. Enter the following two lines shown in boldface:

```
//----------------------------------
#include <vcl\vcl.h>
#include <Dir.h>
#include <Dos.h>
#pragma hdrstop
```

16. Press F9 to run the application.

17. Select the BUTTONS folder in which the button images are held.

Figure 6-9 gives you a big clue as to where that folder resides: It's in the Images folder within the Program Files\Common Files\Borland Shared folder.

Figure 6-9: Impress your users with StringGrids that display images as well as text strings.

18. Click the Load button.

You've just built the form shown in Figure 6-9.

This form shows the contents of each of the files that you can use for button graphics in C++Builder 3 applications — just in case you were wondering what the graphic behind each of these titles looks like. With the click of a button, this program shows both the name of the file and the graphic that's contained in the file — cool, huh?

Chapter 7

Dishing Up Menus

● ●

● ●

Menus of many sorts have long been part of computer programs. If you ever worked with DOS programming (think way back), you probably cringe at the memory of having to create menus by using alphanumeric characters. Fortunately, that's all in the distant past now that you have neat and civilized Windows menus.

Menus provide the means to simplify complicated choices — especially when those choices constantly change according to where you are and what you are doing in a program. The Borland C++Builder 3 main menu alone consists of over 100 items. That menu would make for an intimidating panel of buttons if buttons were the only way a user could make computing choices (and there'd be little space left on the screen for the program to show anything else). Menus offer you not only a method of providing a great many program choices for the user, but also a way to use computer screen "real estate" efficiently.

Among the menu types you can find in C++Builder 3 are these:

✔ The *main menu,* which is typically situated along the top edge of an application's main window (see Figure 7-1).

✔ The *pop-up menu,* so called because it pops up on the screen wherever you click the mouse (see Figure 7-2). You use C++Builder 3 pop-up menus whenever you right-click and a *context-sensitive* menu appears listing the most commonly used actions you can perform in a particular window. (I also refer to pop-up menus as *speed menus* because they appear on demand to help speed things along.)

The PopupMenu component is not displayed in any regular location on a C++Builder 3 form. Pop-up menus are displayed wherever you specify them in your program — typically at the current mouse pointer location.

Figure 7-1:
Check out the friendly and familiar C++Builder 3 main menu.

Figure 7-2:
A C++Builder 3 speed menu appears when you right-click the Code Editor.

Note: When you are trying out the features of C++Builder 3 that are explained in this chapter, you may want to use the examples included on the CD in the back of this book. Refer to the Appendix for instructions on how to install the CD and use its example projects.

The First Course: Main Menu Ingredients

The *MainMenu* component resides in the Component Palette's Standard page. You select a MainMenu component by clicking the MainMenu button and then clicking anywhere on a form.

You can use the MainMenu component to create MenuBars that appear at the top of your forms. Following are some sample steps to place a MainMenu component in a new application:

1. **Choose File➪New Application from the C++Builder 3 main menu to create a new C++Builder 3 form.**

2. **Click the MainMenu button on the Standard page of the Component Palette to select a MainMenu component, and then click anywhere in the new form to place the MainMenu component.**

3. **Click the background of the form.**

   If you look at the Object Inspector, you can see that the form's Menu property is automatically loaded with a reference to the new MainMenu component (MainMenu1). This saves you from having to link the MainMenu component to the form yourself. (You can see these properties by clicking the MainMenu component on the form and clicking the Properties tab on the Object Inspector.)

The MainMenu component's AutoMerge property comes into play only when you develop a MDI-type application in which an application has one main form containing all the other application forms. (See Chapter 3 for more on MDI-type applications.)

The MainMenu component's Items property houses the real action. The Items property is where each of the individual menu items are held. (In the next section of this chapter, you find out about the tools that C++Builder 3 provides to visually manage the individual MenuItem objects within the Items property.)

If you click the Events tab of the Object Inspector with the MainMenu component selected on the form, you may be surprised to see that no events whatsoever are listed there. So how do you accomplish anything with the MainMenu? Think of the MainMenu component as a candy box that just holds the goodies — the goodies in this case being a series of *MenuItem* objects that you add one by one.

Using the Menu Designer

To configure a MainMenu in C++Builder 3, click the MainMenu component on the form, and then click the ellipsis button of the Items property in the Object Inspector (or right-click the MainMenu component and choose the Menu Designer option from the SpeedMenu) to bring up the MainMenu's speed menu. Either way, you get the visual menu creation tool, the *Menu Designer,* shown in Figure 7-3.

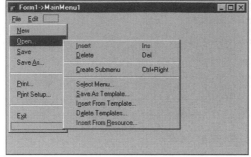

Figure 7-3:
Use the
Menu
Designer to
navigate
and
manage
MenuItems
for the
MainMenu
component.

The name of the MainMenu component that you are viewing (in this example, it's `Form1⇨MainMenu1`) is shown in the title bar of the Menu Designer window.

Figure 7-4 shows the properties for a MenuItem object loaded into the Object Inspector.

Figure 7-4:
Properties
for the
MenuItem
object
currently
selected in
the Menu
Designer
can be
viewed and
edited using
the Object
Inspector.

The following steps show you how to add MenuItems to a MainMenu component:

> 1. **Continuing with the previous example, click the MainMenu component on the form.**

2. **Right-click the MainMenu component to get the MainMenu component's SpeedMenu, and then select the Menu Designer option to open the Menu Designer window.**

   This also loads the Object Inspector with a new MenuItem and places the cursor on the `Caption` property for the new MenuItem.

3. **Using the Object Inspector, enter text into the `Caption` property of the new MenuItem object.**

   This is the text that appears in the first MainMenu item located at the far-left side of the menu bar for your form (for this example, I entered the word `File`, a logical choice).

4. **Press Enter.**

   You are ready to enter the text for the next menu item.

The Menu Designer automatically completes the `Name` property text for the MenuItem object by adding the numeral 1 to the end of the text that you enter into the `Caption` property. For example, if you enter the word `File` into the `Caption` property, C++Builder 3 loads the text `File1` into the MenuItem's `Name` property in the Object Inspector. This saves you the effort of having to compose and enter text for any of the Name properties in your MainMenu component's MenuItem objects.

✔ You can continue adding MenuItems simply by entering the text that you want to appear in the `Caption` property of the new MenuItem in the Object Inspector and then pressing Enter. This process can build the menu section shown earlier in Figure 7-1 in a matter of minutes (or seconds, if you're really dexterous).

✔ You can insert a menu item into a main menu by selecting MenuItem in the Menu Designer and then pressing the Insert key. This action positions a new MenuItem in the Menu Designer before the selected MenuItem.

✔ To remove MenuItems from a main menu, just click the MenuItem in the Menu Designer, and press Delete.

✔ After you add MenuItems, you can move any of them by clicking a MenuItem and dragging it to another MenuItem's position. When you release the mouse button, the MenuItem is placed where you dragged it, and the MenuItem originally there moves down one position in the MainMenu.

TIP

Adding action to a MainMenu

Naturally, you want your MenuItems to do something when selected by the user; however, MenuItems have only one event that can be accessed from the Events tab on the Object Inspector.

You can call on the trusty C++Builder 3 Code Editor to add event-handling code to the MenuItem by using the following steps:

1. With the MainMenu component selected, right-click the component for the speed menu, and select the Menu Designer option to get the Menu Designer window.

2. Go to the MenuItem to which you want to add code.

3. Select the MenuItem component, and then click the Events tab on the Object Inspector.

4. Double-click the empty field next to the OnClick event-handler to get into the Code Editor.

You can now enter the code that is executed when the user selects the MenuItem.

Creating hot keys and shortcuts

By using the Object Inspector to insert an ampersand (&) before a letter in a MenuItem's Caption property, you can create a "hot key" that the user can press to instantly choose a menu option — instead of having to scroll through a list of options — and click when the MainMenu is expanded. (The hot keys are identified by an underscore, so be careful not to use the same character twice in a single menu.) You can also add prefix characters to the MenuItems in the MainMenu on a form by editing the Caption properties in the Object Inspector.

You can easily link shortcut key combinations to each MenuItem object in a MainMenu component. First, using the Menu Designer, navigate to the MenuItem that you want to access. This action loads the MenuItem into the Object Inspector. Then, by using the ShortCut property's drop-down list on the Object Inspector, you can choose from among more than 80 key combinations, as shown in Figure 7-5.

Be careful not to associate the same shortcut with more than one menu option because the user can employ shortcuts at any time in the program, even when menu sections are not expanded. Figure 7-6 shows how the Menu Designer looks when shortcut keys have been associated with MenuItems.

Figure 7-5:
A list of
shortcut key
combinations
for a
MenuItem
is available
in the
Object
Inspector.

Shortcut combinations

Figure 7-6:
Shortcut
key
combinations
show up
alongside
the menu
items that
they trigger.

Grouping menu items

At times, you may want to group menu items together, or to look at it another way, keep menu items apart.

Here's how you insert a dividing line into a form's MainMenu component to group or separate items:

1. **Continuing with the previous example, click the MainMenu component on a form.**

2. **Right-click to bring up the MainMenu SpeedMenu.**

3. **Select the Menu Designer option from the SpeedMenu to show the Menu Designer window.**

4. **Navigate to the menu item that you want to place a dividing line above.**

5. **Press the Insert key to create a blank MenuItem object above the currently selected item in the column of menu items.**

6. **Enter a minus-sign character (–) in the `Caption` property on the Object Inspector.**

   As soon as you move off either the `Caption` property or the current MenuItem object in the Menu Designer by using the arrow keys or by clicking another item, a separator is inserted in the new MenuItem space that was created when you pressed the Insert key in Step 5.

The MenuItem's `Break` property lets you determine when you want to start another column of MenuItems within the same top-level menu item. Three `Break` property options — `mbNone`, `mbBreak`, and `mbBarBreak` — are available in the Object Inspector.

By default, the `Break` property is set to `mbNone`, which has no effect. By changing the `Break` property to either `mbBreak` or `mbBarBreak`, the selected menu section is divided into two columns with the current menu item in the Menu Designer shown at the top of the new column. You can create more than two columns, but then you would need to make the additional columns into subitems. (See the following section for more about subitems.) If you select the `mbBreak` option, empty space is inserted between the two columns. If you select the `mbBarBreak` option, a vertical rule is inserted between the two columns.

Separating menu items

To separate MenuItems within a MainMenu component, follow these steps:

1. **Select the MenuItem that you want to divide.**

2. **Follow Steps 1 through 4 from the section, "Grouping menu items," earlier in this chapter.**

3. **Select the desired `Break` property option from the Object Inspector.**

   I use `mbBarBreak` in the example shown in Figure 7-7.

4. **Press F9 to run the program, which puts the `Break` property into effect.**

With the steps outlined so far in this chapter, I created a menu that looks like the one in Figure 7-7. (In this example, the first MenuItem is called Fish, which expands to show you seafood entree items.)

Figure 7-7:
Dividing a
MainMenu
component
into two
sections is
a matter of
changing
only one
property in
the Object
Inspector.

When you have the Menu Designer displayed (refer to the section, "Using the Menu Designer"), right-clicking any item within the Menu Designer gives you the speed menu shown in Figure 7-8. Selecting the Create Submenu option from this speed menu results in a submenu that appears when you click the associated menu option.

Figure 7-8:
When you
right-click a
MenuItem
within the
Menu
Designer
window, a
speed menu
appears
with
additional
options.

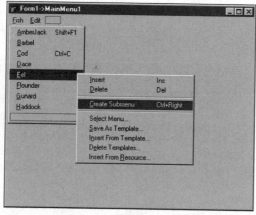

The right-pointing arrow next to the Eel menu option in Figure 7-9 indicates that a submenu exists within this item. If you add submenu items to a menu selection, the results look something like the submenu in Figure 7-9.

Figure 7-9:
Submenus
help you
arrange
menu
items and
save space
in your
windows.

Submenu

If a menu item that you are adding produces a dialog box or window of some sort when the item is selected by the user, indicate this to users by trailing an ellipsis (. . .) after the menu text. (Adding an ellipsis is a convention followed by most Windows programmers.)

Adding check marks to menu items

Each MenuItem object within a MainMenu component is capable of displaying a check mark next to its caption. The check mark is controlled by the MenuItem object's `Checked` property. Setting the `Checked` property to `true` (by using the drop-down list in the Object Inspector) displays a check mark; setting the `Checked` property to `false` removes the check mark.

The `Checked` property enables you to include true/false or on/off settings as part of a program's main menu. An example of this is in C++Builder 3 itself. The last two option items in the View menu can be toggled to make the Toolbar and Component Palette visible or invisible.

Placing radio item buttons in a menu list

Windows menus can be made to behave like radio buttons, which means only one item at a time can be selected from a menu group.

The following steps show you how to use the MenuItem's `GroupIndex` property and `RadioItem` property to create a just-pick-one setup in your MainMenu components:

1. **Add a group of MenuItems to the MainMenu component by following the steps in the section, "Using the Menu Designer," earlier in this chapter.**

2. Divide the MenuItems into groups by following the steps in the section, "Grouping menu items," earlier in this chapter.

3. Use the Object Inspector to set the `GroupIndex` property to the same value (any whole number except 0) and each `RadioItem` property to `true` for each of the new MenuItems.

Tick marks now show up as black dots similar to radio buttons to the left of the MenuItem caption. To determine which one of the MenuItems is selected, examine the `Checked` property in the Object Inspector.

Disabling menu items

At times, you may want to disable menu items when their options aren't currently needed. You can switch MenuItem objects on or off within C++Builder 3 by setting the MenuItem object's `Enabled` property in the Object Inspector to `true` or `false`. You can actually enable and disable MenuItems while the program is running by referencing MenuItem objects by name from anywhere in your code. The following line of code disables a MenuItem called `Options1`:

```
Options1->Enabled = false ;
```

With the MenuItem's `Enabled` property set to `false`, the MenuItem is grayed out, and the user can no longer choose that selection.

Adding and removing menu items

In addition to changing MenuItems at design time, you can also add or delete MenuItems at runtime. Because you have full access to the list of MenuItem objects via the MainMenu component's `Items` property, you can add the MainMenu component at runtime by using these steps:

1. Click the Button component button on the Standard page of the Component Palette, and then click anywhere on a form to place the button.

2. With the Button selected, click the Events tab of the Object Inspector, and then double-click the empty field next to the `onClick` event handler.

You're in the Code Editor, where you enter the following lines:

```
TMenuItem *NewItem=new TMenuItem(this);
NewItem->Caption = "New item";
NewItem->Checked = True ;
MainMenu1->Items->Add(NewItem);
```

3. Press F9 to run the program, and then click the button that you added to the form.

Each time you click the new button, menu items are added alongside the menu bar of the program.

If you want to add menu items within a File menu's drop-down list, just replace the last line of the code in Step 2 with the following line:

```
File1->Add(NewItem);
```

Make sure that you have a MenuItem named File1 in your MainMenu component. (In my example back in Figure 7-7, I actually called the File MenuItem Fish1!) As long as the reference to the MenuItem in the code matches the text entered in the Name property of the MenuItem on your form, you'll be okay.

Standardizing a menu

User-friendliness goes beyond creating versatile menus that are easy to figure out. Smart developers try to make all of their programs work the same way. For example, a user typically expects to exit a Windows application by pressing Alt+F and then X. That's a shortcut convention to include in your program if you want to be a "friendly" developer.

As users move from program to program, common menu headings speed things along, as do uniform captions for menu options and standardized shortcut keys. The following table shows you some standard menu headings and the menu items that go with them.

Menu Heading	Menu Items
File	New, Open, Close, Save, Save All, Exit
Edit	Undo, Cut, Copy, Paste, Delete
Help	Search, Contents, About

Creating menu templates

Standardizing menu items across all your programs doesn't have to mean added work on your part — C++Builder 3 menu templates enable you to store and retrieve menu sections for reuse with other applications. Talk about instant standardization!

You can gain access to the C++Builder 3 menu templates by following these steps:

1. **Select a MainMenu component on a form, and right-click it to bring up its speed menu.**

2. **Choose the Menu Designer option from the speed menu to open the Menu Designer window.**

3. **Right-click one of the MenuItems within the window to open the Menu Designer speed menu, and then choose the Insert From Template option.**

   The Insert Template dialog box, shown in Figure 7-10, appears.

Figure 7-10:
Menu
templates
speed your
development
while giving
your users
recognizable
menu
formats.

4. **Select the Window Menu option from the Insert Template list, and click OK.**

   C++Builder 3 inserts a standard Windows menu section (with options such as New Window, Tile, and Cascade) into your main menu.

The C++Builder 3 menu templates also enable you to store your own menu sections. So, now that you know where the menu templates live, you can add a menu template of your own. Just follow these steps:

1. **Activate the Menu Designer as described in Steps 1 and 2 in the previous list of steps.**

2. **Right-click a menu section to bring up the Menu Designer speed menu, and choose** `Save as Template`.

3. **Enter a name for your new Template into the Template Description edit box.**

4. Click OK.

That's all there is to it!

Before leaving main menus, just remember: If you are not happy with the way your menu is working out, you can easily insert, delete, or drag MenuItems around, reorder them, or move them into completely different menu branches by using your mouse.

Placing PopupMenu Components

Unlike main menus, you can place as many *PopupMenu* components within a form as you desire. PopupMenu components are triggered when a user right-clicks (or left-clicks with a left-handed mouse) into a form. The PopupMenu offers options that are relevant to the item that was clicked (in techno-terminology, it's called *context-sensitive help*).

Every control that's placed on a form has a `PopupMenu` property available. If you associate a `PopupMenu` property with a component, when users right-click the component, they see that specific PopupMenu component (but associating a PopupMenu with a component on a form is not mandatory). You can have a different `PopupMenu` property for each component on a form, but don't get carried away.

The following steps demonstrate how you can build a program using a PopupMenu component:

1. **Drop a PopupMenu component into a form by clicking the PopupMenu button on the Standard page of the Component Palette, and then click anywhere in the form.**

2. **Right-click the PopupMenu component to bring up its speed menu, and then choose the Menu Designer option.**

   You can now add MenuItems to the PopupMenu component in the same way that you'd add them to a MainMenu component (refer to the section, "Using the Menu Designer," earlier in this chapter for steps on how to add items to a main menu).

3. **Enter some text into the `Caption` property of each MenuItem.**

   For this example, "Amanita," "Boletus," "Coprinus," "Dermocybe," and "Entoloma" are used (see Figure 7-11).

4. **Select all the items in the Menu Designer by holding down the Ctrl key and clicking each of them.**

5. **Click the Events tab of the Object Inspector.**

Figure 7-11:
A pop-up menu in action.

6. **Double-click the blank field of the** `OnClick` **event in the Object Inspector to get into the Code Editor, where you enter the following:**

```
if (Sender->ClassNameIs("TMenuItem"))
  Panel1->Caption =
    dynamic_cast<TMenuItem*>(Sender)->Caption ;
```

Each of the menu selections now points to a single event handler.

7. **Click the Panel button on the Standard page of the Component Palette, and then click anywhere in the form to drop in a Panel component.**

8. **With the Panel component selected, click the Properties tab on the Object Inspector, and then click the** `PopupMenu` **property.**

9. **Select the PopupMenu component (**`PopupMenu1` **created in Step 1) from the** `PopupMenu` **property drop-down list on the Object Inspector.**

10. **Press F9 to run the program.**

You should see something like the example in Figure 7-11. When the program is running, right-click the Panel component on the form to bring up the PopupMenu control. As you select items from the PopupMenu, the `Caption` property of the Panel changes according to the code that you entered into the `OnClick` event in Step 6.

When you click a component's `PopupMenu` property drop-down list, you get a choice of not only the pop-up menus that reside on the current form, but also any others in your current C++Builder 3 project, which saves you from having to redefine some menus.

PopupMenu components can be modified at runtime in the same way that main menus are modified (refer to the section, "Adding and removing menu items," earlier in this chapter). You are free to add or remove items to and from pop-up menus as the program is running.

Merging Menus with MDI Applications

Earlier in this chapter, I warn against placing more than one MainMenu in the same form. Although that warning still stands, you may find that you have to work with multiple menus that are in different forms within the same application.

Suppose that you're developing an application that involves both text entry and drawing. You could use a *MDI application* (MDI stands for *M*ulti-*D*ocument *I*nterface). The main form (the *parent* form) of a program contains all the other forms (the *child* forms) in a MDI. For example, one child form may handle drawing and another may deal with word processing. Each of these child forms can contain its own MainMenu component, and sections of the child main menus can be merged with the parent's as they are used in the application.

To see how MainMenus are used in MDI-type applications, follow these steps:

1. **Create a new form in a new project by choosing File⇨ New Application from the C++Builder 3 main menu.**

2. **Set the** FormStyle **property of the new form to** fsMDIForm **using the drop-down list in the Object Inspector.**

3. **Click the MainMenu button on the Standard page of the Component Palette, and then click anywhere in the form to place a MainMenu component.**

4. **Right-click the MainMenu component, and then select the Menu Designer option from the speed menu that appears to open the Menu Designer.**

5. **Right-click the Menu Designer window to bring up its speed menu, and choose the** Insert From Template **option to get the Insert Template dialog box.**

6. **Choose File Menu from the list shown in the Insert Template dialog box, and then click OK.**

   This places a File Menu section in the Menu Designer for your MainMenu component.

7. **With the File Menu item selected in the Menu Designer, change the** GroupIndex **property in the Object Inspector to** 1.

8. **From the Menu Designer, double-click Open in the File menu to get into the Code Editor, where you enter the following:**

```
TForm2 *form2 ;
form2 = new TForm2(this) ;
form2->Show() ;
```

9. **Choose File⇨New Form from the C++Builder 3 main menu to add a second form to the project.**

10. **With the new form selected, choose** fsMDIChild **from the drop-down list of the** FormStyle **property in the Object Inspector.**

   The new form becomes a subform of the form created in Step 1.

11. **Click the Events tab of the Object Inspector, and then double-click the empty field next to the** OnClose **event handler.**

   You're in the Code Editor, where you enter the following:

```
Action = caFree ;
```

12. **Click the form created in Step 1.**

13. **Select File⇨Include Unit Hdr from the main menu to show the Include Unit dialog box.**

14. **Select** Unit2 **from the list, and then click OK.**

15. **Click the form created in Step 9, and then click the Panel button on the Standard page of the Component Palette.**

16. **Click the form, and then set the** Align **property of the Panel component to** alTop **using the Object Inspector.**

17. **Delete the text contents of the Panel component's** Caption **property.**

18. **Click the Memo button on the Standard page of the Component Palette, and then click anywhere in the background of the form created in Step 9 to place a Memo component.**

19. **Using the Object Inspector, set the** Align **property of the Memo component to** alClient.

20. **Click the MainMenu button on the Standard page of the Component Palette, and then click the background of the form created in Step 9 to place a MainMenu component.**

21. **Add an Edit menu template to the MainMenu component using the method described in the "Creating menu templates" section earlier in this chapter.**

22. **Select the Edit Menu option from the Insert Template window list, and click OK.**

23. **With the new Edit MenuItem selected in the Menu Designer, change the** GroupIndex **property to 3 using the Object Inspector.**

24. **Click the MainMenu component on the form, and then set the MainMenu component's** AutoMerge **property to** true **using the Object Inspector.**

25. **Click the SpeedButton component button on the Additional page of the Component Palette, and then click the Panel placed on the form created in Step 9 to add a SpeedButton component to the Panel.**

26. **You can also load a bitmap graphic into the** Glyph **property, if desired.**

   For this example, I use the graphic called FileOpen.bmp in the Program Files\Common Files\Borland Shared\Images\buttons folder. (Loading graphics into SpeedButton components is covered in Chapter 5.)

27. **Click the OpenDialog button on the Dialogs page, and then click the Panel placed on the form created in Step 9 to add an OpenDialog component to the Panel.**

28. **Double-click the SpeedButton that you placed on the form in Step 25 to get into the Code Editor, where you enter the following:**

```
OpenDialog1->Execute() ;
Memo1->Lines->LoadFromFile(OpenDialog1->FileName) ;
```

29. **Press F9 to run the application.**

   With the program running, click Open from the main menu of the form to show the child form. As the child form appears, so does its main menu, but the menu options that you placed in the MainMenu component on the child form are shown as part of the main form's menu.

That's the *merge* part of this program. Auto-merging offers you an easy way to present consolidated menu options to the user and a low-maintenance way to create an uncluttered menu bar in an application.

The preceding steps should produce a program that looks similar to the one shown in Figure 7-12. If you close the child form, you see that the menu options you placed in the MainMenu component of the second form are no longer displayed on the menu bar.

The values placed in the GroupIndex property of the MenuItem (which can be accessed from the Object Inspector) determine the priority of each MenuItem when auto-merging is performed. The auto-merging process moves from left to right along the menu bar, and the GroupIndex of any menu item must never be less than that of the menu item to its left. If you have matching GroupIndex values for items on the menu bar in your program's forms, when you merge the forms, the top-level menu item for the main form won't be visible.

Merged main menus   Child forms

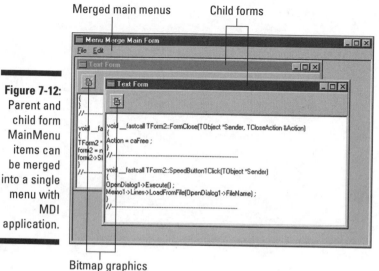

Figure 7-12:
Parent and
child form
MainMenu
items can
be merged
into a single
menu with
MDI
application.

Bitmap graphics

To take a stab at prioritizing MenuItems when auto-merging, try these steps
using the example program built in the preceding steps (Steps 1 through 29):

1. **Bring up the Menu Designer by double-clicking the MainMenu
   component on the first form built in the preceding list of steps.**

2. **Select the** File **MenuItem in the Menu Designer, and then change the**
   GroupIndex **property value to 2 in the Object Inspector.**

3. **Using the Object Inspector, double-click the** MainMenuClick **event for
   the second form built in the previous list of steps, and set the** Edit
   menu value of the child form to 2.

   When you run the application and start a child form, the main menu
   changes from File to Edit. It changes back to File again when the child
   form is closed.

If you start to get weird things going on during the merging of MDI menus,
don't blame some supernatural menu monster; the culprit's more likely to
be clashing GroupIndex values.

If you use the Object Inspector to set the AutoMerge property to true in the
MDI parent form, you won't see the menu for that form in your program; you
see the menu only at design time. Set the AutoMerge to true for only the
application's child forms.

Chapter 8
Building with Win32 Components

• •

In This Chapter

▶ Tracking program status using the ProgressBar component

▶ Conveying information with the StatusBar component

▶ Discovering a wealth of control with the RichEdit component

▶ Adding images with the ImageList component

▶ Viewing and organizing data entries with the ListView and TreeView components

▶ Creating multipage forms with the PageControl component

• •

*A*t the risk of stating the obvious, the Win32 page of the C++Builder 3 Component Palette houses controls that make it easy to construct (surprise!) a Windows 95- and Windows NT 4-style user interface.

In the interest of space, not every resident of the Win32 page gets coverage in this chapter. But I do make sure to include sample programs using the Win32 components that turn up most often in C++Builder 3 applications. You find out how to create Windows mainstays, such as progress bars, status bars, and "tree" structures for organizing files.

This chapter contains examples of some of the finest C++Builder 3 components. To get you up and running with these fine components, you may want to take a look at the C++Builder 3 project files for the examples in this chapter that are included on the CD at the back of this book. For instructions on how to install the CD source code, please refer to the Appendix.

Adding a Progress Bar to an Application

Keeping end users informed of what's going on is more than just a matter of being polite, especially when users have to wait for one program operation to end before they can continue with another. Ideally, a user should never have to wait too long for anything, but some tasks just aren't done in a hurry. Some users even resort to the "three-finger salute" (Ctrl+Alt+Delete) when an application appears to be ignoring them, when, in fact, the program is simply finishing up a long procedure.

Whether you're loading files, saving files, performing calculations, or conducting any other operation that takes a while to finish, think about adding a *ProgressBar* component to your application. A ProgressBar component displays exactly how much of a task is completed so the user isn't left wondering if the program will ever finish.

To add a ProgressBar component to an application, follow these example steps:

1. **Choose File⇨New Application to open a new form in a new project.**

2. **Click the ProgressBar button on the Win32 page of the Component Palette, and then click anywhere on the form to drop in the component.**

3. **Click the Label button on the Standard page of the Component Palette, and then click directly below the ProgressBar to place a Label on the form.**

4. **Click the Button component button on the Standard page of the Component Palette, and then click next to the Label component dropped onto the form in Step 3.**

5. **While the Button component is selected, change the** Caption **property of the Button to** Go To It! **in the Object Inspector.**

6. **With the Button component still selected, click the Events tab on the Object Inspector, and then double-click the empty field next to the** OnClick **event handler.**

   This action puts you in the Code Editor, where you enter the following lines of code:

```
for ( ProgressBar1->Position = 0;
      ProgressBar1->Position < ProgressBar1->Max ;
      ProgressBar1->Position++)
{
Label1->Caption =
   String(ProgressBar1->Position) + "%" ;
Application->ProcessMessages();
Sleep(100) ;    // simulates some real work!
}
```

7. **Press F9 to compile and run the program.**

   The end product should look like Figure 8-1. If you click the "Go To It!" button, you can see the progress bar gradually fill as the program whizzes around the for loop created in the code.

Figure 8-1:
Progress
bars, such
as this one,
tell users
how much
of a task is
completed.

And While You're at It, Add a Status Bar

Status bars are a handy way to provide pertinent information about an application to the user. You can create separate message compartments in a status bar by using the `Panels` property to convey information to the user unobtrusively. Status bars normally sit along the bottom of a form. In fact, the *StatusBar* component automatically drops to the bottom of a form when you first place it.

StatusBar components aren't to be confused with ProgressBar components. If a progress bar is running, the user has to wait for it to finish before doing anything else with the program. StatusBar components, on the other hand, provide information about the whole application in general and not just a single operation. (For example, if you click the C drive icon in the Window Explorer, a status bar tells you how much free disk space is available, what files are selected, and so on.)

The following steps use a StatusBar component to create an example status bar that welcomes users and tells the time:

1. **Click the StatusBar button on the Win32 page, and then click anywhere on a form (created using Step 1 in the previous section) to drop a StatusBar component onto the form.**

2. **Using the Object Inspector, double-click the `Panels` property of the StatusBar component.**

    The StatusBar Panels Editor dialog box appears.

3. **Click the Add button in the dialog box to add a panel to the form.**

4. **Type the text HH:MM:SS in the `Text` property using the Object Inspector to represent the time, set the `Width` property in the Panel's properties to `70`, and then choose the `Raised` setting from the `Bevel` property drop-down list in the Object Inspector.**

5. **Add a second panel to the StatusBar component by clicking the Add button, and then enter some text into the** Text **property using the Object Inspector.**

   In this example, Welcome... was entered into the text box.

6. **Click the Timer component button on the System page of the Component Palette, and then click anywhere on the form to drop in a Timer component.**

7. **Click the Events tab on the Object Inspector, and then double-click the empty field next to the** onTimer **event handler.**

   This puts you in the Code Editor, where you enter the following:

   ```
   StatusBar1->Panels->Items[0]->Text =
       Now().TimeString() ;
   ```

8. **Press F9 to run the application.**

   You should end up with a form similar to the one shown in Figure 8-2. The left panel contains the clock, which keeps time through the Timer component, and the Welcome... text sits in the right panel to show how easily you can display a message for users.

Figure 8-2:
Panels
made
with the
StatusBar
component
can be used
to convey
information
to the user
at a glance.

Adding Text with the RichEdit Component

By using the *RichEdit* component, you can allow the user not only to enter an unlimited amount of text, but also to make changes to the style of that text. In fact, the RichEdit component goes even further and provides paragraph formatting and built-in printing.

Much of the functionality in the RichEdit component shines through at runtime, which the following steps show you. Use these steps to build a simple word-processing form of your own:

1. Choose File⇨New from the main menu to get the New Items dialog box.

2. Select the Projects tab in the dialog box, and then click the SDI Application icon.

3. Click OK, and the Select Directory dialog box appears.

4. In the Directories tree view box, select the folder you want the files for this new project to be saved in, and then click OK.

5. Click the RichEdit component button on the Win32 page, and then click anywhere on the form to drop in a RichEdit component.

6. Using the Object Inspector, set the Align property of the RichEdit component to alClient.

7. Click the SpeedButton component button on the Additional page of the Component Palette, and then click the speed bar at the top of the form to place the newly selected SpeedButton component; repeat this step six more times.

8. Click and drag the SpeedButton components dropped onto the form in Step 7 to cluster the SpeedButton components in two groups of three and one individual button.

9. Using the Object Inspector, set the SpeedButton property values to those shown in the following table, using a different property name for each button.

Property Name	GroupIndex	Caption	AllowAllUp Setting
btnBold	1	B	true
btnUnderline	2	U	true
btnItalic	3	I	true
btnLeftJust	4	|<	false
btnCenter	4	=	false
btnRightJust	4	>|	false
btnPrint	0	None	false

Even though btPrint doesn't have its Caption property set here, you can assign SpeedButton components a graphic. Click the ellipsis button of the Glyph property using the Object Inspector to see the Picture Editor dialog box, and then click the Load button. You will find a selection of images in the \Program Files\Common Files\Borland Shared\Images\ Buttons folder.

10. Select the first three SpeedButton components on the form as listed in the table in Step 9 (btnBold, btnUnderline, and btnItalic) by clicking each while holding down the Shift key.

11. Click the Object Inspector's Events tab, and then double-click the empty OnClick event name field.

You're now in the Code Editor, where you enter the following lines:

```
TFontStyles fsThis ;

if (btnBold->Down)
  fsThis << fsBold ;
if (btnUnderline->Down)
  fsThis << fsUnderline ;
if (btnItalic->Down)
  fsThis << fsItalic ;

RichEdit1->SelAttributes->Style =
  TFontStyles(fsThis);
```

These lines of code make sure that the RichEdit component's text style is set according to the user's button selection at runtime.

12. **Select the second group of three buttons listed in the table in Step 9 (`btnLeftJust`, `btnCenter`, and `btnRightJust`).**

13. **Click the Events tab on the Object Inspector, double-click the empty field next to the `OnClick` event handler, and then enter the following in the Code Editor:**

```
if (btnLeftJust->Down)
  RichEdit1->Paragraph->Alignment = taLeftJustify ;
if (btnCenter->Down)
  RichEdit1->Paragraph->Alignment = taCenter ;
if (btnRightJust->Down)
  RichEdit1->Paragraph->Alignment = taRightJustify ;
```

These lines of code ensure that the proper text alignment is assigned to the appropriate RichEdit component. For example, you set `btnLeftJust` so that the text aligns left-justified.

At this point, the core of the application is complete. But to make this application look more polished, you can make the buttons reflect the current style of the text at the cursor location as the cursor moves around the RichEdit component.

14. **Click the RichEdit component, then click the Events tab of the Object Inspector, and then double-click the empty field next to the `OnSelectionChange` event handler.**

You're now in the Code Editor, where you enter the following:

```
btnBold->Down =
  RichEdit1->SelAttributes->
    Style.Contains(fsBold) ;
btnUnderline->Down =
  RichEdit1->SelAttributes->
    Style.Contains(fsUnderline);
```

```
btnItalic->Down =
  RichEdit1->SelAttributes->
    Style.Contains(fsItalic);

switch (RichEdit1->Paragraph->Alignment)
  {
  case taLeftJustify :
    btnLeftJust->Down = true ;
    break ;
  case taCenter :
    btnCenter->Down = true ;
    break ;
  case taRightJustify :
    btnRightJust->Down = true ;
    break ;
  }
```

Each button now reflects the font style and paragraph-alignment properties of the RichEdit component at the current cursor location as the user moves around the text.

To continue with the RichEdit example, you can add a printing feature to your program and save the text from the RichEdit component to a text file on your hard disk, and vice versa.

15. **Press F9 to run the program.**

16. **Double-click the Print SpeedButton component on the form (the last button that you added in Step 7).**

   You're now in the Code Editor, where you enter the following line:

```
RichEdit1->Print(Caption) ;
```

   Now you can add file-opening and file-saving features.

17. **Press F12 to move from the Code Editor to the Form Designer.**

   Next, you're adding some functionality to one of the program's menu options.

18. **Choose File⇨Open from the main menu in the Form Designer (not from the C++Builder 3 main menu).**

   You are now in the Code Editor and ready to modify the code that the C++Builder 3 template provides for you.

19. **Add the following lines (those shown in bold) to the event handler in the Code Editor:**

```
OpenDialog->Execute();
if (OpenDialog->FileName!= "")
  RichEdit1->Lines->LoadFromFile(
    OpenDialog->FileName) ;
```

Adding this code takes care of loading text from disk files into the program's RichEdit component. The user can select the file that he or she wants to load (open) by using the Open File dialog box that has been included in the OpenDialog component in the forms part of the application template.

20. Click the form, and choose File⇨Save.

Again, you go directly to the menu option's `OnClick` event handler in the Code Editor.

21. Add the following lines (those shown in bold):

```
SaveDialog->Execute();
if (SaveDialog->FileName!= "")
  RichEdit1->Lines->SaveToFile(
    SaveDialog->FileName) ;
```

22. Press F9 to run the program.

Enter any text that you like into the RichEdit control's area, and then use the program's speed buttons to change the appearance (bold, underline, and so on) and alignment of the text. Watch how the speed button settings change as you move the cursor from one style of text to another by pressing the arrow keys.

Figure 8-3 shows you what the program should look like. Choose File⇨Save and File⇨Open to save text to disk and then read the text by opening the file from the disk again. Don't forget that you can also print your text. How's that for functionality!

Figure 8-3:
Use the C++Builder 3 project template and the RichEdit component to create speed buttons that change the appearance of text.

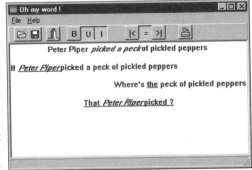

Getting the Picture with the ImageList Component

As its name implies, the *ImageList* component holds a collection of images — all of which are the same size. But you, the developer, won't see the images when using this component because ImageList is a nonvisual component (which means that the program's end user won't see the component directly either). However, the end user does see the actual images, which are usually small bitmap and icon files. This ImageList component must be placed on a form in order to be used by the components covered next — *ListView* and *TreeView*.

Use the following steps to load some sample graphics into an ImageList component:

1. **Click the ImageList button on the Win32 page, and then drop the component into the form by clicking anywhere on the form.**

2. **Right-click the ImageList component, and choose the ImageList editor option from the speed menu that appears.**

   The ImageList editor dialog box shown in Figure 8-4 appears. By using the Add, Delete, and Clear buttons in the ImageList editor, you can manage the images held in the ImageList component.

You can add a few images to the ImageList by clicking the Add button and then selecting image files using the Open dialog box that appears. (Most of the graphics that I use in Figure 8-4 are available in the C++Builder 3 subfolder, Program Files\Common Files\Borland Shared\Images\Icons.)

You can use the Delete button to remove the currently selected image within the ImageList editor, or if you want to completely start over, you can remove all images from the ImageList by pressing the ImageList editor's Clear button.

Figure 8-4:
The ImageList editor refines the appearance of graphic images.

If you choose a graphic that clearly shows the background color the image is displayed on, you can hide the background color by selecting it from the Transparent Color drop-down list. Your image then looks more natural when it's used in your program.

Organizing Data Items with the ListView and TreeView Components

The ListView and TreeView components make your applications even more user-friendly by allowing your end user to browse information visually.

The ListView component

The *ListView* component provides a way of presenting a list of data items to the user. You can associate a list of images with the data items in the ListView by using an ImageList component. The images are shown alongside each item in the ListView component.

Component properties

The descriptions for each data item in the ListView component are held in the `Items` property, which has its own property editor (the ListView Items Editor). This property editor, shown in Figure 8-5, allows you to view individual items within your ListView component at design time — these *items* are intuitively called ListItems!

ListItems contain a caption and data defined by your application. The caption contains a string, and the data (which can be an image) contains a pointer to a data structure associated with each ListItem.

Figure 8-5:
Use the ListView Items Editor to add items and associate graphics with them.

ListView Items Editor

Items: Earth, Chemical, Earth Station, Industry

New Item | New SubItem | Delete

Item Properties
Caption: Earth
Image Index: 0
State Index: -1

OK | Cancel | Apply | Help

To make sure the ListView operates as intended, each item in the list needs a picture. Enter the ImageList index number of the associated image into the Image Index text box (refer to Figure 8-5).

The graphic part of a ListView component is handled by an ImageList component that's loaded with the images that you want to use in a ListView (see the section, "Getting the Picture with the ImageList Component," earlier in this chapter).

The ImageList component serves as an image container for the ListView component and is associated with the ListView component by either the LargeImages property or SmallImages property. Both of these properties have drop-down lists on the Object Inspector from which you can select any ImageList component that has previously been set up on the form. Which of these two properties you use depends on the ViewStyle property setting from the Object Inspector.

The ViewStyle property has four settings — vsIcon (which uses the LargeImages property) and vsList, vsReport, and vsSmallIcon, all three of which use the SmallImages property. LargeImages shows items in the ListView as complete icons, whereas SmallImages shows columns of entries with a less-detailed icon next to the item's text.

If you want the user to be able to select an entry in the ListView, but not make any changes to data items in a ListView component, set the ReadOnly property of a ListView component to true using the Object Inspector. The user won't be able to change the caption of a selected data item.

Component events

The ListView component's onChange event can be used to find out which item the user selected, and the onChanging event can be used to hold code that you want executed prior to moving from the currently selected data item to the new data item.

Try these steps to construct a working program that shows three different ways of using a ListView component:

1. **Select File⇨New Application from the main menu to open a new application.**

2. **Use the steps outlined in the "Getting the Picture with the ImageList Component" section of this chapter to drop an ImageList component into the new form.**

3. **Click the ListView button on the Win32 page, and then click anywhere on the form to drop a ListView component onto the form.**

4. **Click the Panel button on the Standard page of the Component Palette, and then click anywhere on the form to drop a Panel component onto the form.**

5. **Using the Object Inspector, select** alBottom **from the Panel's** Align **property drop-down list.**

6. **Click the ListView, and use the Object Inspector to select the** ImageList1 **value from the** SmallImages **property drop-down list.**

7. **Using the Object Inspector, select the** vsList **option from the** ViewStyle **property drop-down list.**

   Now to create the data items that will populate the ListView.

8. **Still using the Object Inspector, double-click the ListView component's** Items **property to open the ListView Items Editor dialog box.**

9. **Click the New Item button in the dialog box, and then type any text you like for the caption of the new data item being created.**

10. **Enter a number in the Image Index text box in the ListView Items Editor dialog box according to the index of the graphic that you want to display.**

    The graphic appears next to the text entered in Step 9 in the corresponding ImageList component.

    When you add images to an ImageList, the image is assigned a number according to its order in the list. That number is the *index* of the graphic. When you add the images to the ListView, you can click the Apply button to see which image you're associating to the list.

11. **Repeat Steps 9 and 10 for as many items (such as text that corresponds to the image or data) that you want to add to your ListView component.**

12. **With the ListView component selected, press Ctrl+C to place a copy of the component on the C++Builder 3 Clipboard.**

13. **Press Ctrl+V twice to place two copies of the component on the form.**

14. **Click and drag the ListView components and arrange them in a horizontal row on the form.**

15. **Click the middle ListView component in the row; then using the Object Inspector, select** vsReport **from the** ViewStyle **property's drop-down list.**

16. **Add one column header to the second ListView component by double-clicking the** Columns **property on the Object Inspector to activate the ListView Editing dialog box.**

17. **Click the Add button in the ListView Columns Editor dialog box to add a column entry called** 0 – TListColumn **to the ListView component, and then click the new column entry with the mouse and type** Items **in the** Caption **property text box on the Object Inspector.**

18. **Click the far-right ListView component in the row, and then use the Object Inspector to select the** vsIcon **option from the** ViewStyle **property's drop-down list.**

19. **Use the Object Inspector again to choose the ImageList component from the** LargeImages **property drop-down list.**

20. **Select all three ListView components, click the Events tab of the Object Inspector, and then double-click the blank event name field for the** OnChange **event.**

    This action takes you into the Code Editor, where you enter the following line:

    ```
    Panel1->Caption = Item->Caption ;
    ```

21. **Press F9 to see the ListView components in action.**

    You should end up with a form like the one in Figure 8-6.

Figure 8-6:
C++Builder 3
lets
you add
graphics to
ListView
components.

The TreeView component

The *TreeView* component expands on the ListView component by allowing you to also visually organize program data. If you examine the Windows Explorer, you can see that it uses a branching "tree" structure that allows users to navigate to folders within folders, and files within folders, with just a click. (This functionality is what the TreeView component adds to your applications.) By building these trees into your applications, you can visually represent hierarchical relationships to make it easy for users to choose and manipulate any type of data item.

TreeView component properties

The TreeView component boasts 36 properties, so I'm limiting myself to discussing the most important ones here.

But first, follow these steps to add a TreeView component to a program:

1. **Select File⇨New Application from the main menu to create a new application with a blank form.**

2. **Click the TreeView button on the Win32 page, and then click anywhere on the form to drop in a TreeView component.**

3. **Use the steps in the section, "Getting the Picture with the ImageList Component," earlier in this chapter to populate an ImageList component with images associated with the TreeView component.**

4. **To load the ImageList with three images associated with the TreeView component, first click the** Images **property of the TreeView component on the Object Inspector, and then click the down arrow to select** ImageList1.

   You can find the images you need in the Program Files\Common Files\ Borland Shared\Images\Icons folder.

5. **Double-click the TreeView's** Items **property on the Object Inspector to enter data into the TreeView.**

   This action displays the TreeView Items Editor shown in Figure 8-7.

Figure 8-7: The TreeView Items Editor enables you to manage TreeView items.

6. **Click the New Item button in the TreeView Items Editor dialog box to add a blank item to the Items ListBox.**

7. **Enter the text associated with the new tree item into the Text box.**

   For the example in Figure 8-7, England was entered at the highest level of the tree. (If this tree item has an image, the Image Index setting should be 0; if no image is assigned to the tree item, it should be -1. The negative value is used to indicate that no image is associated with this item; a value of 0 refers to the first image in the ImageList component list.)

8. **Click the New SubItem button in the TreeView Items Editor dialog box.**

   This action creates a blank field below the item that you just created.

9. **Enter a name for the blank field in the Text box, and then enter 1 in the Image Index box.**

   In this example, I entered London and typed 1 in the Image Index box because I want the city item to display a different graphic than the country item. (You would not necessarily enter 0 for the first level image setting and then 1 for the next branch; it depends on how the images are organized in the ImageList.)

10. **Once again, click the New SubItem button in the TreeView Items Editor dialog box.**

    This action takes you down to the next item level, where you can enter a name for the blank SubItem. For this example, I entered a street name.

11. **Repeat Steps 6 through 10 to add more TreeView items to the TreeView component on the form, and then click OK to close the Items Editor.**

    You can add more items and set different properties as you like from the TreeView Items Editor dialog box.

12. **Press F9 to run the program.**

After making a start with the preceding steps, you can examine some of the more important TreeView component properties in greater depth.

When you set the SortType property to true, the tree is sorted in alphabetical order. If you use the drop-down list in the Object Inspector for this property (as opposed to setting the property in your code), your options are stNone, stText, stData, and stBoth. Selecting one of these choices triggers the TreeView component to check that the tree is in alphabetical order.

The StateImages property allows you to associate an ImageList component with the TreeView component so that you can display an image with an item's text that reveals the status of that TreeView item. Suppose that you have a customer whose account has been placed on hold. You can use a suitable image to reveal that this customer's account needs attention.

Figure 8-8 shows how setting TreeView component properties can dramatically change the look of the TreeView in your programs.

Figure 8-8:
By using
the Object
Inspector
and
TreeView
Items
Editor,
you can
vary the
presentation
of the
TreeView
compo-
nents.

The Selected property, which is available only at runtime, holds the TreeView item that is currently highlighted or selected by the user's having clicked on it. (You need to know which item the user has chosen at runtime when you are using the TreeView event handlers, which I discuss in the next section.)

TreeView component events

Select a TreeView component, and then click the Events tab on the Object Inspector. More than 25 TreeView event handlers appear. You can read about some of these event handlers in this section.

The OnChange event

The OnChange event is triggered any time that the user changes anything in a TreeView component. For example, this event can be used for code that loads text in other components (such as EditBoxes and Labels) on a form. You can also use this event to place the contents of a data table field into other components on a form according to the selected item on the TreeView component.

The following steps use the form created in the earlier section, "TreeView component properties," to show you how the onChange event can be used to control other components on a form:

1. **Click the Label button on the Standard page of the Component Palette, and then click anywhere on the form to place a Label component.**

2. **Click the TreeView that was placed on the form created in the earlier section, "TreeView component properties."**

3. **Click the Events tab of the Object Inspector, and then double-click the empty field next to the** OnChange **event handler.**

   You end up in the Code Editor, where you enter the following line:

   ```
   Label1->Caption = Node->Text ;
   ```

4. **Press F9 to run the application.**

   As you move from item to item, the text in the Label component that you just placed on the form changes to the text of the currently selected TreeView item.

The OnChanging event

Another useful TreeView event is the OnChanging event. The OnChanging event is called prior to leaving a TreeView item after the user has selected another TreeView item.

You can use the argument AllowChange in the OnChanging event handler to decide whether the program will allow the user to move from the current TreeView item. The following code example shows how you can use the OnChanging event handler to enforce *user-entry validation*. (If a user clicks one item in a tree and then wants to click another item, before C++Builder 3 highlights the second item, you can place code in the onChanging event handler to check whether the user is allowed to view details of the item they have clicked. Such safety features are easily accomplished by entering code in the OnChanging event.)

```
//------------------------------------------------
void __fastcall TForm1::TreeView1Changing(
    TObject *Sender, TTreeNode *Node,
        bool &AllowChange)
  {
  if (Edit1->Text == "")
    AllowChange = false ;
  }
```

The OnExpanded event

The OnExpanded event can be invaluable for building trees "on demand" — that is, when the user decides to expand a particular TreeView item. TreeViews can be slow if they load up all the many branches of the tree, especially when just a few are going to be used. Loading subitems on demand through the OnExpanded event can save time when the program initially loads your TreeView data.

Adding TreeView items using code

If you want to add items to your trees on the fly, you can use the following steps:

1. **Click the Button component button, and then click the form that was created in the earlier section, "TreeView component properties," to drop a new Button component onto the form.**

2. **Click the Events tab on the Object Inspector, and then double-click the empty field next to the** OnClick **event handler.**

3. **Enter the following lines in the Code Editor:**

```
TreeView1->Items->Add(
   TreeView1->Selected, "New Node");
TreeView1->Items->AddChild(
   TreeView1->Selected, "New Child Node");
```

4. **Press F9 to run the program.**

   Every time you click the new button, two new items are added to the TreeView component. One TreeView subitem is added to the currently selected item, and one new item is added on the same level and directly after the currently selected item.

Creating a Multilayer Form with the PageControl Component

The *PageControl* component gives you the means to create multiple-layer forms so that you can pack far more components into a form than you could otherwise. You can access these form layers, called *pages,* by selecting a *tab* or label at the top of the component. (This is something you've done numerous times already; the pages of a Component Palette are accessed this way.)

Components can be added to each PageControl page in the same way that you add components to any form. By using a PageControl component, you can neatly pack the functionality of many forms into a single, easy-to-use form.

The following set of steps shows you how to use a PageControl component to add a number of pages to a single form:

1. **Choose File⇨New Application from the C++Builder 3 main menu to get a blank form.**

2. **Click the PageControl button on the Win32 page, and then click anywhere on the form to drop in a PageControl component.**

   Initially, the PageControl looks just like a panel.

3. **Using the Object Inspector, select** `alClient` **from the** `Align` **property's drop-down list, and then right-click the PageControl component.**

4. **Select the New Page option from the speed menu that appears.**

   A new page is added to the PageControl component. The Object Inspector is now loaded with a new tabbed page called `TabSheet1`; these tabbed pages are objects with their own set of properties and events.

5. **Using the Object Inspector, change the text in the** `Caption` **property to something more meaningful than the default name** `TabSheet1`.

   For this example, the page was labeled `Page 1`.

6. **Repeat Steps 4 and 5 twice to add a couple more pages to the form.**

7. **Click the PageControl component.**

   When a PageControl component contains pages, you must click in the top section of the PageControl component next to the tab headers to select the component.

8. **Press F9 to run the application.**

Now you can click from page tab to page tab to view the contents of various pages on the form. In Figure 8-9, see how you can make use of this multipage application.

Figure 8-9: The PageControl component lets you build multiple pages on a form to make the most of the limited screen space.

Part III
Wiring Your Building with More Components

The 5th Wave   **By Rich Tennant**

THE FIRST GRAPHICAL USER INTERFACE COPYRIGHT LAWSUIT.

OH HEY—GREAT STUFF, MERLIN! SWIRLING VORTEX, FLAMING SKULL, HARBINGER TOAD—JUST LIKE THE CALDRON USED BY THOSE THREE WITCHES UP ON THE HILL.

In this part . . .

C++Builder 3 offers even more components that you can use "right off the rack" to turbocharge your programs. With the step-by-step example format, you find out how to choose the right components for the job and then how to link them together to create robust applications.

This part guides you through building dialog boxes and applications for managing files and folders (then you'll really feel like a Windows programmer). You get the powerful Borland Database Engine really revving so that you can visually integrate database functionality into your programs.

When you know how to access your data, you'll want to show the information to the end user in a presentable way. C++Builder 3's integrated QuickReport components provide a smooth path to constructing reports that you can connect to databases. Want to add some multimedia files to your programs? That's covered here, too, plus you can find out how to link and embed OLE objects (some high-end developing for when you get really brave).

Chapter 9

Talking about Dialog Box Components

*T*he Dialogs page of the Component Palette is home to ten components that won't knock you out when you place them on a form at design time, but watch out — these performers have talents that really shine come runtime when you activate them.

Dialog box components provide easy ways for you to get your application users opening and saving files, accessing fonts, and choosing colors, as well as the many aspects of printing and printer handling. Using these dialog components not only speeds up your application development, but also provides consistency in the way your programs look and work. When your users need to perform a task of some kind using a dialog box, they won't have to wonder how Box A works versus how Box B works. In addition, the dialog box components let you to create intuitive programs that allow your end users to manipulate files without a lot of fumbling around.

Accessing Dialog Box Components

When you place a dialog box component on a form, you need a way of telling the dialog box when to make its appearance in the program. You can display a dialog box at any point in your program; you just need to execute it by placing a line of code such as the following in your program:

```
OpenDialog1->Execute() ;
```

All dialog boxes have the same call — `Execute()`. The name of the dialog box component in the call varies, of course, depending on the type of dialog box involved. (For example, a Font dialog box call is `FontDialog1-> Execute();.`)

If you have not already ventured into the goodies that are on the CD that's in the back of this book, you might want to take a look at the three C++ Builder 3 project files that are included on this CD specifically for the examples that are in this chapter. For instructions on how to install the CD source code, please refer to the About the CD Appendix.

Adding an OpenDialog Component to a Form

Most applications involve a user accessing data from a disk, making changes to the data in some way, storing the work back to a disk, and then keeping the whole conglomeration organized through a system of files and folders. The *OpenDialog* component provides an easy way for you, the programmer, to provide file access in your programs. Most Windows applications follow a standard layout in order to open files, so it just makes sense that yours should, too. Figure 9-1 shows you what an *OpenDialog* component looks like when it's running.

Figure 9-1: Check out an OpenDialog component in action.

To try out an OpenDialog component in a program, create this sample application using the following steps:

1. **Click the OpenDialog button on the Dialogs page of the Component Palette.**

2. **With the OpenDialog button selected, click anywhere on a form to place an OpenDialog component on the form.**

   The OpenDialog component is the first in the line of components on the Dialogs page.

3. **With the DialogBox component still selected and using the Object Inspector, enter** txt **into the** DefaultExt **property of the OpenDialog component.**

This step determines the file extension that will be automatically appended to any filename that your program user enters. If the user gets specific enough to add a file extension, the user is calling the shots — the file extension the user enters overrides your original one.

Using the Filter property, you can stipulate a list of file types that an OpenDialog component is most likely to use within the context of your program. To set up a list of the most likely candidates, follow these steps:

1. **With the OpenDialog component selected on a form, click the** Filter **property, and then click the ellipsis (. . .) button on the Object Inspector.**

You get the Filter Editor dialog box as shown in Figure 9-2, which is the editor for the Filter property.

Figure 9-2:
Open only
the files
that you
want by
using the
Filter Editor.

Filter Editor	
Filter Name	Filter
Text File	*.txt
Rich Text Files	*.rtf
Mystery Files	*.X
Rank and File	*.rnk
Data File	*.dat

OK   Cancel   Help

In the Filter Name column of the Filter Editor dialog box, you have room for a brief description of the file type; you enter the actual filter in the right column. (For more details on how to use filters, see Chapter 12.)

2. **Add the following filters to the Filter list, and then click OK.**

Filter Name	*Filter*	*Index*
Text files	*.txt	1
Rich Text files	*.rtf	2
Mystery files	*.X	3
Rank and Files	*.rnk	4

The user can choose from one of the listed filters in the OpenDialog component while the program is running. The Open dialog box then displays only the files of the selected filter type.

3. **Set the** `FilterIndex` **property value to** 2 **in the Object Inspector.**

   After you fill up the Filter Edit dialog box in Step 2, the `FilterIndex` property is set to a value of 1 — the default filter that is used initially by the DialogBox at runtime. But in this example, the `FilterIndex` property is set to 2, so the filter with an Index of 2 becomes the Rich Text files as declared in the table in Step 2.

   Just to keep you on your toes, the `FilterIndex` property index starts at 1 (the default) and not 0, as you might expect.

4. **Click the Memo button on the Standard page of the Component Palette, and then click anywhere on the form to drop in a Memo component.**

5. **Using the Object Inspector, set the** `Align` **property of the Memo component to** `alBottom`**.**

6. **Click the Button component button on the Standard page of the Component Palette, and then click the form above the Memo component that was placed in Step 4.**

   This step places a Button on the form.

7. **Using the Object Inspector, set the** `Caption` **property of the Button component to** &Open**.**

8. **Click the Events tab of the Object Inspector, and then double-click the empty field next to the** `OnClick` **event handler.**

   You're in the Code Editor, where you enter these lines:

   ```
   if ( OpenDialog1->Execute() )
     Memo1->Lines->LoadFromFile(OpenDialog1->FileName) ;
   ```

   The first line of the previous snippet of code shows the OpenDialog component to the user. If the user clicks OK in the Open dialog box, a return value of `true` is passed back from the dialog box (it's checked using the `if` statement). To explain this example code in plain English (or *pseudo-code,* as it's called):

   ```
   If the OpenDialog returns true then
     load the memo component with the file named in the
           OpenDialog
   ```

9. **Press F9 to run the program.**

10. **Click the button to kick the OpenDialog component into action; then select any file, and click OK on the OpenDialog component.**

    The contents of the Open dialog box's chosen file are loaded into the Memo component.

Adding a SaveDialog Component to a Form

The *SaveDialog* component button sits next to its partner, the OpenDialog button, on the Dialogs tab page of the Component Palette and is used in much the same fashion.

In this section, you build on the example program steps listed in the previous section of this chapter. The steps that follow demonstrate how you can add file-saving capability to your programs by using the SaveDialog component:

1. **Click the SaveDialog button on the Dialogs page of the Component Palette, and then click the form created in the previous section to drop a SaveDialog component onto the form.**

2. **Using the Object Inspector, set the SaveDialog component's properties as shown in the following table:**

Property	Setting
DefaultExt	txt
Filter	Text Files, *.txt
Options ofOverwritePrompt	true
Title	My Save Dialog

3. **Click the Button component button on the Standard page of the Component Palette, and then click next to the Button on the form created in the previous section to place a new Button on the form.**

4. **Using the Object Inspector, enter &Save into the** Caption **property of the new Button component.**

5. **Click the Events tab of the Object Inspector, and then double-click the empty field next to the** OnClick **event handler.**

   You end up in the Code Editor, where you enter the following:

   ```
   if ( SaveDialog1->Execute() )
     Memo1->Lines->SaveToFile(
       SaveDialog1->FileName) ;
   ```

6. **Press F9 to run the program.**

You now have a simple text editor. Figure 9-3 shows an example of how your program may look with some text entered into it. Have a go at loading and saving some files.

Figure 9-3:
You can
create a
basic text
editor
almost as
fast as you
can say
"Open" and
"Save."

Styling Text with a FontDialog Component

The fifth button on the Dialogs tab page of the Component Palette leads you to the *FontDialog* component. A Font dialog box enables you to incorporate font changes within your applications and gives your application users the ability to choose from any of the available Windows fonts. Figure 9-4 shows you how much action is packed inside one little dialog box.

Figure 9-4:
The Font
dialog box
is a familiar
sight to
Windows
users.

The FontDialog component loads the fonts that are available for your particular Windows installation. Where does it get this list of fonts? That depends on the setting of the `Device` property. The fonts that the user can select varies according to the device where fonts are viewed — a screen, a printer, or both. You can place some restrictions on the fonts that users may select by employing the `MaxFontSize` and `MinFontSize` properties. (Or check out the property options that are available in the C++Builder 3 online help system.)

Sixteen font setting options can be included in the Font dialog box, such as check boxes to turn type styles on and off and options to show or hide the font example window.

When you set the `fdApplyButton` subproperty of the `Options` property to `true` using the Object Inspector, you enable a runtime Apply button in the FontDialog component. You can then use the `OnApply` event in the Events page of the Object Inspector to place some code. Then when you click the Apply button, a relevant action occurs according to the settings that are available. The `OnApply` event is typically used to make the font of a component or set of components the currently selected font for the FontDialog.

Use the following steps to put the FontDialog component to work to build a simple font-selection application:

1. **Choose File⇨New Application from the main menu to open a new form.**

2. **Click the FontDialog component button on the Dialogs page of the Component Palette, and then click anywhere on the form to place a FontDialog component.**

3. **Click the Panel button on the Standard page of the Component Palette, and then click anywhere on the form to drop in a Panel component.**

4. **Using the Object Inspector, set the `Align` property of the Panel component to `alTop`, and enter some text in its `Caption` property.**

   In Figure 9-5, you can see that the popular adage (courtesy of Noël Coward) "Mad dogs and Englishmen. . . ." is used.

5. **Using the Object Inspector, change the Button component `Caption` property to `Set Font`.**

6. **Click the Events tab on the Object Inspector, and then double-click the empty field next to the `OnClick` event handler. When you're in the Code Editor, enter the following lines:**

```
if (FontDialog1->Execute())
  Panel1->Font = FontDialog1->Font ;
```

7. **Click the FontDialog component, double-click the `Options` property to expand the list within the Object Inspector, and then from the drop-down lists for the `fdApplyButton` and `fdEffects` subproperties, select `true`.**

8. **Click the FontDialog component, click the Events tab on the Object Inspector, and then double-click the empty `OnApply` event field.**

   You're in the Code Editor, where you enter the following line:

```
Panel1->Font = FontDialog1->Font ;
```

9. Press F9 to run the program.

The program in this example should end up looking something like mine in Figure 9-5.

Figure 9-5:
You will find
it's much
easier to
change
a font
using the
FontDialog
component.

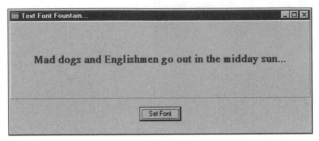

You can try out all the fonts and color combinations that you like from the Font dialog box that appears when you click the Set Font Button, but don't forget to try out the Apply button in the dialog box to see what effect that has.

Adding a ColorDialog Component to a Form

What's your favorite color? If you answer green, do you mean jade green, lime green, or the color of the Chicago River?

Whenever you need to offer a color choice within a program, you can allow your end users to pick their favorite tint by offering them the fully functional *ColorDialog* component.

 The button for the ColorDialog component (shown in the margin) sits next to the FontDialog button on the Dialogs page of the Component Palette. It spawns the rather fabulous Color dialog box, shown in Figure 9-6.

The `Color` property designates one color setting in the dialog box, and a handful of options is available through the `Options` property — the most interesting of which are listed in the following table.

Figure 9-6:
The
ColorDialog
component
shows its
true colors.

Option	Description
cdFullOpen	Gives the ColorDialog component access to an extended color palette (the custom color selector in Figure 9-6).
cdPreventFullOpen	Restricts the ColorDialog component to a set palette of colors.
cdShowHelp	Adds a Help button to the ColorDialog component.

To see how applications can perform with pigments, use the following steps:

1. **Choose File⇨New Application from the main menu to open a new form.**

2. **Click a Panel button, a Memo button, and a Button component button on the Standard page of the Component Palette, and then click anywhere on the form after clicking each button to place these components.**

3. **Click the Memo component, click the** ScrollBars **property in the Object Inspector, and then click the down arrow and select** ssVertical.

4. **Click the ColorDialog button on the Dialogs page, and then click anywhere on the form.**

5. **Click the Panel component and in the Object inspector, set the** Align **property to** alTop, **and clear the Panel's** Caption **property.**

Custom colors and hexadecimals

The CustomColor property controls all those tints, tones, and shades that have no names, but seem to be limitless in number.

The color information is stored in the CustomColor property using a string format with one line holding one color. Here's how you create the string format:

Enter the name of the string and then an equal sign (=), followed by the color's six-character *hexadecimal* equivalent.

The hexadecimal is broken down into three groups of two numerals with each group representing the amount of blue, green, and red (respectively) that, when mixed, result in the desired color. To make these combinations easier for the computer to process, each number is held in a hexadecimal format (base 16). The numerals 10 through 15 are represented by the letters A through E, and certain letter and color combinations equate to a numeric value that represents a color. It would take pages of this chapter to explain the many details of the base-16 numbering system, but you can try using the following hexadecimal CustomColor property colors:

```
white=FFFFFF
blue=FF0000
green=00FF00
red=0000FF
black=000000
```

The right section of the Color dialog box is where the user can concoct custom colors at runtime (refer to Figure 9-6). You can set up 16 custom colors at a time, indicated in the grid near the lower-left corner of the Color dialog box.

---

6. **Click the Memo component, and then set its Align property to** alTop **in the Object Inspector.**

7. **Click the Button component button on the Standard page of the Component Palette, and then click the lower part of the form to place a Button component.**

8. **Click the Button component, and then change the** Caption **property of the Button to** Set Color **using the Object Inspector.**

9. **With the Button component selected, click the Events tab on the Object Inspector, and then double-click the empty field next to the** OnClick **event handler to get into the Code Editor, where you enter the following lines:**

```
if ( ColorDialog1->Execute() )
  {
  Panel1->Color = ColorDialog1->Color ;
  Memo1->Lines->Assign(ColorDialog1->CustomColors);
  }
```

10. **Click the ColorDialog component, expand the** `Options` **property in the Object Inspector by double-clicking it, and set** `cdFullOpen` **within the** `Options` **property to** `true`**.**

11. **Press F9 to run the program.**

    The form's custom color information is contained in the Memo component, which I call Favorite Color Form for this example (see Figure 9-7).

Figure 9-7:
The behind-
the-scenes
code for
creating
some
custom
colors.

12. **Click the Set Color button on the form to invoke the Color dialog box, and then choose a color.**

13. **Click the Define Custom Colors button (grayed out in Figure 9-6) to select several custom colors on the right side of the Color dialog box, and then click the Add to Custom Colors button.**

14. **Close the Color dialog box by clicking OK.**

Printing with the PrintDialog and PrinterSetupDialog Components

Before Windows came along, adding another printer to a DOS program could be a developer's worst nightmare. You were forced to deal with all the nuances and quirks of each printer yourself!

Two components in the Dialogs tab — *PrintDialog* and *PrinterSetupDialog* — make printer setup torture a thing of the past.

Using the printer components in an application

The following steps make use of the PrintDialog and PrinterSetupDialog components within an application:

1. **Choose File⇨New Application from the main menu to open a new form.**

2. **Click the Panel button on the Standard page of the Component Palette, and then click anywhere on the form to drop in a Panel. Using the Object Inspector, remove the text from the** Caption **property of the Panel, and set the** Align **property of the Panel to** alTop.

3. **Click the SpeedButton component button on the Additional page, and then click the Panel you just placed; then repeat this step to place a second SpeedButton component onto the Panel.**

4. **Click the PrinterSetupDialog button on the Dialogs page, and then click anywhere on the form.**

5. **Click the PrintDialog button on the Dialogs page, and then click anywhere on the form.**

   You could also add a graphic to each of the SpeedButtons by assigning their Glyph properties. (See Chapter 5 for more information on Glyphs.)

6. **Click one of the SpeedButton components, click the Events tab on the Object Inspector, and then double-click the empty field next to the** OnClick **event handler.**

   This step puts you in the Code Editor, where you enter the following line:

   ```
   PrinterSetupDialog1->Execute() ;
   ```

7. **Click the other SpeedButton, click the Events tab on the Object Inspector, and double-click the empty** OnClick **event handler field. Then enter the following line in the Code Editor:**

   ```
   PrintDialog1->Execute() ;
   ```

8. **Press F9 to run the application.**

   When you run the program, you can start each of the dialog boxes by clicking their corresponding buttons. For example, when you click the button associated with the PrinterSetupDialog component, you get the dialog box shown in Figure 9-8.

After the PrinterSetupDialog component is added to your program, the user gets the Print Setup dialog box shown in Figure 9-8, which displays the name of a printer currently selected as the target printer for any file the user outputs. The Name drop-down list shows the choice of available printers. (If you're connected to a network, a number of printers is shown on the list.)

Figure 9-8:
The
PrintSetup-
Dialog
component
is the place
to pick a
printer.

Clicking the Properties button in the Print Setup dialog box produces a configuration dialog box for the printer that you selected. This dialog box can change according to the current target printer. Other options allow the user to set the size of the paper and the orientation (tall or wide) of the printed image.

More options with the PrintDialog component

After the trial run with the PrintDialog component in the previous section, you may be in the mood for another example of how to put this component to work. If you have a taste for more Print programs, continue on with the example application built in the previous section.

Click the SpeedButton that you associated with the PrintDialog component — the dialog box shown in Figure 9-9 appears. This dialog box is used for setting up a print job before it's handed over to the Windows 95 Print Manager.

Figure 9-9:
Here's
where the
print job
setup takes
place.

The top section of the dialog box shown in Figure 9-9 refers to the printer itself, so if you need to redirect a print job at the last minute, you can do so. (The Properties button is also thrown in for good measure for a more complete printer dialog box configuration.)

The various subproperties of the `Options` property of a PrintDialog component, which you can view on the Object Inspector at design time, define how the dialog box appears to your program users. These subproperties are listed in the following table.

Option	*Action*
`poPrintToFile`	Shows the Print To File check box.
`poPageNums`	When set to `true` from the Object Inspector at design time, provides a Pages radio button (refer to Figure 9-9). From and To edit boxes are enabled to allow the user to set a page range for printing on the Print dialog box.
`poSelection`	Enables the Selection radio button for printing only highlighted text.
`poWarning`	Generates a warning message if you try to print to an uninstalled printer.
`poHelp`	Displays a Help button in the Print dialog box.
`poDisablePrintToFile`	If PrintToFile is set to `true`, you can temporarily disable the check box by using this setting.

The PrintDialog component's `PrintToFile` property is set to `true` whenever the Print To File check box is selected by the end user.

The drop-down list of options available in the Object Inspector for the `PrintRange` property refer directly to the All, Page, or Selection radio buttons on the Print dialog box that the user sees. You, as a programmer, would need to know the setting of this property (if the user has selected all pages or a range of pages) when the user closes the Print dialog box. To determine the status of these properties, you can use code such as

```
if ( PrintDialog1->PrintRange == prAllPages )
  {
  // Take appropriate action to print all pages here
  }
```

The FromPage and ToPage properties refer to the corresponding edit boxes of the Print dialog box. Use these properties according to which pages of a document are to be output or printed. After the user closes the Print dialog box, you can use the FromPage and ToPage properties in your code as follows to handle the current printing job:

```
for (int i=PrintDialog1->FromPage;
    i < PrintDialog1->ToPage+1; i++)
  {
  // Code to print each page here
  }
```

The following steps extend the example program created earlier in this section to get some actual text on paper:

1. **Click the RichEdit component button on the Win32 tab of the Component Palette, and then click anywhere on the form.**

2. **Using the Object Inspector, set the RichEdit component's** Align **property to** alClient.

3. **Click the button associated with the PrintDialog component, click the Events tab on the Object Inspector, and then double-click the** OnClick **event-handler name and change the code to the following:**

```
if ( PrintDialog1->Execute() )
  RichEdit1->Print(Caption) ;
```

4. **Press F9 to run the program, and then enter some text in the Rich Text editor.**

   After you enter text into the RichEdit component on the form and set the print options in the Print dialog box in the program, when you close the Print dialog box, a printed page of the text you entered is output.

Chapter 10

Creating Database Applications

· ·

· ·

*T*he data components in C++Builder 3 offer you an easy way to retrieve, manipulate, and store data in a robust application that knows its way around databases. More than one dozen database-related components fill two whole pages of the Component Palette — the Data Access and Data Controls pages. In the interest of space, I picked out the "workhorse" data components — Table, Query, DataSource, DBLabel, DBEdit, DBMemo, DBGrid, and DBNavigator — to cover in this chapter.

The C++Builder 3 data controls speed your development *and* supply all-important functionality to applications that include database tables. Components that your program users work with directly, such as the Labels, DataGrids, and EditBoxes, are located on the Data Controls page. Those components depend on certain other components from the Data Access page to provide the actual data from the databases.

Integrating database access within your applications is one of the really cool features of C++Builder 3. You can get a jump-start on the road of success with database access by using the several example projects included on the CD that's in the back of this book. Please refer to the Appendix for more details on how to use your *C++Builder For Dummies* CD.

A distinction needs to be made between two groups of components. Data Control components are *visual* components — you actually see them at design time, and your end user sees them when working with your application. Data Access components are *nonvisual*. When you drop one onto a form, what you see is an icon in place of the component; your end user doesn't actually see the component, but the program gains some behind-the-scenes functionality from the addition of the component. (You find more about this topic a bit later in this chapter.)

Before you can dive into building database applications, you need a brief introduction to the Borland Database Engine and the C++Builder 3 SQL Explorer.

Revving Up the Borland Database Engine

In the bad old days of programming, your program had to recognize the exact format that its data was in to gain access to that data. Then the program was restricted to using only that particular data format, unless you wanted to do a major rewrite of your program!

The Borland Database Engine (BDE) liberates you from this data communication confinement. The BDE acts as a go-between for your applications and databases. Essentially, it's a set of files that enables C++Builder 3 to access databases. Whether your data is held in Paradox or dBASE tables, or any other type of format, all of that data are basically just fields that contain raw data that are held in records that are held in tables.

The BDE needs to know which types of tables you want to access, however, and for this purpose, it requires a *driver* (a single piece of software that can access a certain type of data-file format). Most of the drivers that you're ever going to need are provided with C++Builder 3, especially those drivers for accessing data stored locally on your hard disk, which is what you read about throughout this chapter.

So, how do you get to see these drivers? You can easily configure the BDE for the databases that you want to access from your application. To access database objects from C++Builder 3, you need to define BDE *alias.* An alias acts as an intermediary between your program and your database tables. (An alias can also be used by more than one program on your machine.)

The following steps show how to configure the BDE to use a database:

1. **Choose Start⇨Programs⇨Borland C++Builder 3 from the Windows 95 taskbar.**

   You then see a program called BDE Administrator.

2. Click the name of the program to run it.

You get a window similar to one shown in Figure 10-1.

3. If Databases are not already visible, expand the Databases tree view by clicking the + sign, and then click BCDEMOS.

Each database entry is called an *alias* and represents a particular folder where your data is stored. Instead of having to remember long path names that reference databases, you can simply refer to the alias, which will connect you to the database. Figure 10-1 shows how aliases in the BDE Administrator represent short names or nicknames for folders that hold data tables. The folder information is held in the PATH entry.

4. Select Object⇨New from the BDE Administrator's main menu to bring up the New Database Alias dialog box with STANDARD as default, and then click OK.

A new database alias entry called STANDARD1 will be added to the Databases window of the BDE Administrator.

Database Alias names   Alias database driver type   Alias folder path

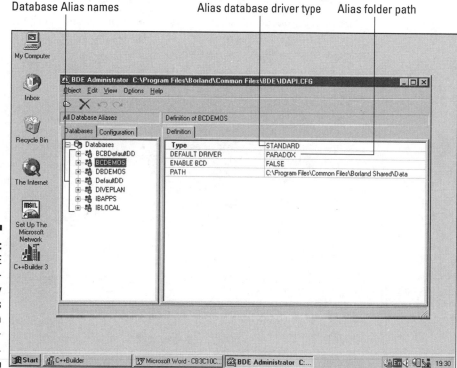

Figure 10-1:
The BDE Administrator Utility provides you with ready-to-use drivers.

5. **Change the text from** STANDARD1 **to something more meaningful (and interesting!), an then press Enter.**

6. **Click the blank Path field in the Definition page of the BDE Administrator, and then enter the path where your dBASE or Paradox database files reside.**

   If you're not sure of the exact location of data files on your drives, you can bring up a Select Directory dialog box by clicking the ellipsis button.

7. **Having completed the alias name and** PATH **details, select** Object⇨Apply **from the BDE Administrator's main menu.**

8. **Finally, from the main menu, choose** File⇨Exit **to close up.**

Discovering the Explorer

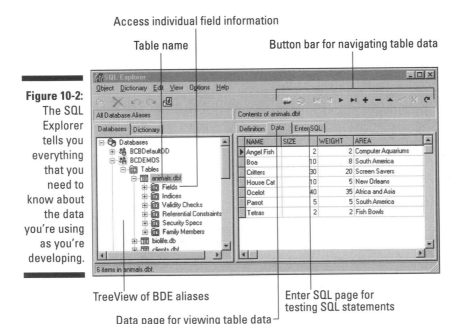

To experience the most powerful data viewing and manipulation tool that C++Builder 3 has to offer, just follow these steps:

1. **Choose** Database⇨Explore **from the main menu.**

   The SQL Explorer allows you to access, modify, test, and, in general, manage data held in tables that you use within your application *while* you're developing (see Figure 10-2).

Access individual field information

Table name

Button bar for navigating table data

Figure 10-2:
The SQL
Explorer
tells you
everything
that you
need to
know about
the data
you're using
as you're
developing.

TreeView of BDE aliases

Data page for viewing table data

Enter SQL page for
testing SQL statements

2. **Click the Databases tab of the Explorer, and then click the + button to the left of Databases to view all database items.**

   The aliases shown earlier in Figure 10-1 are also presented in the Database hierarchy of the Explorer.

When you click the plus sign next to an item's icon, you can see all the details of the tables within an alias. You can view and modify the information about the tables by clicking the tables and then selecting one of the three pages on the right side of the SQL Explorer screen. You can modify the information shown just by clicking in the appropriate edit boxes and adding or removing the information.

Conjuring Up the Database Form Wizard

C++Builder 3 comes equipped with some productivity tools called w*izards.* One in particular, the Database Form Wizard, almost does the form creation for you by automatically placing and linking the components on a form to the fields and tables in a particular database. The wizard provides you with an instant form for editing and saving data that's ready for use in your program.

Before getting into some of the details of database-application development, check out just how easily you can get a data-editing application off the ground using C++Builder 3. Just follow these steps to create an example program:

1. **Choose File⇨New Application to create a blank form in a new application.**

2. **Choose Database⇨Form Wizard.**

   The first screen of the Database Form Wizard appears.

3. **Click the Next button.**

4. **In the next screen, select** BCDEMOS **as the Drive or Alias name and** biolife.db **as the Table Name (as shown in Figure 10-3).**

   C++Builder 3 supplies a ready-made data file.

5. **Click Next.**

6. **Click the >> button (between the two list boxes on the third option screen of the Database Form Wizard) to select all fields for the** biolife **table selected in Step 4.**

7. **Click Next, and then click Next again.**

8. **Click the Finish button.**

Figure 10-3:
The first
screen of
the
Database
Form
Wizard
makes it
easy to
choose a
database
table.

9. **Choose Project⇨Remove From Project; then select** Form1, **and click OK.**

10. **Press F9 to run the program you just created.**

Yes, you have just created your first database application. Easy, wasn't it? Figure 10-4 shows the sample program that C++Builder 3 automatically titled Form2.

Figure 10-4:
You can
conjure up
database
forms such
as this one
almost as
fast as you
can say
"Follow the
Yellow
Brick
Road."

Have a play with this program; it does everything that you need to manage a single table. Try out the button bar (this is a Navigator component) at the top of the form. The program allows you to navigate, edit, add, and remove records. ("The DBNavigator component" section later in this chapter has more information on this control.)

Accessing Data Modules

One type of form that handles data access in your programs is called a *data module.* Your program users won't ever see a data module at runtime because it is a nonvisual component. The data module can hold any type of nonvisual components that a program requires. Don't bother trying to place a visual component in one of these because you'd waste your time; C++Builder 3 won't allow it!

Note: Components fall into the category of *visual* or *nonvisual.* A visual component is visible or can be made visible on a form at runtime; you know what the component will look like when the program runs. A nonvisual component doesn't reveal itself at runtime, but helps other visual components to do their job when the end user uses visual components. Examples of visual components include the Edit, Label, and Memo components. Examples of nonvisual components include all the components from the Data Access and Dialogs pages on the Component Palette. A nonvisual component is represented by an icon at design time so that you're not flying blind as you're building — you can still change the nonvisual components' properties by using their icons.

To see what a data module looks like, choose File⇨New Data Module from the main menu. A data module looks just like a form except that it has far fewer properties and events. With the data module selected, if you click the Events tab on the Object Inspector, you see two events that you can use: the OnCreate event to place code, for opening tables and connecting to the databases that are used in your program; and the OnDestroy event, for closing tables that may have been used in the data module.

Building an Application with the Table Component

The *Table* component resides on the Data Access page of the Component Palette and can be accessed by clicking the Table button. The Table component represents a single data table. With this component, you control all aspects of how data file tables are used in your programs.

The following steps demonstrate how to drop a Table component onto a form, associate it with a data table file, and then open the table ready to use.

1. **Click the Table button on the Data Access page of the Component Palette, and then click anywhere on a form to drop in a Table component.**

   You can now see some of the Table component's properties if you examine the Object Inspector.

2. **Click the Object Inspector's Properties tab, and using the drop-down list from the** DatabaseName **property, select the ready-made** BCDEMOS **value.**

   Next, you need to select the table that you want the Table component to represent in your program.

3. **Using the Object Inspector, select the** CUSTOMER.DB **value from the drop-down list in the** TableName **property.**

4. **Again, using the Object Inspector, set the** Active **property of the Table component to** true.

   Step 4 opens the ready-made customer table in the Table component; the data in the table can now be accessed. Before you use a Table component in the example that follows, here are some more details about Table components:

   - The Table component's Exclusive property prevents programs that might be running on other computers from using a table while you have it open. The Exclusive property is used primarily when you store your tables on a network drive where multiple users may be trying to access the table at the same time. The Active property must be set to false before setting the Exclusive property to true; otherwise, you get an error message saying Cannot perform this operation on an open dataset when you try to set the Exclusive property to true while the Active property is true.

   - The ReadOnly property needs to be set before setting the Active property to true. (Setting the Active property to true is also called *opening* the table.) As its name suggests, the ReadOnly property prevents data changes that the user may make from being written to the table.

   - The Filter property provides a quick way to restrict the view of the data in a table. For example, if you are interested in the records for just one customer in particular, you can assign the Filter property to something like CustNo = 5. Then when you set the Filtered property to true, you can restrict your view of the table to those records that have a value of 5 in the CustNo field.

The following example program shows you how to use some of the built-in methods of the Table component to navigate through a data table. Just run through these steps:

1. **Select File⇨Application from the main menu to create a blank form in a new application.**

2. **Follow Steps 1 through 4 described earlier in this section of the chapter.**

3. **Holding the Shift key, click the Button component button on the Standard page of the Component palette, and then click four times in a horizontal row at the top of the form to drop in four Button components.**

   You're aiming to have four buttons in a row at the top of the form, such as in Figure 10-5.

4. **Click the Memo button on the Standard page of the Component Palette, and then click anywhere on the form to place the component.**

5. **Click the far-left Button component that you placed on the form in Step 3, and then enter |< into the** Caption **property on the Object Inspector.**

6. **Click the Events tab of the Object Inspector, and then double-click the empty** OnClick **event-handler field.**

   You're then in the Code Editor, where you enter the following:

   ```
   Table1->First() ;
   LoadMemo() ;
   ```

   Clicking the far-left button (now with the |< caption) at this point moves the Table1 component (created in Steps 1 through 5) with the function call First() to look at the first record in the table, which shows you the Memo component that was dropped onto the form.

7. **Click the second button from the left and then enter < in the button's** Caption **property on the Object Inspector.**

8. **Click the Events tab on the Object Inspector, double-click the empty field next to the** OnClick **event handler, and then enter the following in the Code Editor:**

   ```
   Table1->Prior() ;
   if (Table1->Bof)
      ShowMessage("You're at the start!") ;
   LoadMemo() ;
   ```

Clicking the second button in the program now moves the component to the previous record in the table.

9. **Next, click the third button from the left, and using the Object Inspector enter > into the** `Caption` **property.**

10. **Click the Events tab on the Object Inspector, double-click the empty field next to the** `OnClick` **event-handler, and then enter the following in the Code Editor:**

```
Table1->Next();
if (Table1->Eof)
  ShowMessage("You've hit the end!") ;
LoadMemo() ;
```

Clicking the third button now moves the component to the next record in the table.

11. **Using the Object Inspector, set the right button's** `Caption` **property to** >| .

12. **Click the Events tab of the Object Inspector, double-click the empty** `OnClick` **event handler field, and then enter this code in the Code Editor:**

```
Table1->Last() ;
LoadMemo() ;
```

Clicking the far-right button now moves the Table1 component to look at the last record in the table.

13. **While still within the Code Editor, press Ctrl+End, and then press Enter to drop to the end of the file. Now enter the entire** `LoadMemo` **function, as follows, into the Code Editor:**

```
void TForm1::LoadMemo()
{
Memo1->Clear() ;
for (int i=0; i < Table1->FieldCount-1; i++)
  Memo1->Lines->Add(Table1->Fields[i]->FieldName
    + ": " + Table1->Fields[i]->Text) ;
}
```

14. **Right-click the Code Editor, and choose the Open Source/Header File option from the speed menu that appears.**

15. **Use the arrow keys to cursor down the file and enter the following boldface line where shown:**

```
private:  // User declarations
          void LoadMemo();
public:  // User declarations
```

16. **Press F9 to run the program.**

The field details displayed in the Memo component change as you click the buttons on the form to navigate through the customer table. A message appears to tell you when you reach the last record. This program should look something like the one shown in Figure 10-5.

Figure 10-5:
You can navigate a table's records by using buttons to access the Table component's methods.

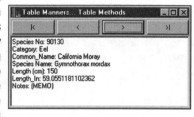

Species No: 90130
Category: Eel
Common_Name: California Moray
Species Name: Gymnothorax mordax
Length (cm): 150
Length_In: 59.0551181102362
Notes: (MEMO)

Linking a DataSource Component to a Table

Before you let yourself loose on the components in the Component Palette's Data Controls page, you need to know about another control on the Data Access page — the *DataSource* component.

The data held within the Table components must be accessed by the Data Controls components so that the end user can interact with your programs. But Data Controls components can't be linked directly to Table components without the help of the DataSource component. The DataSource functions as a "matchmaker" of sorts between a Table and any Data Controls components that you drop onto a form.

The following steps show you how to place a DataSource component on a form and how to link a DataSource component to a Table component:

1. **Using the form constructed in Steps 1 through 16 in the previous section of this chapter, click the DataSource button on the Data Access page of the Component Palette, and then click the form next to the Table component form to drop in a DataSource component.**

2. **Using the Object Inspector, select the existing Table component name from the drop-down list of the** `DataSet` **property of the DataSource component.**

The Table component name is already there, waiting to be selected, so do it!

Setting a DataSource component's `Enabled` property to `false` blanks out the Data Controls component's contents, which, in effect, puts the "big freeze" on any Data Controls components that are linked to the DataSource component.

Creating Applications with Data Controls Components

Data Controls components rely on the components from the Data Access page (described in previous sections of this chapter) to provide the data from a database. Then the Data Controls components allow the user to view and manipulate the data on a form.

Data Controls components feature a `DataSource` property that links the components to a database table. Most of the components covered in this section also have a `DataField` property that links them to a particular field within a table. These components are sometimes known as *data-aware controls*. These controls are linked to database tables and are rigged so that they can send and receive data to and from those tables. Every component on the Data Control page is data-aware because it has a `DataField` property that inherently knows about all data types. When you set the `DataField` property to any field in a table, the property gets the data type from the table without you writing any code.

The DBGrid component

The *DBGrid* is a powerful data-aware component that enables your program to view many rows in the DBGrid component table at once. As you can see in the next set of steps, you can use a grid to create an instant table-maintenance program with a handful of mouse clicks with no coding whatsoever.

The following steps show you how to create a data-aware program:

1. **Select <u>F</u>ile⇨<u>N</u>ew Application from the main menu to create a blank form in a new application.**

2. **Follow Steps 1 through 4 from the first set of steps in the section, "Building an Application with the Table Component," earlier in this chapter to place and open a Table component in the form.**

3. **Click the DBGrid button on the Data Controls page of the Component Palette, and then click the form to place it.**

4. **Click the DataSource button on the Data Access page of the Component Palette, and then click the form next to the Table component that was dropped onto the form in Step 2.**

5. **With the DataSource component still selected, select the** `Table1` **value from the drop-down list of the** `DataSet` **property on the Object Inspector (make sure that you first clicked the Properties tab).**

6. **Click the DBGrid component on the form, and then select the** `DataSource1` **value from the** `DataSource` **property's drop-down list on the Object Inspector.**

7. **Press F9 to run the application.**

   You can use the DBGrid to move around the records in the table and even edit them, as long as the `AutoEdit` property of the DataSource is set to `true`.

You don't have to leave this example program yet. DBGrids offer far more than a view of a data table. You can add more pizzazz to the grids that you use in your programs.

The next couple of steps show you how to select which columns the user sees:

1. **Continuing from the preceding steps, make sure the DBGrid component is selected by clicking it with the mouse, and then right-click to show the speed menu. Select the Columns Editor option from the speed menu.**

   You get the DBGrid Columns editor dialog box, which is initially shown with no entries.

2. **Click the Add All Fields button in the dialog box.**

   The Columns list box fills with all the fields for the table linked to the DBGrid via the DBGrid component.

   To remove a field from the DBGrid, select the field by name in the Columns ListBox, and then press Delete.

   You can change the way that each column in your DBGrid looks in the program by selecting the field by name in the DBGrid Columns editor dialog box and then setting the properties of that column using the Object Inspector. (Figure 10-6 shows a DBGrid column being edited in the Object Inspector.)

Modify column font properties

Figure 10-6:
Use the
Object
Inspector to
jazz up your
DBGrid
Columns.

Find Column Header
properties under
Title property

**3. When you finish customizing your DBGrid columns, click the X
button in the upper-right corner of the DBGrid Columns editor to
close the dialog box.**

The following bullet points show ways to make DBGrids less conventional:

- ✔ By default, DBGrid columns are displayed according to the order in
  which the fields that they represent are held in the linked table. To
  reorder columns, open the DBGrid Columns editor (as shown previously in Steps 1 through 3), click and drag the field names within the
  Columns editor, and then drop the names into their new positions.

- ✔ Click the ellipsis button of the PickList property. You get the String
  List editor dialog box, which you can use to enter a list of items that
  can be selected for a particular field.

- ✔ Use the Title property to modify the column header. C++Builder 3
  titles each column by its data table field name.

- ✔ Experiment with the different settings in the Columns editor, such as
  the Font property and the Color property drop-down lists. You may
  end up with some interesting design effects like those in Figure 10-7.

DBGrid components can be used to convey loads of information and are useful
for showing an entire table all in one shot, but you may want to focus on a single
field. That's when some of the other data-aware components come in handy.

Figure 10-7:
Try experi-
menting
with the
settings in
the DBGrid
Column
properties
to change
the
appearance
of the grid.

CustNo	Company	City	Phone
1221	Kauai Dive Shoppe	Kapaa Kauai	808-555-0269
1231	Unisco	Freeport	809-555-3915
1351	Sight Diver	Kato Paphos	357-6-876708
1354	Cayman Divers World Unlimited	Grand Cayman	011-5-697044
1356	Tom Sawyer Diving Centre	Christiansted	504-798-3022
1380	Blue Jack Aqua Center	Waipahu	401-609-7623
1384	VIP Divers Club	Christiansted	809-453-5976
1510	Ocean Paradise	Kailua-Kona	808-555-8231
1513	Fantastique Aquatica	Bogota	057-1-773434
1551	Marmot Divers Club	Kitchener	416-698-0399
1560	The Depth Charge	Marathon	800-555-3798
1563	Blue Sports	Giribaldi	610-772-6704
1624	Makai SCUBA Club	Kailua-Kona	317-649-9098
1645	Action Club	Sarasota	813-870-0239
1651	Jamaica SCUBA Centre	Negril	011-3-697043
1680	Island Finders	St Simons Isle	713-423-5675

Customized Data Grid

The DBLabel component

The *DBLabel* component, like other Data Controls components covered in this chapter, has a `DataField` property in addition to a `DataSet` property. The `DataField` property enables the DBLabel component to be linked to a single field or column in a table. (The DBLabel component has similar properties and exactly the same events as the regular Label component on the Standard page of the Component Palette, which is discussed in Chapter 4.)

The following steps show you how the DBLabel component operates:

1. **Continuing with the example program created in "The DBGrid component" section earlier in this chapter, increase the size of the form by clicking it and dragging to allow room for another component.**

2. **Click the DBLabel button on the Data Controls page of the Component Palette, and then click anywhere in the newly created space in the form to place a new DBLabel component.**

3. **Select the `DataSource1` value from the DBLabel component's `DataSource` property drop-down list in the Object Inspector.**

4. **Select a field name from the `DataField` property's drop-down list.**

   The DataField property is directly above the `DataSource` property on the Object Inspector.

5. **Click the Table component in the form, and then using the Object Inspector, make sure the `Active` property is set to `true`.**

   You can see the data in the field that you chose in Step 4 for the first record in the table.

6. **Press F9 to run the application.**

   Use the arrow keys on the DBGrid component to move down the records of the table; you can see that the contents of the DBLabel component correspond to the contents of the field for the currently selected row on the DBGrid.

The DBLabel automatically updates its contents when the row in the table changes. DBLabel components are fine for showing data, but what component do you use to change values in fields? That's covered in the next section.

The DBEdit component

The *DBEdit* component's properties and events are much the same as those of the Edit component on the Standard page of the Component Palette (refer to Chapter 4). This section focuses on how to link the DBEdit component to a data table. As with the DBLabel component, you link a DBEdit component to a single field within a record.

Add the following set of steps to the previous example to see how you can put the DBEdit component into operation:

1. **Continuing with the example in the previous section, click the DBEdit button on the Data Controls page of the Component Palette, and then click anywhere in the empty space in the form to drop in a DBEdit component.**

2. **Use the Object Inspector to select the** `DataSource1` **value from the drop-down list of the** `DataSource` **property of the DBEdit component.**

3. **Using the Object Inspector again, select a field name from the** `DataField` **property's drop-down list of the DBEdit component; then press F9 to run the application.**

   Use the arrow keys to scroll down the DBGrid; you can see the contents of the edit control change. Try entering some different text into the contents of the DBEdit. As you leave the field (by pressing the Tab key), the same value in the DBGrid also changes. All these components are now linked by the DataSource component.

The DBMemo component

Like the components on the Standard page of the Component Palette, a DBEdit component is not always capable of displaying multiple lines of text — it's designed to handle only a single line of text at a time. What you need is a *DBMemo* component to give the user *memo fields* (multiple lines of text).

To see the DBMemo component in action, use the following steps, building on the example program created in the previous section of this chapter:

1. **Select File⇨Application from the main menu to create a blank form in a new application.**

2. **Follow Steps 1 through 5 described in "The DBLabel component" section earlier in this chapter.**

3. **Click the Table component in the form, and use the Object Inspector to set the** `Active` **property to** `false`**.**

4. **Click the DBMemo button on the Data Controls page of the Component Palette, and then click anywhere in the form to drop in a DBMemo component.**

5. **Using the Object Inspector, set the** `DataSource` **property of the DBMemo component to** `DataSource1` **and its** `DataField` **property to** `Notes`**.**

6. **Click the** `Table` **property, and using the Object Inspector, set the** `Active` **property to** `true`**; then press F9 to run the application.**

When you run this example program, multiple lines of text are automatically read in from the `Notes` field in the `biolife` table and displayed in the DBMemo component on the form.

The DBNavigator component

Using grids to navigate the records of a table may not offer you all the control that you want. The *DBNavigator* component gives your programs navigational and editing control through an integrated set of speed buttons.

To drop a DBNavigator component onto the form built with the steps in the previous sections of this chapter, just follow these two steps:

1. **Continuing with the steps in "The DBEdit component" section earlier in this chapter, click the DBNavigator button on the Data Controls page, and then click anywhere in the form to drop in a component.**

2. **Set the** `DataSource` **property of the DBNavigator component to** `DataSource1` **using the Object Inspector; then press F9.**

See Figure 10-8 for the results.

The buttons on the DBNavigator component resemble the buttons you'd see on a VCR or CD player, with a few extra buttons thrown in for added functionality (refer to Figure 10-8). You can decide which buttons you want available in this component by setting them to either `true` or `false` within the expandable `VisibleButtons` property in the Object Inspector.

Move to first record in table

Move to previous record in table

Move to next record in table

Move to last record in table

Insert new record before current record

Figure 10-8:
The DBNavigator component provides a ready-made way of moving through the data on the data-aware controls.

Remove current record

Place table in edit mode

Save changes made while editing or inserting

Cancel changes made while editing

Refresh all table data from database

Filtering Data with the Query Component

At times, you may need to analyze data from multiple tables simultaneously to acquire information that a single table just can't provide. By using a *Query* component instead of a Table component, you can filter information from a single table *and* merge columns from many tables to give you the view of the data you need to solve your problem.

Query components have a number of properties and methods in common with the Table component. Queries have both records and fields, but a Query is more dynamic than a Table component, thanks to its SQL (Structured Query Language) property. *SQL* is an industry-standard language specifically designed to let users create databases, add new data to databases, maintain the data, and retrieve selected parts of the data.

So how do you go about setting up a Query? You can follow these steps to manufacture an example program that uses the Query component:

1. Select File⇨New Application from the main menu to create a blank form in a new application.

 2. Click the Query button on the Data Access page of the Component Palette, and then click anywhere on the form.

 3. Click the DataSource button on the Data Access page, and then click next to the Query component just dropped onto the form.

4. Click the DBGrid button on the Data Controls page, and then click anywhere on the form to drop in a new DBGrid component.

5. Click the DataSource component in the form, and select Query1 from the DataSet property's drop-down list on the Object Inspector.

6. Click the DBGrid component, and then use the Object Inspector to select DataSource1 from the drop-down list in the DataSource property.

7. With the DBGrid still selected, use the Object Inspector to set the Align property of the DBGrid to alBottom.

The Query is now linked to the DataSource in exactly the same way that you hook a DataSource to a Table (as shown in the "Linking a DataSource Component to a Table" section earlier in this chapter).

8. Click the Query component, and using the Object Inspector, set the DatabaseName property to BCDEMOS.

9. Double-click the SQL property on the Object Inspector to start the String List editor for the SQL property, and then enter the following line of SQL text into the Code editor:

```
SELECT * FROM EVENTS
```

This single line of SQL code results in the Query component displaying every field from the Events table. (The asterisk is a *wildcard,* or substitute, that stands for "all fields" when placed in this position in an SQL statement.)

10. Click OK to close the String List editor.

11. Using the Object Inspector, set the Active property of the Query component to true.

These steps place a Query component onto a form and link the Query, via a DataSource component, to a DBGrid. When you set the Active property to true, an exact match for the Events table (in the BCDEMOS database) appears in the DBGrid that you placed in the form.

At the beginning of this section, you find out how to use a Query to filter data from a table. In the following steps, you see how to specify criteria that data fields in a record must match before the record is included in the set of records for the Query:

1. **Continuing with the previous set of steps, double-click the** SQL **property on the Object Inspector to open the SQL String List editor.**

2. **Extend the SQL code in the editor to the following:**

```
SELECT * FROM EVENTS WHERE VENUENO = 5 ;
```

3. **Click OK to close the String List editor.**

4. **Reactivate the Query component by using the Object Inspector to set the** Active **property to** true.

   C++Builder 3 closes the query when you close the String List editor because you can't change an active Query. You then see a subset of the Events table data in which only the records that have a venueno field value of 5 are shown in the data set.

The preceding example program provides you with an introduction on using the Query component in conjunction with other components in the form (such as the DBGrid, in this case). The secret behind successful use of Query components is to get the most out of the SQL language. For more information, you may want to pick up *SQL For Dummies,* 2nd Edition, by Allen G. Taylor (published by IDG Books Worldwide, Inc.).

Chapter 11

Constructing Reports

● ●

In This Chapter

▶ Dropping a QuickReport component into a form

▶ Connecting a QuickReport component to a database

▶ Getting rapid report results with Report Wizards

▶ Calling reports from within your programs

▶ Using band properties to format reports

▶ Building master/detail reports

▶ Grouping records and summarizing report columns

● ●

*Y*ou really have your hands full when it comes to creating a report program. The whole process involves retrieving information stored in a database, presenting the information in a concise and meaningful way, and then formatting the information so that the end user can understand what all those rows, columns, fields, entries, and labels are all about.

C++Builder 3 has gone a long way to help you manage your report generation by dedicating a chunk of the Component Palette entirely to report-building controls. You can find the QuickReport components stashed away on the QReport page of the Component Palette. The components on the QReport Component Palette page work together to enable you to intuitively and visually design reports within C++Builder 3 forms. By using the components on the QReport page in your application development, you can create all kinds of quality reports (in full color, too). Most, but not all, of the QuickReport components get some coverage in this chapter. But you can still get a feel for how to incorporate these components into your applications.

As you may have seen elsewhere in the book, many of the source code examples are on the CD included in the back of this book. So, if you can't get the hang of it as soon as you'd like, take a look at the QuickReport project. All of the reports in this chapter are included. More details on how to use the material on the CD is in the Appendix.

Adding a QuickReport Component to a Form

QuickReport components, by and large, control your reports and any print and preview methods that go along with them. The fact is that you can't create reports in C++Builder 3 without reaching for a QuickReport component.

Dropping a QuickReport component into a form changes the nature of the form so that its sole purpose is to hold report components. The form is no longer a regular application form. It becomes, in effect, a read-only reporting and browsing part of the program because you're limited to reading data rather than adding, removing, or changing data on the form.

To add a QuickReport component to a form, just follow these steps:

1. **Choose File➪New Application from the main menu to create a blank form in a new application.**

2. **Click the QuickReport button on the QReport page of the Component Palette, and then click anywhere on the new form to drop in a QuickReport component.**

   A large grid area appears on the form.

The QuickReport component houses an army of properties that, once you place the QuickReport component on a form, can be accessed through the Object Inspector. Here's a rundown of some of those properties:

- ✔ The `ReportTitle` property holds the text (which you enter using the Object Inspector) that's used to identify a report when it's sent to either the Print Manager or a network printer queue. So try to make this text meaningful and relatively polite!

- ✔ The `Page.Orientation` property settings determine whether the report prints tall (the `poPortrait` setting, which is the default) or wide (the `poLandscape` setting).

- ✔ The `Page.PaperLength` and `Page.PaperWidth` properties are set to 0 by default. With that setting, the properties use one of three standard paper-size dimensions in the `Page.PaperSize` property. If you want to specify a custom paper size (by using the Object Inspector), you need to set both the length and width properties.

- ✔ Use the `Page.Columns` property when you need to specify multiple-column reports (once again, using the Object Inspector). Here's an example of when this comes in handy: If you need to print addresses for a mass mailing onto sheets of adhesive labels, you can increase the `Page.Columns` property setting to account for the number of labels that you're printing across a page.

To load a QuickReport labels form (just to get a look at a multicolumn report template), select File⇨New from the main menu to get the New Items dialog box. Click the Forms page tab, and then click the QuickReport labels icon to load up the QuickReport Labels report example.

✔ The `Page.LeftMargin`, `Page.RightMargin`, `Page.TopMargin`, and `Page.BottomMargin` properties take effect when the `Columns` property is set to greater than 1. For example, to make sure that your printed report text doesn't run off the edges of your expensive adhesive mailing labels, you can set a gap between rows of labels by changing either of these properties. You need to change the value for only one of these properties; the value is automatically converted to the other measurement and loaded into the corresponding property on the Object Inspector.

QuickReport Control Example

Now, dive right in and create a report application. C++ Builder 3 enables you to do this by providing "bare-bones" QuickReport forms; all you need to do is format the report and link to a database.

Before creating a simple list report form (a list report here means a report that lists the field details of a single table), follow these steps to create a small program that allows you to control the QuickReports created in this chapter:

1. **Select File⇨New Application from the main menu.**

2. **Click the Button component button on the Standard page of the Component Palette, and then click anywhere in the form.**

3. **Using the Object Inspector, set the** `Caption` **property of the button to** `List Report`.

4. **Repeat Step 2 to place a second button component alongside the first one.**

5. **Using the Object Inspector, set the** `Caption` **property of the second button to** `Master/Detail Report`.

6. **Select the CheckBox button from the Standard page of the Component Palette, and then click the form, below the two buttons, to place a CheckBox component.**

7. **Using the Object Inspector, set the** `Caption` **property of the CheckBox component to** `Preview`.

Great! That sets the scene for creating some cool QuickReports. Now let's party!

Create a QuickReport — Fast!

Continuing from the preceding set of steps, you are now ready to add a QuickReport form to the example program. These steps take you through the stages of creating a simple list report using live data:

1. **Select File⇨New from the main menu to bring up the New Items dialog box.**

2. **Click the Forms tab, and then double click the** QuickReport List **icon.**

   A new form called QRListForm appears.

3. **Click the Table component on the QRListForm, and select** BCDEMOS **from the** DatabaseName **property drop-down list.**

4. **Using the Object Inspector, select** customer.db **from the** TableName **property drop-down list.**

5. **Using the Object Inspector, set the** Active **property of the Table component to** true.

6. **Click the** Report title **object on the QuickReport form that you created in Step 5.**

7. **Using the Object Inspector, set the** Text **property to** Customer List Report.

8. **Click the QRLabel component with the text** Put column headings on this band **on the QuickReport form.**

   The Label component is placed on the QuickReport form as a guide to remind you of the report band's purpose. (Report bands are covered in more detail later in this chapter in the section, "Striking Up the QuickReport Band Properties.")

9. **Using the Object Inspector, change the** Caption **property of the QRLabel component that you just placed on the form to** Customer Name.

10. **To make the report heading more distinct, adjust the QRLabel component, and using the Object Inspector, change the** Font.Style.fsBold **property to** true **and the** Font.Size **property to** 12.

11. **Click the QRLabel button on the QReport page of the Component Palette, and then click the Report form about halfway across the Column Header band.**

12. **Using the Object Inspector, change the** Caption **property of the QRLabel placed in the form in Step 11 to** Phone No.

13. **Repeat Step 10 for the second QRLabel component to make this a more distinct report heading.**

You have now placed the column header labels into your report. Continuing from the preceding steps, follow these steps to connect the data fields themselves:

1. **Using the mouse, click the text** Put data components on this band, **and then press delete to remove the QRLabel component.**

2. **Select the QRDBText button from the QReport page on the Component Palette, and then click the Detail band of the Report form to place a QRDBText component underneath the** Customer Name **QRLabel component.**

3. **While QRDBText is selected, using the Object Inspector, select** MasterTable **from the** DataSet **property drop-down list, and then select** Company **from the** DataField **property drop-down list.**

4. **Select the QRDBText button from the QReport page on the Component Palette, and then click the Detail band of the Report form to place another QRDBText component; this time, click the mouse underneath the** Phone No. **QRLabel component.**

5. **Using the Object Inspector, select** MasterTable **from the** DataSet **property drop-down list, and then select** Phone **from the** DataField **property drop-down list.**

6. **Right-click the QuickReport component to get the QuickReport speed menu, and then choose the Preview option.**

The QuickReport component then gives you a WYSIWYG (what you see is what you get) report preview on your screen. (The report should look similar to the one shown in Figure 11-1.) Reports are typically output to a printer, but many of today's Windows applications offer users a sneak peek of how a report's going to look before it hits the page. This option saves paper because you don't have to keep on printing a report to get it right.

The rows of information in the report shown in Figure 11-1 are courtesy of the *QRBand* component called *rbDetail*. Each column refers to data-aware QRDBText components. These components are associated with a particular column of the customer table through the DataField property.

Figure 11-1:
Report
previews
show you
what your
report looks
like before
it's printed.

Using a QuickReport Form in Your Program

After creating the report in the previous set of steps, you have a report that you can preview at design time, and I bet you are itching to show off your new-found talent to your users! However, doing so begs the question, "How do I hook QuickReports into my programs?" As you will see in this section, the answer is . . . with one line of code!

If you want to show a screen preview of the report to the user, use the `Preview` method of the QuickReport. If you just want to print the report directly, use QuickReport's `Print` method.

Using the control program created in the steps in the earlier section, "QuickReport Control Example," follow these steps to integrate the report:

1. **Double-click the** `List Report` **button to transfer you to the Code Editor where you can type the following lines of code:**

```
if (CheckBox1->Checked)
  QRListForm->Preview() ;
else
  QRListForm->Print() ;
```

2. **So that the main form can use the list report's form, select** <u>F</u>ile⇨ **<u>I</u>nclude Unit Hdr from the main menu, select** ufrmQRList **from the Include Unit dialog box, and then click OK.**

3. **Press F9 to compile, link, and run the program.**

With the program running, if you select the Preview check box and then press the List Report button, the user sees a preview of the report. If you have a printer connected to your computer, you can deselect the Preview check box on the main form of your example program and click the List Report button. You then get a printout of your first C++Builder 3 report. Congratulations!

Striking Up the QuickReport Band Properties

If you ever wanted to play with a band, here's your opportunity. (You don't have to be able to play a musical instrument, and it doesn't matter if you sing off-key.) QuickReport components feature *bands* — not the country or heavy-metal kind, but strips of space within a report form that hold form headers or details about the report. The *QRBand* component plays an important role in formatting reports, so here I focus on that one for a bit.

 If you drop a QRBand component onto a form (by clicking the QRBand button on the QReport page of the Component Palette and then clicking anywhere in the form), you can get a look at how this component works.

The most important property for the QRBand component is BandType, which determines where and when the band is printed. You use the drop-down list in the Object Inspector to select the contents of the BandType property. The following table lists the most commonly used BandType properties and what they do.

BandType Property Setting	*Description*
rbTitle	Prints automatically at the start of the report. You can place more than one title band in a QuickReport form; the bands are printed sequentially in the order that you place them on the form.
rbPageHeader	Used for placing specific information such as the date or time.
rbPageFooter	Used for page footers, such as report page numbers. Appears at the base of every page.

(continued)

BandType Property Setting	Description
rbGroupHeader	Used to set up master/detail relationships within reports. (Master/detail reports are covered later in this chapter.)
rbGroupFooter	Used for placing subtotals or report flags as group trailers within table master/detail relationships.
rbColumnHeader	Similar to a page header; used for multiple-column reports because it can be repeated for each column across the width of a page.
rbDetail	Used for each detail record in a report that holds the actual table data; several can be used at one time. (A report can have multiple bands, and each can hold anything from actual data to the title of the report.)
rbSubDetail	Holds the fields shown in a report for a detail table's records when a master/detail arrangement is used. In the example built in the later section, "Mastering Master/Detail Reports," a subdetail band is used to hold the order table fields for each vendor.
rbOverlay	Used to create bands that "float" over the report page independent of the positions of other bands on the page.
rbSummary	Used for summaries tagged onto the end of a report. (This band typically contains fields and text that help to explain the contents or to draw conclusions from the report.)

The Frame property adds boundary areas to your band components. The Frame property is expandable, with a bunch of subproperties you can use to set attributes such as width, color style, and boundary placement. For reports with multiple columns, use this property to provide separators between the report fields.

Mastering Master/Detail Reports

Reports can become quite complex forms to create; often reports will require information from more than one data table. In this case, the *master/detail form* browses two related tables, displaying one table in one portion of the form and the second table in another portion.

The next section leads you through the steps for constructing an example Master/Detail QuickReport form. (If you haven't read the previous sections of this chapter, you may want to do so before tackling the following project.) C++Builder 3 takes the sting out of creating these more complex master/detail reports by offering a "ready-cut" QuickReport Master/Detail form for you to utilize and modify.

Setting up a master/detail report

You can use the steps in this section as your personal hands-on introduction to master/detail report generation. To begin your groundwork for building a complete report, start with these steps:

1. **Choose File⇨New from the main menu to show the New Items dialog.**

2. **Select the Forms tab, and then double-click the QuickReport Master/ Detail form.**

   C++Builder 3 creates a new form called QRMDForm. The form contains two Table components.

3. **Use the Object Inspector to set the following properties for each of the two Table components.**

Property	*Value*
DatabaseName	BCDEMOS
TableName	customer.db
Active	True

Property	*Value*
DatabaseName	BCDEMOS
TableName	orders.db
Active	True

4. **With the second Table component selected, click the ellipsis (. . .) button on the MasterField property on the Object Inspector. This action accesses the Field Link Designer dialog box.**

5. **Select CustNo from the Available Indexes drop-down list.**

6. **Click CustNo in both the Detail Fields and the Master Fields list boxes, and then click the Add button.**

   CustNo-> CustNo appears in the Joined Fields box, as shown in Figure 11-2.

Figure 11-2:
Use the
Field Link
Designer
dialog box
to state
master/
detail
relation-
ships
between
data tables.

7. **Click OK to close the dialog box.**

8. **Click the** Report title **object on the QuickReport form that you created in Step 2.**

9. **Using the Object Inspector, set the** Text **property to** Customer/ Orders Report.

10. **Using the Object Inspector, change the** Caption **property of the QRLabel1 component from Put Column Headings on this band to** Customer Name.

11. **Click the QRLabel button on the QReport page of the Component Palette, and then click on the Report form about halfway across the Column Header band.**

12. **Using the Object Inspector, change the** Caption **property of the QRLabel that you placed onto the form in Step 11 to** Phone No.

13. **Using the mouse, click the text that says** Put master data components on this band, **and then press delete to remove the QRLabel2 component.**

14. **Select the QRDBText button from the QReport page on the Component Palette, and then click the Detail band of the Report form under the** Customer Name **QRLabel component.**

15. **Using the Object Inspector, select** MasterTable **from the** DataSet **property drop-down list, and then select** Company **from the** DataField **property drop-down list.**

16. **To make the QRDBText component more distinct, use the Object Inspector to change the** Font.Style.fsBold **property to** true **and the** Font.Size **property to** 12.

17. **Select the QRDBText button from the QReport page on the Compo-nent Palette, and then click the Detail band of the Report form to place another QRDBText component — this time under the** `Phone No.` **QRLabel component.**

18. **Using the Object Inspector, select** `MasterTable` **from the** `DataSet` **property drop-down list, and then select** `Phone` **from the** `DataField` **property drop-down list.**

19. **Repeat Step 16 to make the second QRDBText component more distinct.**

That completes the fields for the master table; now to get the detail table fields placed on the form:

1. **Using the mouse, click the text** `Put detail data components on this band`, **and then press delete to remove the QRLabel component.**

2. **Select the QRDBText button from the QReport page on the Compo-nent Palette, and then click the Sub Detail QuickReport band of the report form.**

3. **Repeat the previous step twice so that you end up with three QRDBText components on the Sub Detail QuickReport band.**

4. **Using the Object Inspector, set the** `DataSet` **property of each of the QRDBText components to** `DetailTable`.

5. **Set the** `DataField` **properties of the three QRDBText components on the Sub Detail band to the following field names:**

```
OrderNo
ItemsTotal
AmountPaid
```

6. **Select the Sub Detail band by clicking it with the mouse. Using the Object Inspector, set the** `DataSet` **property to** `DetailTable` **and the** `Master` **property to** `QRMDForm`.

7. **To view your master detail report, right click the form to show the speed menu, and then select Preview.**

   Figure 11-3 shows the report produced in this example. You can see that the orders are listed within their corresponding customers' names.

Figure 11-3:
Master/
detail
reports
offer an
effective
way to
present
related
information
in your
reports.

Customer/Orders Report

Customer Name		Phone No.
Kauai Dive Shoppe		**808-555-0269**
1023	£4,674.00	£4,674.00
1076	£17,781.00	£17,781.00
1123	£13,945.00	£13,945.00
1169	£9,471.95	£9,471.95
1176	£4,178.85	£4,178.85
1269	£1,400.00	£1,400.00
Unisco		**809-555-3915**
1060	£16,355.00	£16,355.00
1073	£19,414.00	£19,414.00
1102	£2,844.00	£2,844.00
1160	£2,206.85	£2,206.85
1173	£54.00	£54.00
1176	£5,511.75	£5,511.75
1202	£4,205.00	£4,205.00
1278	£11,568.00	£11,568.00
1302	£24,485.00	£24,485.00
Sight Diver		**357-6-876708**
1003	£1,250.00	£0.00
1052	£16,788.00	£16,788.00
1055	£23,408.00	£23,408.00

Page 1 of 7

After you approve your new master/detail report, you may want to include it
in the report control program created in the earlier section, "QuickReport
Control Example." Use the following steps to do so:

1. **Double-click the Master/Detail Report button on the QuickReport
   control form.**

2. **This action takes you to the Code Editor, where you type the
   following code:**

```
if (CheckBox1->Checked)
  QRMDForm->Preview() ;
else
  QRMDForm->Print() ;
```

3. **Select File➪Include Unit Hdr from the main menu.**

   The Include Unit dialog box appears.

4. **Select the master/detail form from the Include Unit list box, and then
   click OK.**

5. **Press F9 to run the application.**

Subtotaling columns on a master/detail report

After completing the structure, you're ready to extend the report by maybe including some automatic in-report calculations. The *QRExpr* component can perform a wide range of calculations on any of the data fields of the tables included in your report, from simple column addition to averages, minimum and maximum values, and string manipulation.

Continuing from the previous steps, use the following steps to add QRExpr components to the master/detail report:

1. **Select the form created in the section, "Setting up a master/detail report," earlier in this chapter.**

2. **Click the QRBand button on the QReport page on the Component Palette, and then click below the last QRBand component placed on the form to add another QRBand component.**

3. **Using the Object Inspector, set the** Name **property of the new QRBand component to** bndGroupFooter **and its** BandType **property to** rbGroupFooter.

4. **Click the Sub Detail band, and using the Object Inspector, set the** FooterBand **property to** qrbndGroupFooter.

   The Group Footer band moves up to be directly below the Sub Detail band.

5. **Click the QRExpr button on the QReport page of the Component Palette, and then click the Group Footer band below the ItemsTotal QRDBText component on the Sub Detail band.**

6. **Click the ellipsis (. . .) button of the** Expression **property in the Object Inspector to show the Expression Builder dialog box.**

   Even though you could type expressions directly into the Expression property in the Object Inspector, the Expression builder property editor enables you to create complex expressions easily.

7. **Click SUM from the Available functions list, and then press the Add button in the Function group box.**

8. **Select DetailTable from the Dataset drop-down list, and then select ItemsTotal from the Field list.**

9. **Click the Add button in the Data field group box.**

10. **Click the OK button, and** SUM(DetailTable.ItemsTotal) **is added to the Expression Builder dialog box, as shown in Figure 11-4.**

Select operation to perform from
this list on the chosen data field

Figure 11-4:
Use the
Expression
builder
window to
make light
work of
handling
report data
in a variety
of ways.

Select table

Choose data field
from selected table

Expression
view window

11. **Using the Object Inspector, make the following changes to the QRExpr component: Set the** Master **property to** QRSubDetail1, **the** Mask **property to** ######.00, **and the** ResetAfterPrint **property to** true.

12. **Repeat Steps 5 through 11, this time placing the QRExpr component under the QRDBText component called AmountPaid and selecting** AmountPaid **from the Field list in the Expression builder dialog box.**

Adding a group header to a master/detail report

You want to make the information in your reports as clear and accessible as possible, and one way is to clearly and sensibly identify your columns. To add column headings to the Sub Detail band in the master/detail report built in the previous steps in this chapter, you can follow these steps:

1. **Add one more band by clicking the QRBand button on the QReport page of the Component Palette and then clicking the QuickReport component on the form.**

2. **Use the Object Inspector to set the QRBand component's** BandType **property to** rbGroupHeader **and** Name **property to** qrGroupHeader.

3. **Click the Sub Detail band, and using the Object Inspector, select** qrGroupHeader **from the** HeaderBand **property's drop-down list.**

4. **Click the QRLabel button on the QReport page of the Component Palette, and click the qrGroupHeader band above the OrderNo QRDBText component. Using the Object Inspector, set the** Caption **property to** Order No.

5. **Repeat Step 3 twice, placing the QRLabel components above the other two detail columns, and using the Object Inspector, set the corresponding** Caption **properties of the QRLabel components to** Items Total **and** Amount Paid.

The report is done! Now to call the new master/detail report from the report control form (the one with two buttons and a check box built earlier in this chapter).

Better looking reports with QRShape and QRImage components

You can use a couple of QuickReport components on the QReport page to make your reports visually pleasing, not to mention more professional. These components are *QRShape* and *QRImage*.

Adding QRShape to a report

QRShape has a great deal in common with the *Shape* component that is covered in Chapter 6. To improve the report built so far in this chapter, follow these steps, which use QRShape to underline group headings:

1. **Click the QRShape button on the QReport page of the Component Palette.**

2. **Click the Detail band of the form created in the previous steps in this chapter.**

3. **Using the Object Inspector, set the** Height **property of the QRShape component to 2, and set the** Width **so that the component is wide enough to underline the** Company **and** PhoneNo **fields.**

4. **Using the mouse, click the QRShape component, and place it under the column headings.**

Adding QRImage to a report

Image is all important these days, and if you have a company image, it's important to get that image in your applications wherever appropriate. Printed material, especially reports, are often a prime target for a company logo, and C++Builder 3 makes it very easy to add graphics to a report. Use the following steps to add a graphic to a QuickReport form:

1. **Click the QRImage button on the QReport page of the Component Palette.**

2. **Click the left side of the Title band of the report.**

3. **Using the Object Inspector, click the ellipsis (. . .) button of the `Picture` property.**

   The Picture Editor dialog box appears.

4. **Click the Load button, and then use the Load Picture dialog to browse for your graphics file.**

   You can find some graphics files in the Program Files\Common Files\Borland Shared Files\Images\Icons folder.

5. **Click the graphics file, and then click Open.**

6. **Click OK to close the Picture Editor dialog box.**

7. **Size your image by clicking and dragging the square tabs around the QRImage component's edge, and use the Object Inspector to set the `Stretch` property to `true`.**

Adding cool report graphics is really that easy!

Calling a master/detail report from a program

You access master/detail reports exactly the same way you access any other QuickReport. The following steps lead you through the process of calling the master/detail report from the example program constructed in the earlier section, "QuickReport Control Example":

1. **Double-click the Master/Detail Report button on the control form to get into the Code Editor, where you can enter the following:**

   ```
   if (cbPreview->Checked == True)
     frmMasterDetail->QuickReport1->Preview() ;
   else
     frmMasterDetail->QuickReport1->Print() ;
   ```

2. **While in the Code Editor, choose File⇨Include Unit Hdr from the main menu to get the Include Unit dialog box.**

3. **Select the unit name `ufrmMasterDetailReport` from the Include Unit dialog box.**

4. **To run the program and see your handiwork, press F9.**

Click the Master/Detail Report button to summon your master/detail report. Your report should look something like the report shown in Figure 11-5.

Figure 11-5:
Use
QuickReports
to generate
great-
looking,
functional
reports in a
matter of
minutes.

The QRSysData Component

The *QRSysData* component offers some very useful reporting features. If you place the QRSysData component in a band and use the Object Inspector to set up some properties, the QRSysData needs no further intervention from you.

The QRSysData component's Data property is the property you will use most often. In the Data property drop-down list (within the Object Inspector), you will find its seven functional settings, which are described in the following table.

Setting	Function
qrsDate	Shows the current date in short format (for example, 5/20/97), depending on your Windows setting.
qrsDateTime	Provides both date and time in the same component.
qrsDetailCount	Provides a count of all the records that appear in a band, group, or report.

(continued)

Setting	Function
qrsDetailNo	Provides a number that increases as the report outputs the detail records (useful if you want a counter alongside each detail record).
qrsPageNumber	Prints the current page number of the report.
qsReportTitle	Outputs the string from the QuickReport component's ReportTitle property wherever you place a QRSysData component with the Data property set to this type.
qrsTime	Outputs the time in a hh:mm:ss format (hours, minutes, seconds) into the report when the Data property of the QRSysData component is at this setting.

If you want to include some text to identify a QRSysData component placed on a report, enter the text in the Text property using the Object Inspector. The text is then always used as a prefix to the actual field value, whether it's the current time, date, or whatever else you set the Data property to output.

You may have noticed the QRSysData component placed on the QuickReport example forms used in this chapter. The QRSysData component on the QuickReport example forms is on the Page Footer and provides automatic report page numbering.

Chapter 12

On the Right Path: Using File and Folder Components

In This Chapter

▶ Placing file and folder components on a form

▶ Using the Drive property

▶ Integrating the Directory property

▶ Filtering through files

▶ Displaying and navigating folders and files

*T*he components covered in this chapter have a common mission — to enable you to quickly get at controls needed to manage drives, folders, or files whenever and wherever you need access to such file-driven features in your applications. By using the components introduced in this chapter, you can provide your programs with a standard interface for any task that requires the user to choose a file.

Using File Components

I like to call these components the "F-team" (the *F* can stand for *file* or *folder;* that's up to you). Each of the file components has properties that allow the team to stick together. When combined, each component plays its part to make your file-accessing plans happen.

The file components include the following:

- ✔ **FileListBox:** Provides a list box specifically for listing files.
- ✔ **DirectoryListBox:** Shows the folders for the currently selected drive.
- ✔ **DriveComboBox:** Displays all the drives available to your computer.
- ✔ **FilterComboBox:** Allows you to apply filters to the files that are listed in the FileListBox.

The file components reside on the Win 3.1 page of the Component Palette (see Figure 12-1). As with the other components in the C++Builder 3 palette, you can place them on a form by clicking any corresponding button and then clicking in the form at the location where you want the component.

Note: All the code examples in this chapter are on the CD in the back of this book. You can find more information about the CD in the Appendix.

Figure 12-1:
The F-Team:
The
C++Builder 3
file
component
buttons
on the
Component
Palette.

The DriveComboBox component

The first step in selecting a file is to figure out on which disk drive the file resides. The next step is to access that drive and then find the file on that drive. The following steps are designed to help you do that:

1. **Choose File⇨New Application from the main menu to create a new form for a new program.**

2. **Click the DriveComboBox button on the Win 3.1 page of the Component Palette, and then click anywhere on the new form.**

3. **Press F9 to run the program.**

4. **Click the down arrow on the DriveComboBox component.**

   A list of the drives available on your machine is displayed in the DriveComboBox's drop-down list (see Figure 12-2).

   If you are on a stand-alone machine (that is, not connected to a network), you more than likely have three drives — the A drive being your floppy disk drive, C being your hard disk drive, and D being your CD-ROM drive. You can have quite a few more if you're connected to a network.

5. **Choose the desired drive from the drop-down list (refer to Figure 12-2).**

Figure 12-2:
You can
select a
drive by
employing
the Drive-
ComboBox
component.

This looks all well and good, but there's not much doing yet. The DriveComboBox's `Drive` property changes that (it contains the letter of the drive that's chosen by the user). You won't find the `Drive` property in the Object Inspector; it's a runtime property only.

The `Drive` property enables you to determine from your program code which drive has been chosen from the DriveComboBox drop-down list. So it stands to reason that you use the `Drive` property when users are making selections from a DriveComboBox. The following line of code shows how you can access the `Drive` property:

```
ShowMessage("You selected drive " +
    String(DriveComboBox1->Drive) ) ;
```

You can place your own code for the `OnChange` event handler of the DriveComboBox (accessed from the Events tab on the Object Inspector) to set values when the user selects another drive from the drop-down list.

Another property worth knowing about for the DriveComboBox component is the `TextCase` property. If you set the `TextCase` property to `tcUpperCase`, the drives are displayed in all uppercase letters.

The DirectoryListBox component

The previous section shows you how to select a drive from within a program; this section takes the next step and shows you how to select a folder within a drive by using the *DirectoryListBox* component.

You can expect to use the DirectoryListBox component most often in conjunction with a DriveComboBox component. With that in mind, check out the following steps, which give you an example of how to link together a DirectoryListBox and a DriveComboBox in a program:

1. **Click the DirectoryListBox button on the Win 3.1 page of the Compo-nent Palette, and then click the form created in the previous section of this chapter.**

2. **Select the DriveComboBox component by clicking it.**

3. **Using the Object Inspector, select** `DirectoryListBox1` **from the drop-down list of the** `DirList` **property.**

   This action links the DriveComboBox and the DirectoryListBox.

4. **Press F9 to see how the program built in the earlier steps is transformed.**

   Now, you can click all the folders for the drive that is currently selected in the DriveComboBox.

The DirectoryListBox is an important team player, and now you can see why: Select another drive. (If you choose the A or CD-ROM drive, make sure that you have a disk or CD-ROM inserted in your computer, or you get an error message.) The DirectoryListBox follows the selection in the DriveComboBox by updating itself with the list of folders in the newly selected drive.

To find out which folder the user selected in a DirectoryListBox, use the `Directory` property. This is a runtime property, so you won't see it on the Properties tab on the Object Inspector; you need to access it in your program code.

The `Directory` property contains a string that holds the full directory path of the selected folder, so you don't have to worry about entering the drive letter.

The following steps show you how to integrate the `Directory` property into the example program described earlier in this chapter:

1. **Click the Label button on the Standard page of the Component Palette, and then click anywhere on the form that's been built in the previous steps in this chapter.**

2. **Using the Object Inspector, select the DirectoryListBox component in the form by clicking its name, and then select** `Label1` **from the drop-down list in the** `DirLabel` **property.**

   The Label component is then loaded with the contents of the directory that's chosen in the DirectoryListBox.

3. **Press F9 to kick your program back to life.**

   The DriveComboBox and DirectoryListBox can be linked together so that the DirectoryListBox reflects the folder structure for the currently selected drive (see Figure 12-3).

Figure 12-3:
The
components
added to
this form
exhibit C++
teamwork.

When you set the Label component's AutoSize property to false, if the path name doesn't fit within the width of the Label component, a middle portion of the path name is substituted with an ellipsis (. . .).

The FileListBox component

After you've dealt with applications for choosing drives and folders, you can get down to the actual selection of files within those folders. This section introduces you to *FileListBox,* another component that's used in conjunction with the other F-team components. The FileListBox component shows users the list of files available within a selected folder.

You can use the following steps to incorporate a FileListBox component into the example program built in the previous steps of this chapter:

1. **Click the FileListBox button on the Win 3.1 page, and then click anywhere on the form.**

2. **Click the FileListBox on the form, and then drag it to position it directly below the DirectoryListBox component in the form.**

3. **Click the DirectoryListBox component, and using the Object Inspector, select** FileListBox1 **from the drop-down list of the** FileList **property.**

The FileList property acts as the link for the "F-team" components. You now have a FileListBox powered by a DirectoryListBox that's controlled by a DriveComboBox.

To check out the FileEdit property of the FileListBox component, drop an EditBox component (from the Standard page) into the form created in previous sections of this chapter. You find the EditBox ready to be selected in the FileEdit drop-down list on the Object Inspector. The FileEdit property enables you to filter out the type of files you want to select.

The FileName property in the next example provides you with the full path of the file that's selected from the FileListBox component (it's a runtime property, by the way). This saves you from having to do lots of up-front work before your program can use the file that the user selects.

Filtering Files

The *FilterComboBox* component offers users a choice of file *filters.* (A filter lets users exclude any file types they're not interested in seeing listed in the FileListBox.)

The following steps demonstrate how to add a FilterComboBox to the example program developed in previous sections of this chapter:

1. **Click the FilterComboBox button on the Win 3.1 page, and then click anywhere in the form to drop in a FilterComboBox component.**

2. **Using the Object Inspector, select** FileListBox1 **from the drop-down list in the FilterComboBox component** FileList **property.**

3. **Click the ellipsis button (. . .) in the** Filter **property on the Object Inspector.**

   Now, you've put the Filter property — the most important FilterComboBox property — into service. You can enter a list of file types, and you can restrict the view in the FileListBox to only those selected file types.

4. **Enter a brief description of the filter name in the left column of the Filter Editor (as shown in Figure 12-4).**

Figure 12-4:
Use the
Filter Editor
to set up
filters.

Filter Name	Filter
All files (*.*)	*.*
Text Files	*.txt
Incremental Linker Files	*.il?

5. **In the right column of the Filter Editor, enter the wildcard that you want to apply (see the sidebar on wildcards later in this chapter).**

6. **Click OK to close the Filter Editor.**

After you're introduced to the idea of filtering, you can more fully integrate the EditBox component into your programs. The following steps allow the user to employ the EditBox to add their own file filters at runtime. (In this example, I'm sticking with the sample form developed throughout earlier sections of this chapter.)

 1. Select the EditBox component on the form by clicking it.

2. In the Events tab of the Object Inspector, double-click the empty field next to the `OnExit` **event handler.**

This puts you into the Code Editor, where you enter the following lines of code:

```
FileListBox1->Mask = Edit1->Text ;
FileListBox1->Invalidate() ;
```

This action loads the FileListBox with the contents of the EditBox whenever the user leaves the EditBox while using the program.

You can now enter a file filter at runtime. The filter is applied whenever you move from the EditBox to another component on the form while using the program.

3. Press F9 to run the program.

You now have a whole load of functionality in a small area of form real estate. Your program should look something like the form called "The F Team" shown in Figure 12-5.

Figure 12-5:
Multiple functions can be packed into a compact form.

Play around with this application to get the feel of how it works. Notice that as you select filters from the FilterComboBox, the FileEdit changes, too.

Dealing wildcards

A *wildcard* is not the King of Diamonds in a rage over catching the Jack of Hearts with the Queen. It's a term used to describe a method of filtering out a group of files according to selected criteria.

Consider the example program found in the "Filtering Files" section earlier in this chapter. When the FileListBox initially has the EditBox hooked to it, the EditBox contains the string *.*. This string is a universal wildcard. The asterisks on either side of the period refer to any characters that could be entered in their place. The period between the two asterisks serves the same purpose as the period between any other filename and extension.

If you use the wildcard *.cpp, you get a list of every C++ source file that has a .cpp file extension. If you use the wild-card *.?pp, you'll include every file with an .hpp extension as well as any file with a .cpp extension.

The question mark in a wildcard substitutes for any single character. You can use the * and ? characters as stand-ins for other characters, as you would a joker in card games. In the example programs in this chapter, the files that match the filter (or wildcard) are the only files that are visible and that can be chosen from the FileListBox component.

Chapter 13

It's in Your System: Using System Components

. . . .

In This Chapter

▶ Building timed applications using the Timer component

▶ Embedding and linking files with the OLEContainer component

▶ Adding sound and video with the MediaPlayer component

. . . .

*I*n the coming pages of this chapter, I delve into the deep, dark secrets of applications that are timed to run themselves in the middle of the night, applications that link different files created in separate applications, and techniques for adding video and sound to your otherwise still and silent programs.

The components used to manufacture the sample applications in this chapter are all located on the System page of the Component Palette. They're nonvisual components, which means you see them at design time, but your users won't see them when the programs are run. For the example programs in this chapter, I picked out the System components that I have found to have the most impact in my development.

Because these components are nonvisual, exactly where you drop them into the form doesn't really matter because the component works *behind* the scenes at runtime.

Note: All the code examples in this chapter are on the CD in the back of this book. You can find more information about the CD in the Appendix.

Making Applications Tell Time with the Timer Component

Wouldn't it be nice if you could get your PC to wake you up in the morning or tell you when an egg is done cooking? If that sounds just too frivolous, how about if you could arrange for office systems to perform housekeeping tasks when no one is around. (Who wants to hang out at the office until midnight to start a backup routine or run out daily reports?) These automatic operations, whether silly or serious, can all be accomplished by means of the *Timer* component.

To find out what makes the Timer component tick, you have to put it to use. In the following example, the Timer component is used to create a digital clock and to animate objects on a form:

1. **Choose File⇨New Application from the main menu to open a blank form in a new application.**

2. **Click the Timer button on the System page of the Component Palette, and then click anywhere on the form to place a new Timer component on the form.**

   Use the `Interval` property of the Timer component to state how often you want the `OnTimer` event to be triggered and enter the code you want the Timer component to execute in the `OnTimer` event handler of the Object Inspector. The default value for the `Interval` property is 1,000 milliseconds, which means that the `OnTimer` event is triggered once every second.

   The smaller the value you place in the `Interval` property, the more frequently the `OnTimer` event executes. If you set the `Interval` property value too low, your program will appear sluggish to the user because the program will spend a major part of its time running the `OnTimer` event code.

3. **Using the Object Inspector, set the value in the `Interval` property to 500 (just for purposes of this example) to trigger the event twice each second.**

4. **Click the Label button on the Standard page of the Component Palette. Click the mouse anywhere on the form to place a new Label component on the form.**

5. **Click the Shape button on the Additional page of the Component Palette, and then click anywhere on the form to place a new Shape component on the form. Then repeat this step once.**

6. **Using the Object Inspector, set the Shape component's `Shape` property to `stCircle`.**

You can also make the Shape component different colors by using the Color subproperty of the Brush and Pen properties (expand the Brush and Pen properties by clicking the + button in the Object Inspector).

7. **Click the Timer component that was dropped onto the form in Step 2.**

8. **Click the Events tab of the Object Inspector, and then double-click the empty field next to the OnTimer event handler.**

   You're in the Code Editor, where you enter the following lines:

```
Label1->Caption = Now().TimeString() ;
if (Shape1->Visible)
   {
   Shape1->Visible = false ;
   Shape2->Visible = true ;
   }
else
   {
   Shape1->Visible = true ;
   Shape2->Visible = false ;
   }
```

9. **Press F9 to run the program.**

   You should see that you created a digital clock (as shown in Figure 13-1) with the added bonus of a flashing light (trust me; in real life, that black dot is mesmerizing).

Figure 13-1:
Digital clocks are easy to program with the Timer component.

Embedding and Linking Objects Using the OLE Component

The *OLEContainer* component allows you to link or embed *OLE objects* into your applications. OLE stands for *Object Linking and Embedding,* an activity carried out in Windows. OLE allows you to insert a document or part of a document (termed an OLE object) created by one application inside a document created by another application and maintain a live link between the two. For example, you can store a report and a graph in the same file *(embedding)* or in separate files *(linking).*

Although OLE makes it easy for programs to share files, many developers avoid OLE coding for the sake of their sanity. Fortunately, the OLEContainer component makes your life much simpler: It protects you from the complexities of OLE programming by having already done much of the work for you.

Building a basic OLE program

Use the following set of steps to build an example program that employs an OLEContainer component:

1. **Choose File⇨New Application for a new form in a new application.**

2. **Click the OLEContainer button on the System page of the Component Palette, and then set the component's** Align **property to** alClient **using the drop-down list in the Object Inspector.**

   The component expands to fill the whole form.

3. **Click the MainMenu button on the Standard page of the Component Palette, and then click anywhere on the form to drop a MainMenu component on the form.**

4. **Right-click the MainMenu component to get the speed menu, and select the Menu Designer option.**

   This gives you a Menu Designer form with the caption Form1->MainMenu1.

5. **To get into the** Caption **property of the Object Inspector automatically, type** &File **and press Enter; then type** E&xit **into the** Caption **property of the Object Inspector and press Enter.**

   Two menu items are now added to the MainMenu component (the & character in front of a menu item letter adds an underline to that character to make it a "hot key").

6. **Double-click the Exit menu item on the Menu Designer form to get into the Code Editor; then enter the following line in the menu item's event handler:**

   ```
   Close() ;
   ```

7. **Click the dotted square next to the File menu item added to the Menu Designer in Step 5.**

8. **Type the text** &OLE, **and C++Builder 3 takes you automatically to the** Caption **property of the Object Inspector; then press Enter.**

   A second top-level menu item called OLE is added to the main menu.

9. **Add four subitems to the OLE menu item in the Menu Designer by typing the following four items into the** Caption **property of the Object Inspector, pressing Enter after entering each of the four items:** Insert &Object, Object &Properties, Paste &Special, **and** Change &Icon.

10. **From the Menu Designer, double-click the Insert Object menu item to get into the Code Editor, where you enter the following line:**

```
OleContainer1->InsertObjectDialog() ;
```

11. **Double-click the Object Properties menu item, and enter the following line of code:**

```
OleContainer1->ObjectPropertiesDialog() ;
```

12. **Double-click the Paste Special menu item, and enter the following line of code:**

```
OleContainer1->PasteSpecialDialog() ;
```

13. **Double-click the Change Icon menu item, and enter the following line of code:**

```
OleContainer1->ChangeIconDialog() ;
```

14. **Press F9 to run the program.**

In these few steps you can create a surprisingly versatile program. OLE is a very high-end feature in Windows that's mostly suited to advanced development. You can develop really cool applications with OLE, such as applications that run other applications and applications that *talk* to other applications on different computers.

Adding to the basic program

To put the example program built in the preceding section through its paces, continue with that program by performing the following steps:

1. **Choose OLE⇨Insert Object from the main menu of the example program.**

   The dialog box shown in Figure 13-2 appears. You can scroll through a list of numerous OLE object types in the Object Type list box.

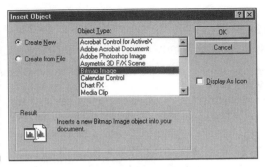

Figure 13-2:
Choose OLE
object
types from
the Insert
Object
dialog box.

2. **Click** `Bitmap Image` **in the Object Type list box.**

3. **Click OK.**

4. **Double-click any part of the OLEContainer object on the form built in the steps in the preceding section of this chapter.**

   The simple menu created in the steps in the preceding section expands to include another five top-level items, and also the color palette, tool palette, and status bar appear. All of these functions are associated with the application — with no code required. If you're feeling arty, you can use your mouse to sketch a graphical masterpiece inside the OLEContainer component.

5. **To see how truly fab the OLEContainer component really is, choose OLE⇨Insert Object again to get the Insert Object dialog box.**

6. **Select an Object Type other than** `Bitmap Image` **from the Object Type list.**

   This time, you might choose a spreadsheet or word-processor object.

7. **Click OK.**

8. **Double-click the OLEContainer object again.**

   Your application adjusts to show the new type of object. The toolbars and menu options change to reflect the object type you've chosen.

As you can see, with a few mouse clicks, this example program can be changed from a drawing package to a fully functioning word processor — just by using the single line of code placed in the Insert Object menu item as shown in Step 10 of the previous section.

To check out the properties of the OLEContainer object, choose OLE⇨Object Properties from the main menu of the example program. You get the dialog box shown in Figure 13-3 (for this example, it's titled Bitmap Image Properties). This dialog box provides the details of the current type of OLE object for the OLEContainer; therefore, its title and contents change with the object type.

Figure 13-3:
Get the
complete
story on an
OLE object
from this
dialog box.

The Change Icon option

The Change Icon option, found in the main menu of the example programs
built in earlier sections of this chapter, lets you change the icon that represents the OLE object type. The Change Icon option comes into play when
you opt for displaying the OLE object as an icon rather than in an editable
format. This can be done by clicking the Display As Icon check box in the
Insert Object dialog box (refer to Figure 13-2). If you opt to display the OLE
object as an icon, you will see only the icon that represents that particular
document type.

The following steps extend the example program built in the previous
sections of this chapter — the program displays an error message if the user
attempts to select the Change Icon menu option before assigning an OLE
object type to the OLEContainer component:

1. **Using the Menu Designer for the Menu1 component (by right-clicking
   the component and selecting Menu Designer from the speed menu
   that appears), select the Change Icon option from the example
   program's main menu option OLE.**

   This step takes you to the Change Icon `OnClick` event handler in the
   Code Editor.

2. **Change the event handler code to the following:**

   ```
   if (OleContainer1->State!= osEmpty)
     OleContainer1->ChangeIconDialog() ;
   else
     ShowMessage("Please select an object type") ;
   ```

The State property has been incorporated into this changed code. Now you can find out what's going on with an OLE object just by checking the State property. Performing a simple check can save you from making function calls that are destined to fail!

The Paste Special option

The Paste Special option goes to work when you have data from another Windows application stashed in the C++Builder 3 Clipboard that you want to place in your OLE object.

To see how Paste Special works, continue with the example program built in the previous sections of this chapter, and then run through the following steps:

1. **Open the Paint application that comes with Windows 95 by choosing Start⇨Programs⇨Accessories⇨Paint from the Windows 95 taskbar.**

2. **Create your own graphic using Paint — feel free to draw whatever comes to mind.**

3. **Choose Edit⇨Select All from the Paint main menu.**

4. **Press Ctrl+C.**

   This places your masterpiece in the Windows 95 Clipboard.

5. **After executing the OLEContainer example application built in the previous sections, choose OLE⇨Paste Special from the application's main menu.**

   You should see the Paste Special dialog box, shown in Figure 13-4.

Figure 13-4:
Choose how you want to paste an object into an OLEContainer component with the Paste Special dialog box.

Paste Special	? X
Source: Bitmap Image	OK / Cancel

As:
○ Paste — Bitmap Image
○ Paste Link — ☐ Display As Icon

Result
Inserts the contents of the clipboard into your document so that you may activate it using Paint.

6. Click OK.

The contents of the Clipboard are placed in the OLE container. You don't even need to choose the appropriate OLE Object Type from the Insert Object dialog box; you can now see how the Paste Special option works. The line of code added to the event handler in Step 12 of the section, "Building a basic OLE program," earlier in this chapter, takes care of handling the object type for you.

7. Double-click the OLEContainer component that was added in the section "Building a basic OLE program."

Your application magically transforms into its very own Paint-type application and displays the graphic that you created using the Paint application in Steps 1 and 2 of this set of steps. You can continue working on your masterpiece from within the OLEContainer component example program, as shown in Figure 13-5.

Figure 13-5:
You can change an OLE application (such as add the Paint program shown here) at any point during runtime.

Adding a speed bar

You can place a Panel component at the top of the form built throughout the earlier section, "Embedding and Linking Objects Using the OLE Component," to act as a handy roost for an application's speed buttons. Just follow these steps:

1. Continuing with the OLEContainer application built throughout the previous sections of this chapter, set the Align **property of the OLEContainer component to** alBottom **using the Object Inspector.**

2. **Click the top edge of the OLEContainer component, and drag it down just enough so that you can see some of the form's background.**

3. **Click the Panel button on the Standard page of the Component Palette, and then click the background section of the form uncovered in Step 2 to add a Panel component to the form.**

4. **Using the Object Inspector, set the** Align **property of the Panel component to** alTop.

   The Panel will act as a speed bar for the program.

5. **Click the SpeedButton Component button on the Additional page of the Component Palette, and then click the Panel component added in Step 3.**

   Repeat this step five times to place a row of six SpeedButton components along the Panel to give it the appearance of a speed bar.

6. **To fill any gap between the Panel component and the OLEContainer component, use the Object Inspector to set the** Align **property of the OLEContainer component back to** alClient.

7. **Press F9 to run the program.**

   The end result should look something like Figure 13-6.

Panel component with Locked property set to true

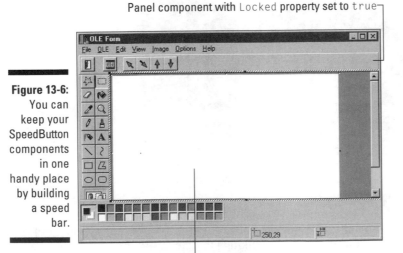

Figure 13-6:
You can keep your SpeedButton components in one handy place by building a speed bar.

Activated OLEContainer component

Curing the component disappearing act

A common problem plagues programmers using OLE objects in real-life programs. When a user activates an OLEContainer component, the other components in the program can disappear from view. The following steps extend the OLEContainer component examples set up in the section, "Embedding and Linking Objects Using the OLE Component," earlier in this chapter.

First, check out how components disappear, and then find out how to avoid this problem:

1. **Choose OLE⇨Insert Object from the main menu of the example program to get the Insert Object dialog box.**

2. **Select an Object type from the Object Type list (for this example, I chose Bitmap Image), and then click OK.**

3. **Double-click the OLEContainer component.**

   The speed bar that you placed into the application in the previous section disappears from sight as the OLE object is activated!

4. **Select File⇨Exit from the main menu to shut down the program.**

Now, you want to make sure that the speed bar remains visible at all times while the program runs. Follow these modifications to the example OLEContainer program built in this chapter:

1. **Click the Panel component dropped on the form created in the section, "Adding a speed bar."**

2. **Using the Object Inspector, set the Locked property of the Panel component to true.**

3. **Press F9 to run the example program again.**

4. **Choose OLE⇨Insert Object from the main menu of the example program to show the Insert Object dialog box.**

5. **Select an Object type from the Object Type list (for this example, I chose Bitmap Image), and click OK.**

6. **Double-click the OLEContainer component on the form.**

Now, with the Locked property set to true, the speed bar stays put when the OLEContainer component is double-clicked.

Grabbing an OLEContainer component from a disk

Use these steps to load an OLE object from a file on disk into an OLEContainer component. (Just continue with the example program developed throughout the section, "Embedding and Linking Objects Using the OLE Component.")

1. **Right-click the OLEContainer component to show the SpeedMenu.**

2. **Choose the Insert Object option from the SpeedMenu to show the Insert Object dialog box.**

3. **Click the Create from File button on the dialog box.**

   This step allows you to select a file to load from disk. This step also changes the dialog box by adding a Browse button and other options such as a Link check box and file path box.

4. **Click the Browse button to show the Browse dialog box, and then select a file to load.**

   I chose a Bitmap (.bmp) file from the Program Files\Common Files\ Borland Shared\images\icons folder for this example.

5. **Click Insert to close the Browse dialog box.**

To embed or to link? OLE!

If you embed OLE objects into your application at design time (by *not* clicking the Link check box in the Insert Object dialog box), a copy of the OLE object's data is added to the application, and the program's executable file then contains all the data for the OLE object. A simple program file can become very large, very quickly.

By linking instead of embedding, a pointer is created telling the client application which file to use; the data stays in the external file. That way, the program file isn't burdened with OLE object data. But remember to keep a copy of the linked file in the location stated when the file was linked into the program; otherwise, C++Builder 3 won't know where to find it.

6. **Click the Link check box in the Insert Object dialog box.**

   Linking the file to the OLEContainer can save on memory resources. Otherwise, the contents of the bitmap file would be embedded within the program no matter how large the file. Embedding the file increases the size of the executable file generated by C++Builder 3, which really slows things down.

7. **Click OK to close the Insert Object dialog box.**

You can see that the graphic you chose is displayed in the OLEContainer component on the form.

Seeing (And Hearing) Is Believing: Using the MediaPlayer Component

Multimedia applications add moving images and sounds to your programs. As a developer, you're probably itching to make your programs a super-sensory experience.

You probably first need to know a few things about multimedia files. Sound and video files are held on your PC's hard disk just like text or graphic files. These files have their own extensions and can consume large amounts of file space. A short video clip alone requires a significant amount of data.

With C++Builder 3, you don't have to run through a complicated maze of programming steps to juice up your programs with multimedia; you just need to drop the right kind of component onto a form and set a few properties.

To place a *MediaPlayer* component onto a form and get a good look at its properties, use the following steps:

1. **Choose File⇨New Application to create a blank form in a new application.**

2. **Click the MediaPlayer button on the System page of the Component Palette, and then click anywhere on the form to drop a MediaPlayer component in the form.**

   The MediaPlayer component appears on your form, as shown in Figure 13-7.

Figure 13-7:
The
MediaPlayer
component
is the
easiest way
to get your
applications
dancing
and
swinging.

The MediaPlayer component features three Auto properties:

✔ When the AutoEnable property is set to true, the component has logic built in to tell the component how to set its buttons according to the component's runtime status. In general, opt for the default setting of true.

✔ The AutoOpen property indicates whether the media file opens automatically at runtime or whether you have to open the media file yourself.

✔ If you set the AutoRewind property to true, the multimedia file always starts from the beginning of the file when its play or record option is selected. If the AutoRewind property isn't set to true, the user must click the component's Prev button to "rewind" the document to the start before playing or recording.

The DeviceType property determines which type of multimedia file you want the component to control. If the DeviceType is set to dtAutoSelect (the default setting), the extension of the file that is specified in the MediaPlayer component's FileName property (.wav for a sound file, .avi for a video file) determines how the MediaPlayer component presents the file to the user.

If you're using a multimedia file for screen display, the MediaPlayer component can be associated with another component that can act as a projection "screen." Panel components, for example, make ideal C++Builder 3 projection screens for video and animation files. You associate them with the MediaPlayer through the Display property.

The MediaPlayer component's `EnabledButtons`, `ColoredButtons`, and `VisibleButtons` properties (accessed from the Object Inspector) each offer the same set of nine buttons for a MediaPlayer component. The `VisibleButtons` property determines whether a certain MediaPlayer button is displayed. If a button is set to `false` in the `EnabledButtons` property, that button is deactivated and appears grayed out on the screen. If you set the `ColoredButtons` property to `false` for a particular MediaPlayer button, the button shows up only in black. (You can see that setting all of these properties to `false` would make for a dull-looking MediaPlayer component.)

The `FileName` property is arguably the most important property for this component. This property holds the full path of the file that's going to be played.

Sounding good — adding sound to a program

This section shows you how the MediaPlayer component can introduce sound into your programs. Go ahead and create an example program of your own:

1. **Use Steps 1 and 2 in the preceding section to place a MediaPlayer component onto a new form.**

2. **Using the Object Inspector, set the properties of the MediaPlayer component on the form to the following values:**

Property	Value
AutoOpen	true
DeviceType	dtWaveAudio
VisibleButtons.btStep	false
VisibleButtons.btBack	false

3. **Using the Object Inspector, click the ellipsis (. . .) button inside the `FileName` property setting of the MediaPlayer component.**

   You get the Open dialog box.

4. **Select `Wave Files` on the Files of type from the drop-down list in the Open dialog box.**

   If you are not sure where to look for a sound file, try the Windows folder or the Windows\Media folder. This saves you from having to hunt through a number of irrelevant files.

5. **Select any .wav file from the Open dialog box to play in this example program.**

6. **Click the ProgressBar button on the Win32 page of the Component Palette, and then click in the middle of the form to drop in a ProgressBar component.**

7. **Click the Timer button on the System page of the Component Palette, and then click anywhere on the form to drop in a Time component.**

8. **Click the ProgressBar component, and use the Object Inspector to set the Align property to alBottom.**

9. **Click the Timer component, and use the Object Inspector to set the Interval property to 100.**

10. **Click the Events tab of the Object Inspector, and then double-click the empty field next to the OnTimer event handler.**

    You end up in the Code Editor, where you enter the following:

    ```
    ProgressBar1->Position = MediaPlayer1->Position ;
    ```

11. **Press F12, and click the background of the form that you're currently constructing.**

12. **Click the Events tab of the Object Inspector, double-click the empty OnCreate event-handler field, and then enter the following two lines in the Code Editor:**

    ```
    ProgressBar1->Position = 0 ;
    ProgressBar1->Max = MediaPlayer1->Length ;
    ```

13. **Press F9 to run the program.**

    You should see a form similar to the one shown in Figure 13-8 titled "Sight 'n' Sound." Click the Play button (refer to Figure 13-7), and the sound file that you selected earlier in the FileName property emanates from your computer's speakers.

And, looking good, too — including video in a program

The preceding section covers the aural side of MediaPlayer; now it's time for some visual treats. You can easily extend the sound program created in the preceding section to convert it to a video screen. Build on Steps 1 through 13 in the preceding section by continuing with the following steps:

1. **Click the lower-right side of the MediaPlayer program form, and drag it out to enlarge the form to allow for another Panel component.**

2. **Click the Panel button on the Standard page of the Component Palette, and then click the lower part of the form to drop in a new Panel component.**

Figure 13-8:
Here's a
MediaPlayer
component
example
program
that's wired
for sound.

3. **Using the Object Inspector, set the** Align **property of the new Panel component to** alBottom, **and remove the text from its** Caption **property.**

   Turn to the MediaPlayer component to change a couple of property values.

4. **Click the MediaPlayer component, and then using the Object Inspector, change the** DeviceType **property to** dtAVIVideo.

5. **Select** Panel1 **from the** Display **property drop-down list in the Object Inspector.**

   The Panel component will act as the projection screen for the video file.

6. **Click the ellipsis button in the** FileName **property value in the Object Inspector, and the Open dialog box appears.**

7. **Select the Video for Windows option from the Files of type list box, and then select a video file to view in the example program.**

8. **Press F9 to run the program.**

9. **Click the MediaPlayer component's Play button (refer to Figure 13-7).**

   Now you have your own movie. Figure 13-9 shows the viewing screen and a still image from a video file.

Figure 13-9:
Here's a
video image
being
played on
Panel
component.

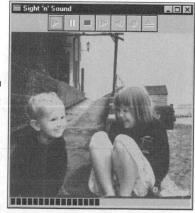

Part IV

Advanced C++Builder 3 Development

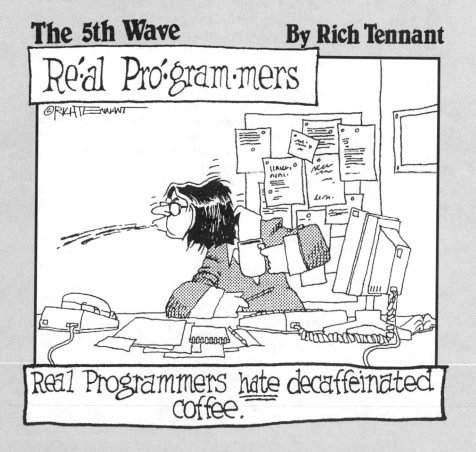

The 5th Wave   By Rich Tennant

Re'al Pro·gram·mers

Real Programmers hate decaffeinated coffee.

In this part . . .

Although all the visual programming stuff really rocks, don't forget you have an industrial-strength C++ compiler working behind the scenes. This section shows you how C++Builder 3 provides you with a code framework from which to launch your applications. You see first-hand the C++ language syntax and the code constructs that you can use to add hidden mega-strength to your programs (may the force be with YOU!).

C++Builder 3 also helps you with some custodial chores. To rid your building of pests, there's a whole chapter on the integrated debugging capabilities of C++Builder 3. And because no one's perfect (not even your end users), Chapter 18 covers exception handling to error-proof your programs. When you've mastered the contents of this section of the book, you'll really start to feel that with C++Builder 3, you can take on the programming world — and win!

Chapter 14

Setting Up Project Files

· ·

In This Chapter

▶ Handling an event handler

▶ Checking out unit code

▶ Examining source code

▶ Changing a `Name` property

▶ Using `#include` statements to include code from another file

· ·

Some developers may be happy to lope along with C++Builder 3, not caring too much about what's happening behind the scenes. But they're missing some valuable insights on not just C++Builder 3, but also how the C++ language works. (I will say, if you're one of those uninquisitive types, you'd better unhand this book right now!) By delving into the nitty-gritty of exactly how C++Builder 3 projects are constructed, you can get the most out of your development work (I promise).

This chapter takes a close look at the contents of the files that C++Builder 3 produces when you create a new application and shows you how those files relate to what's actually happening in your programs. You can also see how C++Builder 3 applications are constructed, how program files work interdependently, and what you, yourself, can and can't change in the files.

Note: All the code examples in this chapter are on the CD in the back of this book. You can find more information about the CD in the Appendix.

Identifying Parts of a Project

When you choose File⇨New Application in C++Builder 3, what actually happens? C++Builder 3 goes off to create a framework or skeleton of a project that becomes your new program. Before you can even scoot your mouse across the main form of a new application, C++Builder 3 is already busy automatically creating the basics of a Windows application for you. I cover those basics — the form, the source code, the header file, and the source file — as well as the C++Builder 3 project files in this section.

When you choose the New Application menu item from the C++Builder 3 main menu, a new project with a blank main form called Form1 (the default name for the new form that C++Builder 3 opens for you) stands ready for components to be dropped into it.

If you choose View⇨Toggle Form/Unit or Press F12, you switch to the Code Editor and can view the contents of the Unit1.cpp file that is associated with Form1.

Checking out the Unit1.cpp file

The Unit1.cpp file holds the *event handlers* and other helper functions for your form. Event handlers are special functions that perform useful actions when something happens in a program (for example, when a user clicks a button).

Here's how the code for the Unit1.cpp file looks as soon as C++Builder 3 creates it for you (line numbers are added to the following code sample to make it easier to follow):

```
1  //---------------------------------------
2  #include <vcl.h>
3  #pragma hdrstop
4
5  #include "Unit1.h"
6  //---------------------------------------
7  #pragma package(smart_init)
8  #pragma resource "*.dfm"
9  TForm1 *Form1;
10 //---------------------------------------
11 __fastcall TForm1::TForm1(TComponent* Owner)
12         : TForm(Owner)
13 {
14 }
15 //---------------------------------------
```

The following paragraphs get under the hood of what's going on in the preceding code example. (I just touch on the "business end" of the code.) Lines 1, 6, 10, and 15 are the comment lines that C++Builder 3 adds.

Line 2 — The #include statement is roughly equivalent to the effect of you pasting entire files of code at the top of the file (see the section, "Including #include Statements," later in this chapter). The file vcl.h gives you access to the most commonly used Visual Component Library (VCL) header files.

Line 3 — This line contains a #pragma statement. (A #pragma statement is a compiler directive that performs useful or time-saving tasks.) This statement marks the end of the list of header files that should be included in the precompiled header file. (A *header file* is a special file that contains declarations of functions and global variables that the program requires.)

C++Builder 3 uses the technique of precompiled headers to store header files in an already-processed format. This cuts down on the time that you have to spend waiting for C++Builder 3 to compile and link your programs. (Not all headers are precompiled to save you disk space.) If the header file is included after the #pragma hdrstop statement, this file won't be included in the already-processed format, and C++Builder 3 takes longer to compile and link your program.

If you won't be making many changes to the header file, include the header file before the #pragma hdrstop statement to speed up the compiling and linking.

Line 5 — This line refers to the header file that acts as the partner to the source file in this example. In C++Builder 3, it takes two source files to hold a form's component details and its event handlers (*source files* contain the main parts of your program). These two files are collectively referred to as the form's *unit source files*.

Line 7 — Here's another pragma statement. It ensures that the packages (*packages* are files that contain the components being used by the form in this case) are initialized in the correct order.

Line 8 — This pragma statement includes the form resources and also states that the source file requires a corresponding form layout file. (A *form layout file* holds the details concerning how and where components have been placed on a form. A form file is identified by a .dfm file extension.)

Line 9 — A variable of type TForm1 is declared here. This variable belongs to the new form type. (You create a new form type every time you open a new form in C++Builder 3.) For a new application, this variable goes by the default name Form1.

Lines 11 and 12 — The constructor for the form starts here. You place any initialization code that you need for your form in this ready-made function. The initialization code includes the variables that you declare and initialize when the variable is first used.

Examples in previous chapters of this book (for example, Chapters 5 through 7) show how the source unit file for a form grows as each event handler (which increases functionality) is tagged onto the end of the file.

Crawling inside C++Builder 3 header files

This section focuses on the C++Builder 3 form header file (identified by the .h file extension) and what C++Builder 3 creates and maintains for you in this file. I also explain how and where you can add your own lines of code to this file.

To check out a form's header file, follow these steps:

1. **Select the form by choosing <u>V</u>iew⇨Toggle Form/Unit.**

2. **If you are not currently in the Code Editor, press F12 to go to the form's unit source file.**

3. **Press Ctrl+F6 to go into the header file.**

   You can see the header file open in the Code Editor.

Following is a copy of the default header file for the blank form (it contains no components) that is created when C++Builder 3 starts a new application. By default, this file is named Unit1.h, which is detailed in the code section that follows (the numbered lines are for easy reference only):

```
1  //---------------------------------------
2  #ifndef Unit1H
3  #define Unit1H
4  //---------------------------------------
5  #include <vcl\Classes.hpp>
6  #include <vcl\Controls.hpp>
7  #include <vcl\StdCtrls.hpp>
8  #include <vcl\Forms.hpp>
9  //---------------------------------------
10 class TForm1 : public TForm
11 {
12 __published:     // IDE-managed Components
13 private:         // User declarations
14 public:          // User declarations
15 __fastcall TForm1(TComponent* Owner);
16 };
17 //---------------------------------------
18 extern PACKAGE TForm1 *Form1;
19 //---------------------------------------
20 #endif
```

Here's a line-by-line account of what this file is doing:

Lines 2 and 3 — These lines prevent the file from being included in the program more than once. The #ifndef and #define code constructs as used here work as a type of protection, so even if the file is placed in many #include statements throughout a program, the actual contents of the file are used only once. (Repeated declarations of a global variable that has already been defined in a header file would cause redefinition errors on that global variable when you go to compile the program.)

The code in Lines 2 and 3 work on the principle that if the word Unit1H has already been defined, then this file has been used elsewhere in the program, and, as such, none of the code between Lines 3 and 20 are needed again. If the definition of the word Unit1H has not yet been made, then #define Unit1H in Line 3 makes the definition (to prevent further redefinitions). The rest of the file is used as you normally would.

Line 5 — The inclusion of the Classes.hpp file provides some of the basic utility C++Builder 3 class declarations.

Line 6 — The Controls.hpp file enables the program to access the C++Builder 3 Visual Component Library.

Line 7 — The StdCtrls.hpp file is included so that standard form component declarations (TEdit, TCheckBox, and so on) can be accessed by the program.

Line 8 — The include statement for the Forms.hpp file tells the form what type it is.

A form is basically just another object at your disposal within C++Builder 3. Watch out for other program-level classes (such as *Application* and *Screen*) in the Forms.hpp file.

Lines 10–16 — The form's *declaration* (the code that tells the compiler what's in the form's structure) is found in these lines. Line 10 tells you that this form is type TForm1 and inherits from a TForm. (The TForm is the basic type of form from which all others spring in C++Builder 3.)

Lines 12 and 13 — As you build a form by dropping components into it, the components become *members* of your form. They are placed inside the form's declaration and are referenced as form variables. C++Builder 3 places the references to these between Lines 12 and 13. If you drop some controls onto the form and go back to the form's header file, you see extra lines added in this section of the form declaration.

Lines 13 and 14 — These lines are *class section headers*. Here you place any extra variables and function declarations that you want to manually add to the form.

Line 15 — Here you find the constructor declaration. (*Constructors* are routines that are automatically called when you create an object.) You need access to the constructor declaration from functions that are not actually part of the form. Any *private declarations* that you make can be referenced only from within member functions of the form. A class is not so secretive about its *public declarations;* public data members and functions are available to the rest of your application. (See Chapter 16 for more on classes.)

Even though you define the functions themselves in the unit source file (with the .cpp file extension), you need to declare the way that you want the rest of the application to view or access those functions. You can do this by placing an entry in the form's header file that states the name of the function, the return type, and the name and type of arguments that it takes, if any. Assume, for example, that you need to add a function of your own to a file that added two numbers. It would look like this:

```
int TForm1::AddNumber(int Number1, int Number2)
{
return(Number1 + Number2) ;
}
```

In the form declaration in the header file, you need to place a line, such as the following one, in either the private or public section to declare the function as a *member* of the form:

```
int AddNumber(int Number1, int Number2) ;
```

Understanding the project source file

In this section, you get an up-close-and-personal visit with the project's main source file — plus some insight on what makes it tick.

To gain access to the project's main source file, Choose View⇨Project Source from the main menu.

You can see part of the "nerve center" in a C++Builder 3 project in a file called Project1.cpp. (This is the default C++Builder 3 name for a newly created project.)

You seldom need to access this file directly; maintaining this file is in C++Builder 3's territory. C++Builder 3 makes changes to this file for you as you change options within its menu selections, such as the Project⇨Options menu selection. When you change Auto-create Forms within the Forms tab, C++Builder 3 modifies the project main source file accordingly.

To let you in on the secret life of the project's main source file (this almost sounds exciting!), the code to come for the source file is followed by a line-by-line description of its significance. (In this example, the project has just been created and the default names still apply. Again, I numbered the lines to make code explanations easier to follow.)

```
1   //------------------------------------------
2   #include <vcl.h>
3   #pragma hdrstop
4   USERES("Project1.res");
5   USEFORM("Unit1.cpp", Form1);
6   //------------------------------------------
7   WINAPI WinMain(HINSTANCE, HINSTANCE, LPSTR, int)
8   {
9   try
10    {
11    Application->Initialize();
12    Application->CreateForm(__classid(TForm1), &Form1);
13    Application->Run();
14    }
15  catch (Exception &exception)
16    {
17    Application->ShowException(&exception);
18    }
19  return 0;
20  }
21  //------------------------------------------
```

Line 2 — The #include statement is roughly equivalent to your pasting entire files of code at the top of the file (see the "Including #include Statements" section later in this chapter). The file vcl.h gives you access to the most commonly used Visual Component Library (VCL) header files.

Line 3 — This line contains a *pragma statement,* which marks the end of the list of headers that should be included in the precompiled header files. (See Line 3 in the first code example in this chapter for more information on precompiled header files.)

Lines 4 and 5 — These lines contain two *macro calls,* which add form resources and units to your project. As the number of forms in your application increases, so does the number of lines in this set of lines.

Lines 7–20 — Here you find what's called the *application entry point.* This is the "boss" function of the program, which means it's always the first function to be executed when the application starts. In this example, the function is WinMain.

Lines 9–15 — These lines contain the exception error control. (See Chapter 18 for more on this subject.)

Lines 11–13 — The program's "starting whistle" is actually sounded in these lines. First, the Application object is initialized, and then the application's main form (Form1, in this case) is created. When the main form has been created, the Application object itself runs.

Changing Name Properties

When you change the Name property of a form from the Object Inspector (see Chapter 1 for information on the Object Inspector), C++Builder 3 automatically changes the references to the form. Always use the Object Inspector, as shown in Figure 14-1, to change Name properties — don't attempt to make the changes on your own. You may bite off more than you can chew if you try to amend the form's name within the code. The Object Inspector is far faster at replacing the necessary references than you can ever be!

Figure 14-1:
Always use the Object Inspector to rename forms — unless you enjoy spending countless hours in front of your screen.

You could use the Object Inspector to change the Name property of the Form1 example described earlier in the chapter to something like "JoeBloggs." You would see that the references to the form in the Code Editor are changed for you in a twinkling.

C++Builder 3 respects your privacy to a fault. As such, if you make any modifications to a form variable directly within one of your functions, you have to modify the form variable name references yourself.

Including #include *Statements*

If you examine the top of any C++Builder 3 source files, you are likely to find #include statements. (You may hear them referred to as *include* or *hash include* commands.) These statements are extremely useful code constructs. They tell the compiler to load an include file. Though some header files are added by C++Builder 3, you can also add your own header files. In this case, the file that's being included is the header file. Just as a reminder, here's an example of what an #include include statement looks like:

```
#include <vcl\vcl.h>
```

Where does C++Builder 3 expect the file that's referenced within the brackets of the #include statement to reside? Here are some simple steps that can help you find out:

1. Choose Project⇨Options from the main menu.

The Project Options dialog box appears (see Figure 14-2).

Figure 14-2:
The Project
Options
dialog box is
where you
can locate
files
referenced
in
#include
statements.

(Screenshot: Project Options dialog box with tabs: Forms, Application, Compiler, Advanced Compiler, C++, Pascal, Linker, Directories/Conditionals, Version Info, Packages, Team. Directories group shows Include path: $(BCB)\include;$(BCB)\include\vcl, Library path: $(BCB)\lib\obj;$(BCB)\lib, Debug source path: $(BCB)\source\vcl, Intermediate output. Conditionals group: Conditional defines: _RTLDLL;USEPACKAGES. Aliases group: Unit aliases. Default checkbox, OK, Cancel, Help buttons.)

2. Click the Directories/Conditionals tab.

The Include path text box in the Directories group furnishes the answer to where C++Builder 3 expects this file to be. This text box contains a list of folders in which the file can be located.

Refer to Figure 14-2 for a moment while I tell you what some of those entries mean. The characters $(BCB) — BCB stands for Borland C++Builder 3 — represent the full folder name where C++Builder 3 is installed (for example, C:\Program Files\Borland\Cbuilder3). That shorthand $(BCB) is called an *environment macro*.

Knowing this, you may guess that the #include statement at the start of this section says, in effect, something like

```
#include "c:\program files\borland\cbuilder3\include\vcl\vcl.h"
```

Notice that in this example, the angle brackets (< >) have been swapped for quotation marks. Because c:\program files\borland\cbuilder3\include\ vcl\vcl.h is the full path of the folder, the #include statement does not need to be processed in order for the compiler to discover the actual location of the folder in question.

The benefit of using the environment macros is that they save you from having to create long lines at the top of every file. What if the files that you need to include in your programs have moved? That would mean that all of the folder references in the #include statements in your code have to be changed. Whatta nightmare! You'd find yourself plowing through all of your source files amending the #include lines, which wouldn't leave you much time for eating, sleeping, or discovering what's in the chapters in the rest of this book.

Chapter 15

Controlling Programs with Data Types

- -

In This Chapter

▶ Declaring variables to put data in its place

▶ Getting a line on character strings

▶ Using pointers to manage data

▶ Adding mathematical expressions

▶ Writing `if`, `else`, and `switch` statements

▶ Building loops to save time

▶ Getting to see some CodeInsight

- -

At some point after writing quite a few programs and experimenting with the available C++Builder 3 components, you start itching to move on to bigger, better, and more challenging projects. When you reach this moment of maturity (or madness), this chapter can provide you with the nitty-gritty details of how C++ code is constructed and empower you to take control over how your programs react to a variety of events.

Of all the chapters in this book, you're likely to find this one to be the heaviest going, but take heart. The amount of effort this chapter requires is directly proportional to the benefits you ultimately get out of it. Feel free to tuck the wisdom of this chapter under your belt piece by piece.

If you feel brain-burn coming on, bookmark your place and go grab yourself one of those sugar-loaded, high-caffeine drinks that constitute a major food group for most developers. Then you can come back ready to continue with another chunk of work and to take on the world (or at least the next C++Builder 3 program).

Declaring Data Types: It's All Variable

When you really get into developing, you may find that you need to store, move, or change data. This data can be numeric, text, or graphical. For example, the values a program maintains to balance your bank account are a different kind of data from the text you use to write letters, and that text is a different sort of data from the scanned photos of your birthday party that you keep meaning to e-mail to a few select friends.

As you create programs, you want to be able to reference various items of data by some sort of meaningful notation. That's where *variables* come into play. A variable is a name that you assign to a piece of information of a certain type. You *declare* a variable (that is, note it properly in code so that the system recognizes it) and then use the variable's name to clear it, cram it with data, or anything else that the language enables you to do to it.

Entry-level variables

Before you give a variable a name, you need to decide what *type* of data the variable is going to hold. Certain basic data types are available to you in C++. You can make up more complicated types of your own that are built on the basic data types; these are explained in Chapter 16. Try the three types listed in Table 15-1 for starters, though.

Table 15-1	Basic C++ Data Types	
C++ Data Type	*What It Holds*	*Valid Values*
char	Exactly one character	Single letters (A, a, B, b, and so on) or punctuation (' or ; or even & and $) are valid.
int	A whole number	Examples of valid numbers are 0, 1, 190, or –10, but not numbers that require a decimal, such as 1.5.
float	Decimal number	Values such as 3.6, 10.0, and –9.9 are valid float numbers.

Declaring variables

So once you know what variables you have to choose from, how do you go about using variables and their respective data types? Read on.

The first stage to using a variable is to *declare* (or create) the variable. A *variable declaration* consists of two parts: the variable type and the variable name. Variable declarations are normally one to each line. The following steps demonstrate how to create a variable:

1. **Enter the data type name (such as** `char` **or** `int`**) on a new line in your code.**

2. **Press Tab.**

3. **Enter the name that you want to give the variable, and end the line with a semicolon (;).**

4. **Press Enter.**

   Way to go! You have one variable ready for action.

The following examples show you how you could declare one variable for each of the basic types of variables:

```
char   cLetter ;
```

```
int  iCounter ;
```

```
float   fPayment ;
```

I chose the words `cLetter`, `iCounter`, and `fPayment` as variable names because they indicate the function of the variable's data. You can name variables as you like, but don't forget that you may have to make quick sense of your code at a later stage! And note that I appended the first letter of the variable type to the variable name just to make it easy for you to recognize the variable type later in the program — without having to go back and look at the variable declaration.

As mentioned earlier in this chapter, choose the names of variables so that they imply what the data refers to or what it is used for. That's just a piece of advice; however, some variable-name rules *are* set in stone. Here are the five don'ts of naming variables:

- Don't start variable names with numbers.

- Don't use spaces in variable names.

- Don't use certain special characters (+, –, and ! are some examples) in variable names. Use only letters, numbers, and the underscore character (_).

- Don't use words, such as *if* and *while,* that are reserved by the C++ language (explained later in this chapter).

- Don't use C++ library function names (for example, `printf`, `scanf`, `getchar`, and others).

Here are some examples of valid variable names (even if their appropriateness is questionable):

```
nice_one_deb_it's_a_boy
```

```
Take5
```

```
HaveABeer
```

These are examples of variable names that the compiler will bounce back at you for sure:

    1ForTheMoney — **starts with a number**

    C++Builder 3! — **contains illegal characters**

    switch — **a C++ reserved word**

    No Way — **has a space in it**

If you plan to use a variable in more than one file, declare that variable in a header file (see Chapter 2 for more on header files). You can then reference the variable from any unit that includes that header file. Such variables are called *global* variables because they can potentially be used in any of the program's other code units.

A variable's declaration also offers an ideal opportunity to set the starting value. This is called *initializing* a variable. If you don't set your own initial value for a variable, there's the danger that the variable can contain just about any old value, which could cause some unexpected results for your program. The following code shows how you can extend the variable declarations listed earlier in this chapter so that the variables hold valid data:

```
char    cLetter = 'X' ;
```

```
int     iCounter, i = 0 ;
```

```
float   fPayment = 99.99 ;
```

Notice that in the second line, I use a comma to declare multiple variables of the same type in one statement. It is the same as entering

```
int    iCounter = 0;
int    i = 0 ;
```

so you can save yourself a line of code. In this case, both variables are also initialized to zero — cool! (As you may know, initializing the variables to zero removes any "garbage" that may be left over in the variable, making it ready to be used.) If you want to initialize the variables to different values, you could use the following line:

```
int iCounter = 1, i = 0 ;
```

The following steps give you an example of how to initialize a variable:

1. **Create a new application by choosing File⇨New Application from the main menu.**

2. **Drop one Button and three Label components onto the form. (See Chapters 4 and 5 for steps on how to do this.)**

3. **In the OnClick event for the Button, add the following lines:**

```
char Letter = 'X' ;
int     iCounter = 0 ;
float   fPayment = 99.99 ;
Label1->Caption = cLetter ;
Label2->Caption = iCounter ;
Label3->Caption = fPayment ;
```

4. **Press F9 to run the application, and then click the Button component on the form.**

   The Label components display the variables' initialized values.

Advanced data types

You probably won't use the advanced data types listed in Table 15-2 as often as the basic types, but the following data types can help you to get more specific about how your program holds data.

Table 15-2	Additional Data Types
C++ Data Type	*What It Holds*
unsigned char	Values from 0 to 255 in 8 bits
short int	Values from −32,768 to 32,767 in 16 bits
unsigned int	Positive values from 0 to 4,294,967,295 in 32 bits
unsigned long	Positive values from 0 to 4,294,967,295 in 32 bits
long	Negative to positive values from −2,147,483,648 to 2,147,483,647 in 32 bits
double	Values from $1.7 \times 10{-}308$ to $1.7 \times 10{+}308$ in 64 bits
long double	Values from $3.4 \times 10{-}4{,}932$ to $1.1 \times 10{+}4{,}932$

Deciphering digi-dialect

The numbering method used by most humans is the decimal system, which is based on ten numerals with each digit in a numeral calculated in powers of ten. For example, the number 99 equates to 9 x 10 + 9.

This fact may seem incredibly obvious to you, but computers don't understand a system based on ten digits. They speak in a *binary* tongue that uses only the numerals 0 and 1, with each digit in a number calculated by a power of 2. This means the number 11 in the binary system equates to 1 x 2 + 1, or 3 in the decimal system. So, 99 in the decimal system becomes 1100011 in the binary system (1 x 64 + 1 x 32 + 0 x 16 + 0 x 8 + 0 x 4 + 1 x 2 + 1 x 1). Each of these binary digits is called a *bit* and it takes a full seven bits to store the decimal number 99.

Computers group bits into a set of eight digits called a *byte,* and a byte has the capacity to hold up to a 255 decimal value. Two adjoining bytes are called a *word,* which can hold up to a 2,655,535 decimal value.

Keeping Things Constant

You will find that some values in your programs never change. For example, pi will always equal 3.141592 (plus an infinite number of other digits). In C++Builder 3, you can use a special kind of variable that, once assigned, acts like quick-dry cement and from then on can't be changed. These are called (you guessed it) *constants,* and you create them by appending the keyword const in front of the variable name.

Here are some examples of constants in action:

```
const int MaxCount = 999;
```

```
const float pi = 3.141592;
```

```
char * const Str1 =
  "Jason is a dude!"; // no heckling at the back, please!
```

Note: The importance of the * character in the last line is explained later in this chapter.

TECHNICAL STUFF

Null termination — not just for nothing

C++ uses a technique called *null termination* to indicate the last letter within a character array when the text within the array is shorter than the variable's capacity.

If, for example, you place a word four characters long inside an array that can contain ten characters, a special "null" character (\0) is placed in the fifth character position in the array.

This eliminates the need to store a word length inside the array. The null character indicates that the word has ended and the rest of the array is not in use. If you figured out that this means you can actually use only nine of your ten characters, well done! Go and get yourself a cookie! You have only nine characters available to you because you must use the tenth one to prevent overrunning the end of the array.

Stringing Characters Along

One of the basic data types introduced at the start of this chapter is `char`. It is capable of holding a single character. But what about when you need to store whole words or even complete sentences?

Fear not; you can soon take care of this by building upon the humble `char` type. Characters are grouped together to form a *string* that is stored in an *array*. This is a way of saying that you can refer to a bunch of single characters by using just one variable. You can determine how many characters are in your array (that is, how many letters your word can contain) by adding a whole number enclosed in square brackets at the end of the variable name.

The following declaration provides a variable that is capable of holding a word up to ten characters long:

```
char cPlaceName[10] ;
```

You don't have to use all these characters all the time. This declaration simply sets aside a maximum number. I sense a looming question: How do you know when you've come to the end of a word contained in the array if the word is shorter than the number of characters the array can hold? *Null termination* (described in the previous sidebar, "Null termination — not just for nothing") tells you.

You don't have to worry too much about all this null termination stuff because C++Builder 3 provides a special string class called `AnsiString`. This string manages a great deal of the run-of-the-mill string chores for you and allows you to use strings in conjunction with C++Builder 3 controls in a much more natural way. That's because the components that you place in your forms also use `AnsiString` types for their `Caption`, `Text`, and other such string properties. You often see code like the following snippets in C++Builder 3 applications:

```
AnsiString strTemp ;
strTemp = Edit1->Text ;
Label1->Caption = strTemp ;
```

The first line declares a variable called *strTemp* of type *AnsiString*. The second line loads the contents of an edit box into the variable *strTemp,* and the third line passes the contents of a Label component with the same string of characters.

Getting to the Pointer

In an earlier section, "Keeping Things Constant," I use the * (asterisk) character in code. You use this *operator* to say that you want a particular variable to be a *pointer* type. An operator is a sign (+) or combination of signs (+=) that tells the compiler you want a specific action performed on something in your code.

Computer programs hold their data in memory, and variable names are labels that humans can read to find the place in memory where the data is located. This procedure seems like a reasonable way of going about things, but when amounts of data become greater or when you have a group of items that are of the same data type, referring to items directly can become unwieldy. That's when you might look at using *pointers* (variables that reference data locations, but don't actually contain the data) instead to refer to data.

A pointer-type variable does not hold the data of a particular type; it holds the *address* for data of a particular type. It's actually one step removed from the real thing. This characteristic provides pointer-type variables with the flexibility to be redirected to point somewhere else in memory.

The giveaway syntax for a pointer is the * (asterisk) character, which is placed between the variable name and the variable's data type.

The first two of the following lines are character array declarations; the character pointer variable is declared on the third line:

```
char str1[255] = "This is String One" ;
char str2[255] = "This is String Two" ;
char * cPtr ;
```

The `cPtr` pointer variable does not point at anything yet, but it can be made to access either of the character arrays by using this simple assignment:

```
cPtr = str1 ;
```

At any point in your program, you can redirect the pointer to the other string by using the following code:

```
cPtr = str2 ;
```

This is a technique that can be used for any variable type, not just character arrays.

If you look inside a header file for one of your forms, you can see that all the C++Builder 3 components you placed on the form at design time are actually held as pointers to objects.

Pointers are extremely useful when you're holding large amounts of data in your program. If you need to pass this data to a function that you are calling, the laborious process of sending over all the data as a copy becomes a real chore. Instead, you can use a pointer to the data. Essentially, C++Builder 3 is saying "I don't have it, but I know where you can get it!" to the function that you are calling. (See Chapter 16 for more on calling a function.)

The misuse of pointers is probably the single largest cause of problems in C++ programs. Things go awry, especially if you use a pointer that has not been first properly initialized. You can end up sending the program into the memory twilight zone. So be careful, and remember — if in doubt, check it out! (Chapter 17 contains information on how you might go about this.)

Expressing Operators

You're probably not going to declare variables without actually performing operations on them. Why, that would be like pumping up your bicycle tires and then taking the bus!

To perform an operation on variables in C++, you need to build an *expression* (a code statement that actually does something); check out this example:

```
surf_time = have_board + waves_high
```

Doing the math

A simple mathematical expression that springs to mind is

```
a = 1 + 2 ;
```

Here you are using the + symbol (plus sign) to indicate that you want to perform the mathematical operation of adding the two integers. (The + character is an *operator*.) Table 15-3 provides a rundown of the basic operators that you can use in your C++ code.

Table 15-3	Basic C++ Mathematical Operators	
Operator	*Example*	*Action*
+	2 + 2	Adds the two numbers.
-	2 - 2	Subtracts one number from another.
*	2 * 2	Multiplies the two numbers.
/	2 / 2	Divides the first number by the second number.
%	11 % 2	Provides the remainder after dividing the two numbers.

If you use an integer to represent an amount of money and hold the entire value in cents (for example, $79.50 represented as 7950 cents), you can easily isolate just the cents part by using an expression such as this:

```
Cents = Payment % 100
```

This expression discards the dollar amount and assigns just the coinage left over into the variable Cents.

C++ has a diverse and varied selection of operators to make your programming life more exciting. Table 15-4 lists some of the more advanced operators that you can use in your code.

Table 15-4	Advanced Operators	
Operator	*In Action*	*Description*
++	i++	Increments the value of variable i by 1.
–	i–	Decrements the value of i by 1.
>>	i>>j	Performs a bitwise right shift by j bits.
<<	i<<j	Performs a bitwise left shift by j bits.

Comparatively speaking —
Boolean operators

When faced with making a decision in your code, you may not be so concerned about the numeric result of an expression; you may be more concerned with whether the test you are making is actually `true` or `false`. This situation leads you to what are called *Boolean operators,* a special kind of operator that you're sure to use in many of your `if` statements. With Boolean operators, you're mostly concerned with determining whether an expression is `true` or `false`. Table 15-5 lists some Boolean operators.

Table 15-5		Boolean Operators	
Operator	*Name*	*In Action*	*Description*
==	Equal operator	a == b	Returns `true` if these variables contain the same values.
!=	Not-equal operator	a!= b	Returns `true` if these variables do *not* contain the same values.
>	Greater-than operator	a > b	Returns `true` if the expression on the left is greater than the expression on the right.
<	Less-than operator	a < b	Returns `true` if the expression on the left is less than the expression on the right.
>=	Greater-than or equal operator	a >= b	Returns `true` if the expression on the left is greater than or equal to the expression on the right.
<=	Less-than or equal operator	a <= b	Returns `true` if the expression on the left is less than or equal to the expression on the right.
!	Not operator	!a	Returns `false` if the expression is `true`.
&&	Logical *and* operator	a && b	Returns `true` if both expressions are `true`.
||	Logical *or* operator	a || b	Returns `true` if either expression is `true`.

Shift workers and real operators

The shift operators (refer to last two rows of Table 15-4) deserve a tad more explanation. You use these operators to take the binary value of the variable in question and move all the bits along by the number of positions indicated.

If a variable i holds the value 16, its binary representation is

    010000

If you apply the following expression

    i >> 1

all the bits move one place to the right and the value is effectively divided by 2, yielding the following result:

    001000 (8 when converted back into decimal)

The reverse is true of the left-shift operator. Applying this operator shifts the bits to the left and subsequently increases values with each shift by a power of 2.

So the following variable (where the variable i again contains a value of 16)

    i << 2

provides the following binary pattern:

    1000000 (64 in the human-speak decimal system).

Not all are created equal — assignment operators

Use an assignment operator (=) when you want to give a variable a value. Table 15-6 lists C++ assignment operators.

Table 15-6		C++ Assignment Operators
Operator	*In Action*	*Description*
+=	a += b	Adds the value of *b* to *a*, and places result in *a*.
-=	a -= b	Subtracts the value of *b* from *a*, and places result in *a*.
*=	a *= b	Multiplies the value of *a* by *b*, and places result in *a*.
/=	a /= b	Divides *a* by *b*, and leaves the result in *a*.
%=	a %= b	Sets *a* to the value of the modulo (returns the remainder of the division) of *a* and *b*.
<<=	a <<= b	Left-shifts *a* by *b* number of bits.

Operator	In Action	Description
>>=	a >>= b	Right-shifts *a* by *b* number of bits.
&=	a &= b	Performs a bitwise *and* on *a* and *b*, and places the result in *a*.
|=	a |= b	Performs a bitwise *or* on *a* and *b*, and places the result in *a*.
^=	a ^= b	Performs a bitwise *exclusive or* on *a* and *b*, and places the result in *a*.

When an operator performs a *bitwise*, it looks at each variable at a storage bit level. With the &= operator, if the bit on the left and the bit on the right are 1, the result is also assigned as 1. The result is set to 0 if either the left or right bit is 0. With the |= operator, when the bit on the left or the bit on the right is 1, the result is assigned as 1. It's set to 0 only if both left and right are 0. With the ^= operator, when one, but not both, of the bits on the left or the right is 1, the result is assigned as 1.

Flowing with the Go: Channeling Your Program Path

After seeing the operators that you can use for comparing expressions, you will want to be able to change the course of the programming ship according to the results of your comparisons. In this section, I introduce several code constructs (or code keywords) for channeling the execution path of your program so that you can play "program traffic cop."

Making decisions with if statements

The if statement is a powerful little critter that you use to make decisions within the code of your programs.

The following snippet of code shows this "tiny titan" — the if statement — in action. (You see this message only if the variable *i* contains a 0 value):

```
if (i == 0)
  ShowMessage("i has zero value");
```

When you need to use more than one line of code to do a job, use { and } braces to bind your statements together, as in the following example (my preference is to have each brace on a line of its own):

```
if (i == 0)
  {
  ShowMessage("i has zero value") ;
  return(0);
  }
```

Now you can place as much code as you need to in the code section of the if statement. (The assignment operator = is also valid in an if statement.)

The following two code snippets are valid to the compiler, but entering the first one when you mean to enter the second one may trip you up!

```
if (j = 1)
  j++ ;

if (j == 1)
  j++ ;
```

Danger lies in the first two lines. You actually end up with *j* always containing the value of 1 with the first statement. The second if statement, on the other hand, performs just a comparison and does not interfere with the value of the variable *j*.

If not if, *then* else

You can extend the if statement by using its companion else. The else statement is used when you want a particular action (or set of actions) to be performed when the condition that you provide for the if statement is not true. Here's an example of how you do this:

```
if (i == 0)
  ShowMessage("i has zero value") ;
else
  ShowMessage("There's something of value in your i!");
```

In this case, if the variable *i* contains 0, you will see the first message. When the variable *i* contains any value other than 0, the program executes the code segment inside the else statement, and you see the message "There's something of value in your i!"

You can extend the use of if and else by stringing together a number of these code constructs to build more specific control into your program. Consider the following chunk of code. If the variable *i* contained a value of 2, neither of the messages would be shown:

```
if (i == 0)
  ShowMessage("i has zero value") ;
else if (i == 1)
  ShowMessage("There's value 1 in your i!");
```

Try the following example steps. When you implement the if. . .else statement, every time you click the button, the color of the panel changes:

1. **Choose File⇨New Application from the main menu to create a new form.**

2. **Drop a Panel and a Button component onto the form. (See Chapters 4 and 5 for the steps to do this.)**

3. **Select the Button component, and click the Events tab on the C++Builder 3 Object Inspector.**

   If the Object Inspector isn't already showing on the left side of your screen, press F11.

4. **Double-click the empty onClick event handler name to get into the Code Editor, where you enter the following code:**

```
if (Button1->Caption == "Red")
  {
  Panel1->Color = clRed ;
  Button1->Caption = "Green" ;
  }
else if ( Button1->Caption == "Green" )
  {
  Panel1->Color = clGreen ;
  Button1->Caption = "Blue" ;
  }
else
  {
  Panel1->Color = clBlue ;
  Button1->Caption = "Red" ;
  }
```

5. **Press F9 to run the program.**

6. **Click the button.**

   The color of the panel rotates through the colors that you entered in the Code Editor, thanks to the decision-making that you assigned to the OnClick event.

Saving work with a switch *statement*

When you have multiple options to choose from and you don't have the energy to bash in all those if . . . else combination statements, rest assured that you don't have to. C++Builder 3 has a much easier and neater way of building in such decision-making — the switch statement.

The switch statement can be broken into these three main parts:

- ✔ The *test* to see which variable you're examining for your decision
- ✔ The *case statements* to provide comparison values and corresponding code sections
- ✔ The *default code section* to sweep up any loose ends (anything you don't handle in the case statement)

For example, examine this code:

```
switch (expression)
  {
  case value1 :
      statement1 ;
  case value2 :
      statement2 ;
  case value3 :
      statement4 ;
  ...
  default :
      defaultstatement ;
  }
```

In this example code, the expression is first tested and compared against value1. If this doesn't work, the program then checks against the next value in line and so on, until it either finds one that does work or it reaches the *default* statement, which would then be executed.

One thing to remember about switch statements: Once a match has been found, all the statements that follow it are executed. If you don't want this to happen, you must enter a break statement at the end of each case (as shown in the following lines of code).

You could replace Step 3 in the previous list of steps in this section with a switch statement. For example, examine the following chunk of code:

```
switch (Panel1->Color)
  {
  case clBlue :
    Panel1->Color = clRed ;
    Button1->Caption = "Green" ;
    break ;
  case clRed :
    Panel1->Color = clGreen ;
    Button1->Caption = "Blue" ;
    break ;
  case clGreen :
  default :
    Panel1->Color = clBlue ;
    Button1->Caption = "Red" ;
  }
```

Feeling a Bit Loopy: Building Loops

Have you ever had the feeling that you are repeating yourself unnecessarily? Have you ever had the feeling that you are repeating yourself . . . sorry, got carried away!

Computers are very good and very fast at repeating the same task over and over, and unlike humans, they don't get bored. You have two choices when it comes to repeating tasks in your programs:

- ✔ Cut and paste the operation as many times as you think it will need to be performed — not the best option.
- ✔ Start building loops into your code to execute the same line of code as many times as required — a much more sensible way to go.

Several different looping code constructs are provided in C++Builder 3, and this section covers each of them.

The `for` loop

To specify how many times you want a loop to go around executing the same line of code, use the `for` loop.

Here's a generic sample of a `for` loop:

```
for (expression1; expression2; expression3)
  statement1 ;
```

In this example, the loop begins by evaluating expression1 — this is where you initialize the variables that are used in the loop. Next, expression2 is evaluated, and if it's true, statement1 is executed. Once statement1 is executed, expression3 is evaluated (this is usually used to increment counter variables). This process continues until Expression2 is false; execution then continues to the statement following the for loop.

An example of this loop is shown in the following sample code segment:

```
for (int i=0; i < 100; i++)
   strTemp[i] = ' ' ;
```

This for loop places 100 spaces in a character array. First, you need to declare a counter variable, *i* here, and set it to a starting value, 0. You then need to provide the condition that is going to signal that you're dizzy with all this spinning around and are ready to end the loop. The last part of the for loop controls the statement that indicates how large the step is going to be every time the loop is performed, so you can make the jump in steps of two or more, if you need to. Here, the jumps are made one at a time with the i++.

The while *loop*

Use this style of loop when you're not certain how many times the loop must be performed to do the job, but you know what's going to finish it off. The while loop looks simpler than the previous section's for loop and uses the following construction:

```
while (expression1)
   statement1 ;
```

In this example, expression1 is first evaluated; if it's true, statement1 is executed. This testing and executing process continues until expression1 is false. The program execution then moves on to the first statement following the while loop.

Here's a common application for the while loop:

```
Table1->First() ;
while (!Table1->Eof )
   {
   // Do what you need to here!


   .


   Table1->Next() ;
   }
```

Taking control of your loops

Sometimes you need to provide an escape route inside a loop's code. A means of escape can serve either to prevent a chunk of code from being executed unnecessarily or to prevent the code from continuously running around a loop it can't finish. Two C++ keywords — continue and break — offer you this slip road to get more control over loops.

Use the continue keyword inside a loop to jump straight back to the loop test from anywhere inside the loop code. Here's an example of how you might use this keyword:

```
Table1->First() ;
while (!Table1->Eof )
  {
  if (!Table1-
  >FieldByName("Friend")
  ->AsBoolean )
    {
    Table1->Next() ;
    continue ;
    }
  // Invite to birthday party
  code here...
  .
```

```
  .
  .
  Table1->Next() ;
  }     // end while
```

In this case, the rest of the code is skipped if you are not looking at a record that contains details on a Friend of yours.

If you need to actually get out of a loop in a hurry, call on the keyword break for a quick "ejector seat." Here's how you can use a break inside a loop:

```
if ( x >= 50 )
   break ;
```

In this case, should the variable *x* ever return a value of 50 or more, out of the loop you'll leap.

In the preceding code sample, you move to the first row of the table, and then check to see that you are "not at the end row of the table." If that expression is true, the body of the loop is executed. In this case, it will perform some task on each row of the table. At the end of the body of code for the while loop, the Table1 ->Next() ; line moves you on to the next row of the table, and the process is repeated until the end of the table is reached.

The do . . . while *loop*

A variation on the while loop is the do . . . while loop. With this type of loop, you still don't know how many times you need to perform a loop to complete the task, but you do know that you need to perform the code inside the loop at least once. Here's what the do . . . while loop looks like in action:

```
do
  {
  // repeating lines go in here
  x++ ;
  }while( x < y ) ;
```

In this case, the variable *x* is incremented at least once before the test is made to see whether *x* reached the same value as variable *y*. If not, the code is repeated.

Cut your code faster using CodeInsight

When you get to know the C++ language *constructs* (or syntax in techno-babble) a bit better, you have only one barrier to how productive you can become in your C++ Builder 3 application construction: the speed at which you can express your ideas by typing them into the Code Editor (or the speed of your fingers on those keyboard keys!). C++ Builder 3 has a really neat facility to help you get more than 100 percent productivity out of your development time. It's called *CodeInsight*. CodeInsight was developed to help you, the programmer, maximize the C++ code that you can produce, minimize those annoying typing errors, and get around your C++Builder projects with a minimum of fuss and bother. CodeInsight consists of two productivity feature: *Code Templates* and *Code Find*.

Code Templates

The C++ language control constructs introduced so far in this chapter, such as `if`, `switch`, and `while`, among others, are statements that you will use many times in your C++ Builder 3 programs. It would be tedious to type the same thing again and again; that's where *Code Templates* come in — to help save your time and fingers!

Code Templates work like this. You type a keyword, such as `switch`, into the Code Editor for one of the many predefined templates and then press Ctrl-J. This brings up a window that contains the choice of code constructs that C++ Builder 3 has for that keyword (as shown in Figure 15-1).

Select the option that you want using the up and down arrow keys, and then press Enter. C++ Builder 3 types the code into the Code Editor for you and leaves the cursor at the most suitable place for you to continue programming. Figure 15-2 shows how the Code Editor will look after you've selected the first template.

Figure 15-1:
Easily
trigger Code
Templates
from inside
the Code
Editor.

Figure 15-2 :
CodeInsight
saves you
from
needless
typing,
speeding
your coding.

So how many of these templates are there? Well, the answer to that is — as many as you care to set up for yourself. Borland has set the most common C++ language constructs already, but if you think any templates are missing, rest assured that adding new templates is a piece of cake.

Use the following steps to create a Code Template of your own:

1. Select Tools⇨Environment Options from the main menu to bring up the Environment Options dialog box.

2. Select the CodeInsight tab to show the dialog box in Figure 15-3.

Used in debugging when you rest the
cursor over a variable to show its value

Figure 15-3:
Configure
your own
templates
using the
CodeInsight
page of the
Environment
Options
dialog box.

Template shortcut names

Code for each template

3. Press the Add button to show the Add Code Template dialog box, and then enter a Shortcut Name and Description.

In this example, `intf` is used as the Shortcut Name, and `Function that returns an integer value` is used as the description.

4. Press OK, and you return to the Code window.

You are now ready to type the text you want to add in the Code Editor.

5. Type the following text in the Code window:

```
int |()
  {

  return() ;
  }
```

6. Press the OK button.

You have completed configuring your template.

The | character is used to indicate where you want the cursor to be left once the text for the template is inserted. In the case of the previous steps, the cursor will be left so that the programmer can type the name of the function following the initial `int` declaration.

Using Code Templates not only saves you time, it also saves you from those needless compiler error messages that come from typing mistakes.

Code Find

As your C++Builder 3 projects grow, you can soon lose track of all the different files in which you have made references to certain functions, or used a certain variable. *Code Find* is included in C++Builder 3 to save you time navigating around your projects as they get larger.

You gain access to Code Find by using the Search➪Find in Files options from the main menu, which brings up the Find Text dialog box, as shown in Figure 15-4.

┌Options you can use to control your Code Find

Figure 15-4 :
Use Code
Find to
pinpoint
code —
wherever
it is.

Type the text you're looking for here

Choose the scope of your search with these radio buttons

Type the text that you want to locate in the Text to find box, and then select the options that you need. Tell C++ Builder 3 where you want it to look for your text using the check boxes and radio buttons, and then press OK. You are shown a list of where occurrences of the text are found. An example of using Code Find is shown in Figure 15-5. Double-click the lines in the Message Window to be taken directly to the line of code in the file where the occurrence is found.

Code Editor shows currently selected line in Message window

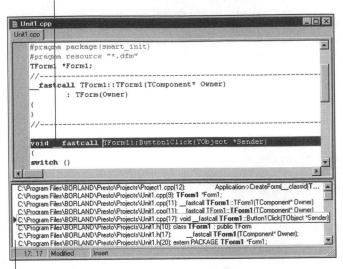

Figure 15-5:
All of the
places your
search text
is referred
to are listed
in the
results of a
Code Find.

Message window shows result of find

Chapter 16

Power Building with More Advanced Data Types

In This Chapter

▶ Using arrays to hold data

▶ Grouping your data with struct and class

▶ Encountering `void` and `return` functions

▶ Passing values to functions using arguments

▶ Handling strings with escape sequences

*B*y now, you're probably developing a taste for ordering code around with C++Builder 3 in your holster. Declaring variables, wielding mathematical operators, controlling the behavior of your programs — it's all pretty heady stuff.

In this chapter, you find out how you can corral your data using arrays, structures, classes, and functions to get more processing power out of your coding and even build your own custom data types. (***Note:*** Chapter 15 introduces you to the basics of data types. If necessary, you may want to familiarize yourself with the material in that chapter before you dive into the following sections.)

Note: All the code examples in this chapter are on the CD in the back of this book. You can find more information about the CD in the Appendix.

Hip-Hip Array: Creating Arrays

Think of an *array* as a "street" lined with data items, and each data item is a house on the street with a number on the front door. You can create arrays of all basic data types (such as int, `float`, or char) and refer to each data item by its numeric *index*. An index is somewhat like a street address — if you know the house number, you can go to that house, knock on the door, and find out who lives there; with an index number, you can get into the array and find out what the data value is at that location. This makes arrays ideal for holding lists of contiguous items such as names, numbers, or other kinds of more complicated data types, such as *struct* (refer to the section about structuring your data in this chapter for more on structs).

Because you can refer directly to each of the data items in an array by its index, arrays are also handy for processing data by using loops. For example, if you held a list of parts prices in any array and wanted to know the price of part Number 1, you would look at the data value at index 1 in the parts prices array. If the price array in this example contained a list of *integers* (whole numbers), it would look something like the following:

Index	Price
0	25
1	32
2	99
3	18
4	59

Because computers consider 0 to be a valid number, array indexes always start at location zero. So, when you create an array with x number of items, the last item will always have an index of $x-1$.

To declare this array of integers in C++, you can use the following code, which gives you an array of five integers:

```
int nPrices[5] ;
```

To access an element in the array, you use the array name followed by the index number of the element that you want. Here's an example of how to declare an integer array, how to assign values to array items, and how to retrieve a value from an array:

```
int nPrices[5] ;

nPrices[0]= 25 ;
nPrices[1]= 32 ;
nPrices[2]= 99 ;
nPrices[3]= 18 ;
nPrices[4]= 59 ;

Label1->Caption =
    nPrices[3]; // 4th element in array 18
```

A five-piece integer array is declared in the first line of this example. The next five code lines load the elements of the array with prices. The bottom line shows how you can access the fourth item in the array (remember that the index starts at 0) and load its contents into a Label component's `Caption` property.

Another method of initializing arrays looks something like this:

```
int nPrices[5] = {25, 32, 99, 18, 59} ;
```

The following example uses another data type in an array called *character pointers* (see Chapter 15 for more on pointers) to hold the name for each day of the week:

```
char *DayNames[7] =
      {"Sunday", "Monday", "Tuesday",
      "Wednesday", "Thursday", "Friday", "Saturday"} ;
```

Given this pointer, you can say that the line

```
Label1->Caption =
    DayNames[5] ; // 6th element in array "Friday"
```

loads the string `"Friday"` into the Label's Caption.

When you have more than one row to organize into a two-dimensional matrix, you can build up what's called a *two-dimensional array*. You create a two-dimensional array just as you would a regular array, except that you add a second index number. In the example line of code that follows, the first bracketed number represents the number of items across one row; the second bracketed number indicates the number of rows. The following two-dimensional array can hold 100 numbers in 10 rows of 10:

```
int Prices[10][10] ;
```

If you have to represent up to ten product ranges with each having up to ten different prices, you can show the third price for Product 2, for example, using this code:

```
Label1->Caption = nPrices[1][2] ;
```

What a handy price-lookup table this array has provided!

Grouping with Structure and a Touch of Class

The ability to group different data types and refer to them under one common type can be very useful. For example, if you maintain information on automobile parts kept in stock, you'll want to hold the price of that part, plus the part number, supplier details, part description, the number in stock, and other details. Chapter 15 tells you how to hold these items individually; the following section shows you how to bind them together.

Structuring your data

An important reserved word used in C++ programs to declare data structures is *struct*. You define struct to bind together various data types that collectively refer to the same object, which makes processing information easier. Structures offer a way of organizing data items so that the whole entity provides greater benefits than the sum of its parts. For example, assume that you need to hold information on your friends to make sure that you don't miss their birthdays. You can create a structure that holds the following information:

Age

Name

Birth date

Street

Home phone number

E-mail address

To create this structure, you can enter the following code:

```
typedef struct MyFriend
  {
  int Age ;
  char Name[30] ;
  char BirthDate[6] ;
  char Street[30] ;
  char HomePhoneNo[20] ;
  char EmailAddress[30] ;
  } TBestFriend;
```

The first line of the code indicates that you are defining a new type of structure — struct MyFriend. You then enter each item as you would if you were declaring them individually (see Chapter 15 for details on simple data types). Notice that the items that compose the structure are contained by braces — { at the beginning, and } at the end. When all of the items are declared, the last line states what the name of the new composite type will be, followed by a semicolon. You can use whatever component items you like to make a struct — even other structs.

When you want to use your new structure inside your code, you are going to need to define it, just as you would with the simpler data types such as int or char. To do this, you can write a line such as the following:

```
TBestFriend bestfriend ;
```

You first enter the new type name TBestFriend, then enter the new variable name bestfriend, and then enter the semicolon. This is the definition of the new variable bestfriend. Just remember that it's the same method you use to define simple data type variables, and you can't go wrong!

After you create your own new data type and have a variable ready to roll, it's pretty likely that you will want to do something with it. The syntax for referring to items within a structure is in this order: first the variable name for the struct, followed by a period, and then the name of the data item within the struct that you want to access. Here are examples of how you can load information into the Name and Street items for your bestfriend struct:

```
bestfriend.Name - "Jake" ;
bestfriend.Street = "CoolCat Crescent" ;
```

You can also gain access to the contents of the structure after it's loaded. To access the internal data, use the same way of referencing (that is, assigning values to) the internal data items as shown in this next line of code:

```
Label1->Caption = bestfriend.Name ;
```

This line of code places the contents of the Name data item into a Label on a form.

Using the same method for creating pointer variables to simple data types (see Chapter 15 for more on this), you can also create pointer variables to structs. One difference is that you place the characters -> between the structure variable name (bestfriend) and the data item name (Name in this example) instead of placing a period between them as was done in the previous example. Here's how it will look when accessing the Name item for a TBestFriend type:

```
TBestFriend *bestfriend=new TBestFriend;
bestfriend->Name = "Jake" ;
```

Getting classy C++ classes

Structures have a serious shortcoming: They leave their contents open to use and abuse from anywhere in the program because of the lack of a mechanism to restrict access. You can alter any data item to any value anytime you want, which is not necessarily a good thing. Because of this, developers now tend to organize and group data items by using *classes* rather than structures.

Because they contain functions as well as data items, classes enable C++ to increase its object-oriented programming power. This, in turn, enables you to build up autonomous data constructs that are more complete because they can contain their own processing rules. It doesn't matter to any code that uses a class how the data is stored internally, as long as you provide a set of "border patrol" functions. Code external to the class calls these functions that retrieve the data. External code is not allowed to access the internal data items.

The data items declared in the structure in the previous section will become data members of the class. (The official name for variables that are part of a class is *data members*.) All actions that need to be performed on the data members can be written as member functions of the class.

A C++ class declaration looks like the following sample code (with pseudo-code explanations):

```
class ClassName
  {
  private :
    // private data members and member functions go here
  public :
    // public data members and member functions go here
  protected:
    // protected data members and member functions go here
  __published:
    // specific to C++Builder 3
  } ;
```

ClassName refers to the type of name that you want to use to identify this kind of class. Following the line that uses the keyword private, you can enter your data items plus any internal class-processing functions. You place the "border patrol" functions that you want your outside code to be able to call so that they follow the line that uses the keyword public. Basically, *public* data members and member functions are accessible from outside the class. Anything declared in the *private* section can't be called from any code outside the class.

Along with public and private, the keyword protected can be used to control class access. All members that are placed in this class are accessible to all member functions of the class and to those classes that *inherit* from this class. Any data member placed in the published section is available through the Object Inspector.

To stay hip in developer circles, you may want to revise the BestFriend structure in the example given earlier in this chapter to the following "classier" version:

```
class TBestFriend
{
private :
  int Age ;
  AnsiString Name ;
  AnsiString BirthDate ;
  AnsiString Street ;
  AnsiString HomePhoneNo ;
  AnsiString EMailAddress ;
public :
  int GetAge(void){return Age;}
  void SetAge(int NewAge){Age = NewAge;}

  AnsiString GetName(void){return Name;}
  void SetName(AnsiString NewName)
    {Name = NewName;}

  AnsiString GetBirthDate(void)
    {return BirthDate;}
  void SetBirthDate(AnsiString NewBirthDate)
    {BirthDate = NewBirthDate;}

  AnsiString GetStreet(void){return Street;}
  void SetStreet(AnsiString NewStreet)
    {Street = NewStreet;}

  AnsiString GetHomePhoneNo(void)
    {return HomePhoneNo;}
```

(continued)

(continued)

```
   void SetHomePhoneNo(AnsiString NewHomePhoneNo)
     {HomePhoneNo = NewHomePhoneNo;}

  AnsiString GetEMailAddress(void)
     {return EMailAddress;}
   void SetEMailAddress(AnsiString NewEMailAddress)
      {EMailAddress = NewEMailAddress;}
};
```

You're probably saying to yourself, now hold on a minute! This is loads more code! How can this approach possibly be an improvement over the earlier `BestFriend` construct? Even though setting up a class initially involves more work than setting up a structure, the benefits abound when you make this leap into object-oriented development.

Notice that the class declaration in this structure has two sections: `private` and `public`.

You can't easily access information on the age of your friends from code external to the class; external code now has to call a function to retrieve the data contained in the age data members. That's what the `GetAge` and `SetAge` functions are used for — to provide a "border patrol" for the class. You don't have to know anything about how the class actually stores the data as you would using structures. You just know that if you call the correct member function (in this case, `GetAge`), the function returns the contents of the age data member as an integer value.

In the `TBestFriend` class created earlier in this chapter, all member functions are defined inside the class declaration. Functions declared in this way are called *inline* functions. For short-class member functions, inline functions are efficient, but as your member functions grow to be more complicated and larger, defining them inline isn't the best method.

Member functions for C++Builder 3 forms are defined outside the class definition because they are expected to become large and complicated; they are even placed in a separate file from their class declaration. A function is defined by the return type first, the class type name is prefixed to the function name with `::` (two colons) separating them, and the parameter list is within the parentheses. Here's how you can define the `TBestFriend` class `GetAge` function outside the class declaration:

```
int TBestFriend::GetAge(void)
{
return Age;
}
```

Function Junction: Adding Functions to Code

If files hold the C++ language code that you write, how is all the code within those files organized? Like other programming languages, C++ splits code within these files into separate clumps, called *functions*. Each function performs a specific task. (You come across functions while constructing the examples in previous chapters in this book.)

Note: C++Builder 3 components have event handlers, which are described in previous chapters of this book, and all of these event handlers are member functions of the forms that you create.

Even though C++Builder 3 creates all the function skeletons that you need to handle component events, you can also add your own functions straight into the Code Editor. C++Builder 3 does not prevent you from diving into the code and creating whatever functions you need.

To increase the likelihood that you can use the functions that you write more than once, write your functions to do the following:

- ✔ **Perform a distinct task:** If a function does just one job, you can add it to your "jobs-I've-got-code-for" list and call this function everytime you need that particular task performed.

- ✔ **Ideally not exceed one screen page in length:** This helps to keep your functions small, which makes them more manageable.

The void function

What if you just want a certain task performed, and you want to place the code for that task in a function of its own? If that's all you need to do, you can use what's called a void function. This construction is called *void* because there is no result to return to the code that called this function; it just performs a task. The following lines show how a void function can be constructed:

```
void FunctionName(void)
{
// Loads of lovely code goes here!
}
```

In this example, the function declaration begins with the word void, followed by the name for the function (which should give an indication of the task that the function performs). The function name is followed by arguments within parentheses. In this example, the word void is placed within the parentheses because no arguments are being passed to the function. (For more on the subject, see the later section, "Don't you just love a good argument?") After the arguments') (closing parenthesis), the *body* of the function starts. This is where the actual coding grunt work of the function is done. The function's body starts with an { (opening brace) and ends with a } (closing brace).

Return to sender functions that return *values*

Some functions *return* values to the calling function as an indication of what the function has been up to while doing its job. This return value can include data of any type. You can define a function that returns a value in the following way:

```
ReturnType FunctionName(arguments)
{
// Loads of lovely code goes here!

return(value of ReturnType) ;
}
```

If you want to define a function that returns an integer, you enter int and then a space prior to the function name.

At some point in the function, you need to say which value you want the function to return. You do this by using the following line:

```
return(value of ReturnType) ;
```

In the case of a function returning an integer, the previous line looks like this:

```
return(1) ;
```

Here's an example of how an integer value is passed back from one function to another:

```
void CallerFunction(void)    // The caller
{
int x ;
x = myFunction() ;          // The call
}


int myFunction(void)     // Well, I Define!
{
// Do lots of things first here!
.
.
return(1) ;    // The pass back
}
```

Here's how this example works: The function `CallerFunction` makes the call to `myFunction` using the line

```
x = myFunction() ;        // The call
```

This line executes `myFunction`, which then does whatever it needs to do (not a lot in this case). When it reaches the return statement, it passes back a value of 1. (You can have as many return statements as you want in a function.) This returns the program execution to the calling function, and the variable *x* is set to the returned value (1 in this case).

Don't you just love a good argument?

You can't get enough of arguments . . . within the context of C++Builder 3, that is! *Arguments* (or parameters, as they are sometimes called) enable you to pass values into functions so that you can make your functions operate on a level that's more commonly used.

You can use arguments to move values around in your programs. In fact, arguments are what the empty brackets that follow the first line of a function declaration yearn for! The following is one example of how you can use arguments in C++:

```
ReturnType FunctionName(
    argType1 argName1, argType2 argName2, .....)
{
// Loads of lovely code goes here!

return(value of ReturnType) ;
}
```

You can see by looking at the preceding sample code snippet that you state the argument type within parentheses (int, char*, and so on), followed by the argument name that you want to use to reference this argument. The argument name appears inside the body of the function, which appears between braces. You want to list arguments in this way within parentheses, separated by commas.

Here's an example that illustrates how to pass an integer and a string into a function:

```
void CallerFunction(void)
{
 int x=99 ;
 AnsiString strThis = "Space. The final frontier..." ;

 myFunction(x, strThis) ;

 // What do you think the variables hold now?

}
```

The call to myFunction in this example passes the values held in the variables x and strThis. This allows myFunction to act on these values after it receives them, as shown in the following lines of code:

```
void myFunction(int x, AnsiString strThis)
{
// Use the arguments in here
strThis = "Highly logical, Captain." ;
x = 0 ;
}
```

In this case, the original variables in CallerFunction in the previous example are not affected by any processing that is done within myFunction because myFunction acts on only copies of these variables. So, in the previous example, the variables still hold the same values (99 and "Space. The final frontier...") they did when they entered myFunction.

Imagine that you are passing a string of characters into a function as an argument, and inside the function you change the first character of every word to an uppercase letter. It would be a bit frustrating if you could not make those changes stick and reap the benefit back in the calling function. You'd be tempted to question the point of making the call in the first place. If you want to keep the changes that are made to your roving variables during their spell inside the called function, you can pass the variables as pointers (see Chapter 15 for more on pointers). To do this, you need to add an & (ampersand) character to the start of each variable when the function is called, which would look something like this:

```
myFunction(&x, &strThis) ;
```

This line of code passes the *address* of each variable in addition to its contents. In this example, you then need to change the first line of your function declaration to look something like this:

```
void myFunction(int *px, AnsiString *pstrThis)
```

Each argument has an * (an asterisk character that's sometimes referred to as a *star*) added between the argument type and argument name. The * turns these arguments into pointer types. Whenever you reference the arguments inside the function, you need to prefix the argument name with an *. The * says to the compiler that you want to gain access to the contents of the variable and not just the address (as passed by the calling function). Take a look at a complete example. Can you spot the difference in this version of the functions?

```
void CallerFunction(void)
{
int x=99 ;
AnsiString strThis = "Space. The final frontier..." ;

myFunction(&x, &strThis) ;

// What do you think the variables hold this time?
}

void myFunction(int *px, AnsiString *pstrThis)
{
// Use the arguments in here
*pstrThis = "Highly logical, Captain." ;
*px = 0 ;
}
```

In this example, pointers to the variables are passed into the function. So, when the program returns to the calling function, the contents of the string and the integer are not what they were. Now, when you refer to the variables inside the called function, you need to place an * character in front of the variable. This is how you eke out the actual variable data that is contained in the argument.

The Great Escape Characters

C++ *strings* (computer-speak for a bunch of contiguous characters) can accept more than just the visible letters of the words and sentences that the user sees. You can embed controlling characters (special characters that format your output), such as the newline character (\n), as well as odd characters, such as quotation marks, into your strings. These special character combinations are called *escape characters*.

An escape character sequence can be placed directly into any of your C++ character strings and consists of two characters, the first always being a \ (backslash). Upon seeing this character, C++Builder 3 knows that it has to do something special with the character that follows.

C++ recognizes a variety of escape characters, as Table 16-1 demonstrates.

Table 16-1   Escape-Sequence Characters and What They Do

Character Sequence	Description
\f	New form or page
\n	New line
\t	Tab character
\b	Backspace
\0	Null character (zero)
\'	' character inside a string
\"	" character inside a string
\\	\ character

To see escape characters in action, imagine that you need to display a message on two lines with quotation marks shown in your program. You can use the following line of code:

```
ShowMessage(
  "\"Feeling Lucky Punk?\"\n\"Make My Day\"") ;
```

Because double quotation marks indicate the beginning and ending of C++ strings, you need to use the \" escape character sequence every time you want to show the quotation mark itself; otherwise, C++ thinks that you are marking the end of the string. To provide a split between two lines in this example, you enter \n, the newline escape sequence. This makes the second part of the message drop down to another line.

Chapter 17

Debugging C++Builder 3 Programs

· ·

In This Chapter

▶ Dealing with compiler errors

▶ Getting inside your program while it's running

▶ Setting up breakpoints

▶ Adding watches to keep an eye on variables

▶ Changing variables to avoid errors

▶ Call stacking to keep track of called functions

· ·

*T*ime to play "Spot the Bug." Choose the type of bugs that this chapter is about:

✔ Hidden microphones in your boss's office

✔ Your colleagues' annoying habits

✔ Defects or unintentional program "features"

If you chose number 3, you win. (You didn't look ahead, did you?)

Computer programmers coined the word *bugs* to mean faults or errors within their programs that can cause nasty problems. So hold off on repellent; you don't need roaches nesting inside your PC to have bug-ridden code (even though you may find yourself repeating "But it worked perfectly last night!" when things mysteriously start to creak and pop).

At some time, you are certain to experience two types of problems (or solution starting points, to put it euphemistically) with your code:

✔ Those that stop your application from compiling (syntax errors)

✔ Those that show up during program operation (runtime or logical errors)

Obviously, you need to remove all of the first kind of bugs from your code before you can move on to finding the runtime kind (real bugs). Puns aside, this chapter's all about getting your program up and running smoothly after you've been stalled by bugs.

To help you along with your exploration of the debugging powers of C++Builder 3, there is a special debugging project with the source code from this chapter on the CD in the back of this book. For instructions on how to install the CD source code, please refer to the Appendix.

Special Delivery: Error Messages and Warnings

It isn't uncommon for your program to fail to run at all when you press the F9 key, especially the first time you press it after a long spell of writing software (what we programmers like to call "code cutting"). The program *compiler* (the part of C++Builder 3 that actually turns your code into an executable program file) often provides a list of messages or warnings (known as *syntax errors*) that tells you when your code is wrong or when you simply typed something incorrectly. C++Builder 3 uses a Message window that appears at the bottom of the Code Editor to convey these errors.

The compiler provides you with more than just the name of the file and the line number on which the problem was detected. C++Builder 3 takes you straight to the problem, as well as providing a description of the error that it found (see Figure 17-1). (Usually compiler error messages are not bugs in the program; they're just syntax errors or typos.)

Figure 17-1: C++Builder 3 takes you to the line of code on which it detected a problem.

```
Unit1.cpp

Unit1.cpp

//------------------------------------

void __fastcall TForm1::Button1Click(TObject *Sender)
{
// int nVeryUsefulCounter = 0 ;
while (nVeryUsefulCounter < 10)
  {
  Memo1->Items->Add(nVeryUsefulCounter) ;
  nVeryUsefulCounter++ ;
  }
}
//------------------------------------

[C++Error] Unit1.cpp(20): Undefined symbol 'nVeryUsefulCounter'.
[C++Error] Unit1.cpp(22): 'Items' is not a member of 'Stdctrls::TMemo'.

20: 28          Insert
```

In the case of the code snippet in Figure 17-1, the declaration for the integer has been left as a commented line by mistake, and the Items property inside Memo1 appears to exist only in the programmer's imagination.

You need to do something about blatantly incorrect code before you can run it past the compiler again. If you don't edit and fix the code by using the Code Editor, the compiler just keeps repeating the cyber equivalent to "Surely, you're joking!" and showing you the door. You need to make changes to the code to remove the syntax problems and then try to rebuild your program (pressing F9 is a quick way of compiling and running a program).

Sometimes the compiler finds that certain lines of your code are *syntactically correct* (meaning that they meet the rules of the programming language), but the compiler still cautions you with a warning. The example warning shown in Figure 17-2 is actually setting the value of the variable, not just checking the value that it contains; so you are asked whether this is really what you intended. You don't have to necessarily change any code when you see a warning message, but be sure to verify that the code that the compiler is highlighting is what you intend it to be.

Figure 17-2:
Warnings are messages in which the compiler draws your attention to code that could produce unexpected results.

License to Kill (Bugs, That Is)

After you get all the compiler errors out of your code, you're in a position to run your program and test that it works as you intended. Code operates somewhat like a car: You may be able to back it out of the driveway, but that doesn't necessarily mean that it's running smoothly or that it's not going to conk out halfway up a hill. (Okay, so I've had some cranky old cars in my time!)

When you do come across runtime problems with your programs, neither the cause nor the solution may be immediately apparent. So how do you go about unraveling the knots that you can tie yourself in? By *debugging*. Debugging is part of the cycle of getting your fare to market, and a *debugger* is a tool that enables you to step through your code, line by line, as your program runs so that you can find those nasty runtime problems.

C++Builder 3 has a fully integrated debugger, so you don't have to go jumping about running other programs to check out your code; it's all part and parcel of C++Builder 3.

Preparing for the hunt: The debug options

Before you can look under the hood of your code, you need to know some things — such as where the catch lever is! You have to make sure that you turn on the debug options for the project. (An application has to be compiled with debug options set to "on" before it is "debuggable.")

Make sure that you have the debug options set by following these steps:

1. **Choose Project⇨Options.**

   The Project Options dialog box appears.

2. **Select the Compiler tab, as shown in Figure 17-3.**

3. **Click the Full debug button in the Speed settings group.**

   C++Builder 3 then saves your activated debug settings in the project make file.

Figure 17-3:
Setting
debugger
options is
one click
away once
you're in
the Project
Options
box.

4. Click OK.

5. Rebuild your program's executable file by choosing Project⇨Build Project1.

By rebuilding the application, you allow the compiler to place extra information in the executable file, which allows C++Builder 3 to perform its debugging operations.

Setting the debug options increases the size of your application's .exe (executable) file, so after you test your application and are sure that it's bug-free and ready to roll out to your users, open the Project Options dialog box again and click the Release button to turn off the debugger settings. (Don't forget that you need to rebuild your application.)

Give your application a break: Setting a breakpoint

After you have your application on the operating table ready to dissect, where do you make the first incision?

You can set any executable line within your application to a *breakpoint*. A breakpoint is a code line that you can highlight in the Code Editor to literally stop your program in its tracks and hand control over to the debugger. Stopping the program gives you the opportunity to start poking around your variables to find out what's going on and what's not happening as you expect. When you think that you've found the section of code that's causing a particular problem, you can place a breakpoint on any line in the code that you suspect is a culprit.

You can set a breakpoint in a line in any one of several ways:

- ✔ Click the first column of the code line in the Code Editor — this toggles the breakpoint on and off. (See Chapter 1 for information on the Code Editor.)

- ✔ Place the cursor in the code line in question, and then press F5 — this also toggles the breakpoint on and off.

- ✔ Choose Run⇨Add Breakpoint to bring up the Edit Breakpoint dialog box. The line loaded into the Edit Source Breakpoint dialog box becomes the Code Editor's current line.

- ✔ Place the cursor in the code line, right-click to bring up the speed menu, and then select Toggle Breakpoint.

When you set a breakpoint in a line of code, that line becomes highlighted, as shown in Figure 17-4.

Figure 17-4:
The program halts at a line with a breakpoint (shown highlighted) and hands control to you and the debugger.

After setting a breakpoint, you can use the Edit Source Breakpoint dialog box shown in Figure 17-5 by doing the following:

Figure 17-5:
The Edit Source Breakpoint dialog box contains the details on a selected breakpoint line.

1. **Choose View➪Breakpoints from the main menu to invoke the Edit Source Breakpoint dialog box.**

2. **Select the breakpoint that you want to inspect by clicking it in the dialog box.**

3. **Right-click the breakpoint in the dialog box to bring up the speed menu.**

4. **Select the Properties option from the speed menu.**

   You can see the Edit Source Breakpoint dialog box with the details of the selected breakpoint line loaded into it.

The Edit Source Breakpoint dialog box provides more options than just a stop-at-this-line command. Suppose that you want to stop at a line only when a particular variable contains a certain value. You may want to enter a condition like the one shown in Figure 17-6. In this example, the condition specifies that the variable *nVeryUsefulCounter* must contain a value of 5 for the program to stop before executing the line in order to allow you to inspect the values currently contained in the variables.

Figure 17-6:
Adding some conditions makes a breakpoint smarter than the average breakpoint.

Another sophisticated feature of the Edit Source Breakpoint dialog box is the Pass count setting. This option is ideal for running through code that requires a great deal of looping, especially when you know you need to execute something a number of times before anything interesting happens. Simply enter into the Pass count text box the number of times the program should execute the line before it stops on the line. C++Builder 3 does the rest for you. For example, if you were to set a Pass count value of 2, the program's execution stops at the breakpoint line after executing it twice.

To view and navigate among all breakpoints, choose View⇨Breakpoints to access the Breakpoint List dialog box. As you can see in Figure 17-7, this dialog box also gives you a neat summary of what's set for each breakpoint.

Figure 17-7:
Surf the breakpoints with this dialog box.

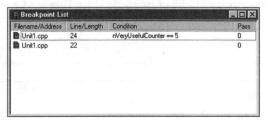

After you use a breakpoint, you may decide not to throw it away completely because you may need it again at a later stage. In this case, choose View➪Breakpoints from the main menu again to show the Breakpoint List dialog box, select the breakpoint from the list, and then right-click to bring up the speed menu. Now, click Enabled to deselect the breakpoint. The breakpoint icon in the first column of the code line in the Code Editor turns gray, and the breakpoint is put on ice for the time being.

To give all these debugging tools a go, follow the steps in this example:

1. **Create a new application by choosing File➪New Application.**

2. **Select Project➪Options from the main menu.**

3. **Select the Compiler tab on the Project Options dialog box.**

4. **Click the Full debug button.**

5. **Click OK.**

6. **Drop a Button and a Memo component (from the Standard page of the Component Palette) onto the form.**

   See Chapters 4 and 5 for the steps on how to do this.

   Two controls are now on the form — Button1 and Memo1.

7. **Click Button1, click the Events tab in the Object Inspector, and then double-click in the empty field next to OnClick.**

   You're in the Code Editor, where you enter the following code in the Button1 event handler:

   ```
   int nVeryUsefulCounter = 0 ;

   while (nVeryUsefulCounter < 10)
      {
      Memo1->Lines->Add(nVeryUsefulCounter) ;
      nVeryUsefulCounter++ ;
      }
   ```

8. **Now, set a breakpoint by clicking the following line and then pressing F5:**

   ```
   while (nVeryUsefulCounter < 10) do
   ```

9. **Choose View➪Breakpoints.**

   The Breakpoint List dialog box appears.

10. **Right-click your new breakpoint in the Breakpoint List dialog box, and select the Properties option from the speed menu that appears.**

    The Edit Breakpoint dialog box appears.

11. **Enter the following code in the Condition edit box of the Edit Breakpoint dialog box:**

```
nVeryUsefulCounter == 0
```

12. **Click the Modify button.**

    You see your condition reflected in the Breakpoint List dialog box.

13. **Move back to the Code Editor by clicking it.**

14. **Add another breakpoint by clicking the following line and then pressing F5:**

```
Memo1->Items->Add(nVeryUsefulCounter) ;
```

15. **Select View⇨Breakpoint from the main menu.**

16. **Right-click the breakpoint you created in Step 14 in the Breakpoint List dialog box.**

17. **To bring up the Edit Source Breakpoint dialog box, select Properties from the speed menu that appears.**

18. **Enter a Pass count value of 2, and then click the Modify button.**

    Well done. You have just set up your first C++Builder 3 debug session.

19. **Press F9, wait until C++Builder 3 rebuilds and runs your application, and then click the Button1 button on the application.**

Notice that the program first settles (that is, stops running temporarily) on the second breakpoint because you set the Pass count value to 2. This line is now called the *execution point* — which is like a "twilight zone" for programs because the program is still loaded, but is "frozen" at the line where you placed the breakpoint.

 If you just want to stop the debugging at this point, choose Run⇨ Program Reset from the main menu, or press Ctrl+F2. Having a program reset option is very handy if you get into one of those horrible situations where your program has stopped responding and you need to exit debugging without rebooting the computer.

Restarting the program

After you create a breakpoint to stop a program, how do you get it going again? You have four choices, as shown in Table 17-1. (See the Cheat Sheet inside the front cover for the button equivalents of pressing the F keys.)

Table 17-1	Running Code that Contains Breakpoints
Key	*Description*
F4	Runs the program up to the line where the cursor is located.
F7	Steps into the function at the execution point.
F8	Executes one line of code at a time: Steps over a function at the execution point, placing you on the next executable code line (also called "stepping through" the program).
F9	Runs the program so that it stops only when it hits a breakpoint or when the program ends.

Your program stops several times in the course of its execution. At this stage, you can't really see what's going on. What you really need is more information, which follows.

Spying on Variables with the Watch Property

When the application has paused at a breakpoint, you've got an ideal opportunity to start poking around under its hood. You can do more than just find out the value of variables at runtime; you can actually *watch* them as they change.

To place a variable under surveillance, place the cursor on the variable in question, and then press Ctrl+F5 or click anywhere on the variable in the Code Editor. Then right-click, and choose Add Watch at Cursor from the speed menu that appears. Both actions display the dialog box shown in Figure 17-8.

If you take your cursor to a variable in the Code Editor while you are debugging, C++Builder 3 instantly shows you the value of that variable in a small tip window. Handy or what?

To view the list of watch values, choose View⇨Watches. Then rerun the application built in Steps 1 through 19 in the latter part the section, "Give your application a break: Setting a breakpoint," earlier in this chapter. As your program stops on the breakpoints that you set up, you can discover the current contents of the watch items at each stage in your program's execution.

Figure 17-8:
I spy with
my little
eye . . . the
Watch
Properties
dialog box.

You can try out this procedure on the *nVeryUsefulCounter* variable in the program in which you just set breakpoints (if you followed the example in the previous section). Use these steps:

1. **Click the Code Editor window.**

2. **Click the *nVeryUsefulCounter* variable, and then press Ctrl+F5.**

   The Watch Properties dialog box appears (refer to Figure 17-8).

3. **Click OK.**

   Your variable is added to the watch list.

4. **Choose View⇨Watches to take a look at your watch list.**

5. **Press F9 to run your application again, and then click its Button component button.**

   Now, when the program stops for the first time, the Watch List dialog box shows the value that is contained in the *nVeryUsefulCounter* variable, as shown in Figure 17-9.

6. **Press F8 to step through the program.**

   You can see that the value of *nVeryUsefulCounter* increases as the loop progresses.

Changing Variable Values While a Program Is Running

C++Builder 3 provides another extremely useful debugging capability — it allows you to not only look at variable values while you are debugging a program, but to also *change* those values. This means that you can prevent potential disasters by being able to load variables with a new value when the program has stopped at a breakpoint.

Figure 17-9:
Watch the
value of
variables
change as
you step
through
your
program's
code.

Before you finish running the sample application built in Steps 1 through 19 in the section, "Give your application a break: Setting a breakpoint," try out this powerful part of C++Builder 3 debugging:

1. **When the application is paused on a breakpoint, set the cursor on any reference to** *nVeryUsefulCounter.*

2. **Press Ctrl+F7 or right-click the variable, and choose Evaluate/Modify from the speed menu that appears.**

   You see the Evaluate/Modify dialog box shown in Figure 17-10.

Figure 17-10:
You can
change a
variable
while the
program is
running by
using the
Evaluate/
Modify
dialog box.

3. **Change the value of the variable by entering any value in the New value text box.**

4. **Click the Modify button.**

   Watch as a change takes effect with the value shown in the Result box.

Continue to step through the program by pressing the F8 key. You can see that the loop terminates when the *nVeryUsefulCounter* variable equals 10.

You can place whole C++ expressions inside the Expression edit box of the Evaluate/Modify dialog box if you need to find the likely outcome of an operation. For example, you could enter a new expression (such as *nVeryUsefulCounter*99* or *nVeryUsefulCounter+45-40*99*) in the Expression edit box, and see the answer in the Result box when you click the Evaluate button.

Using Call Stacking to Keep Track of Called Functions

As your programs become more complex, there may be many calls to a particular function. As such, you may not be certain which route the program took through your code to arrive at a particular breakpoint at a particular time.

You can keep track of which functions have been called within others by using the Call Stack option under View in the C++Builder 3 main menu. Call stacking provides a list of the functions that were called in order for the program to end up at the current line.

When you reach a breakpoint in a function, choose View➪Call Stack from the main menu. In the Call Stack dialog box shown in Figure 17-11, the current function is shown at the top of the list. The parameters that are passed to each function are shown as address values. You need to get a bit technical to interrogate these, so I don't cover the details of address interrogation in this chapter.

In Figure 17-11, values for arguments that are passed into functions are also shown — in this case, you can see address locations. An *address* is a reference to a location within the computer's memory where an application is executing.

Figure 17-11:
The Call
Stack
feature
helps you
keep track
of the
functions
called for a
program.

If you need to skip back to a function that is higher up in the call stack than your current location, follow these steps:

1. **Double-click the line in the Call Stack dialog box that contains the function you want to reach.**

2. **Move the cursor to the first line of the function.**

3. **Press F4 to make the program run to that line.**

Chapter 18

Error-Proofing C++Builder 3 Programs

• •

In This Chapter

▶ Anticipating where your program can go wrong

▶ Catching errors with `try...catch` statements

▶ Protecting code blocks with `try...__finally`

▶ Throwing your own exceptions

▶ Identifying candidates for exceptions

▶ Integrating exception handling into your applications

• •

*Y*ou can always rely on one thing in application development, especially under Windows: You can never rely on anything. You may have spent many hours writing and debugging your program and may be absolutely sure that you've got it 100 percent correct, but the potential for problems always exists.

If you assume that every machine your program runs on is set up in the same way as your own, you're bound to be in for a bumpy ride. Try to think of where your program is most vulnerable, and then look to protect it against the worst.

A program's Achilles' heel can be found in any one of a few places, for example:

✔ **User entry range and type errors:** What if the user enters numbers that your program does not anticipate, such as negative or very large values?

✔ **Lack of disk space:** How will your program react if your hard disk becomes half-full while you're in the process of building something?

✔ **Database access errors:** What happens if a user removes one of your crucial tables or if the database server goes off-line for some reason?

When you want to check out some of the ideas in this chapter, you can use the example projects supplied on the CD in the back of this book.

Taking Some Preventive Measures

If you are looking to add both belt and braces to protect your program against the unexpected (such as dropping down around your ankles), you can go about this in a longhand way. You first need to think of all the ways in which the operations performed in your code can fail and then check every line in every function to see that the task in hand has been performed correctly before moving on to the next line of code. For example, assume you have three simple function calls such as the following:

```
myFunction1() ;
myFunction2() ;
myFunction3() ;
```

To provide any degree of real error protection, you have to change the three previous lines of code to end up looking something like this code section:

```
ret = myFunction1() ;
if (ret == false)
  return(false) ;
ret = myFunction2() ;
if (ret == false)
  return(false) ;
ret = myFunction3() ;
if (ret == false)
  return(false) ;
```

That makes for a lot of return values and a lot of extra code, especially if you think that each line within these functions requires the same level of protection. This code is messy to write as well as to follow when it comes time to enhance further versions. Add to this the fact that you may actually find yourself spending more time writing the error-handling code than writing the actual application, and you're entitled to wrinkle your nose at this method. This leads to the main subject of this chapter: the C++Builder 3 built-in method for effective and efficient error handling.

The following sections give you an introduction to the C++Builder 3 error-protection techniques and then show you how C++Builder 3 provides an error-protection approach at an application level.

Using Exception Handling

An *exception* is another term for an error (or any other unexpected result), and when an exception occurs (such as when you run out of disk space), you need to deal with the error in some way — that's when *exception handling* enters the picture. The implementation of exception handling comes in two parts:

- First, you have to state which areas of code you want to protect so that when an error is detected, details of the exception can be passed to the section of code that can handle that particular problem.

- Depending on the type of exception, the program may be able to continue. At other times (such as the program not being able to locate its main data file), continuing with the program's execution may not be possible; then there may be no choice but to bring down the curtain and close the program.

 A definition is in order here: *Exception handling* can be thought of as controlling the way that your program reacts when an error is encountered or when unexpected results from an application occur at runtime.

Try to protect your functions

You can determine which sections of code you want to place under the custody of exception handling. To do so, use a try { } block, as follows:

```
try
  {
  myFunction1() ;
  myFunction2() ;
  myFunction3() ;
  }
```

The program tries to execute the code contained in the braces, and if an error occurs, the program's normal flow of execution is interrupted and moved to the end of the try section, indicated by the closing brace. An interruption of the normal program flow such as this is called *throwing an exception*.

catch *out any errors*

When normal program execution flow is interrupted by an error, you need a mechanism to see what kind of error has occurred and what to do next.

That's when the `catch` statement is introduced. It has a section of code associated with it that is delimited by opening and closing braces — { and }. The statement looks like the following:

```
catch(...)
  {
  // perform error handling code
  }
```

The (. . .) (three dots in the parentheses after the catch) means that no matter what type of error occurs, the code in the catch is expected to handle it. You can get much more specific by placing object types inside the parentheses of the catch statement. Here are some examples of what you can place within the parentheses:

```
catch(char *Message)
catch(const EDataBaseError &E)
```

In these cases, the program goes into the section of code that follows the catch only if the exception throws an object of the data type declared in the brackets. (See Chapters 15 and 16 for more on data types.)

You can use multiple `catch` sections for a single `try` section to handle several types of exceptions that can be thrown within a single code segment. The program then checks the error that occurs against each `catch` statement to see which one applies.

The following code structure shows how you can implement multiple `catch` sections:

```
try
  {
  // exception handling on
  .
  .
  .
  }
catch( exception_type_1)
  {
  // exception handling code here
  }
catch( exception_type_2)
  {
  // exception handling code here
  }
```

When you use multiple catch statements, start by catching the most specific exceptions first, gradually becoming more and more general. If you don't, the program is always lured into the general exception handler first and never gets to see the catch statements that follow.

try...catch *together*

You can put try and catch expressions together by using the following example of some real code. Assume that you are opening a data table inside a function. You can protect against the table open failing by using something similar to the following:

```
try
   {
   Table1->Open() ;
   }
catch(Exception &E)
   {
   ShowMessage("Bad News! " + E.Message ) ;
   }
```

C++Builder 3 provides you with a whole family of exception objects to ease the job of using exception handling. The Exception referred to in the catch line is a class type in its own right; it's actually at the head of the whole family of exception types. (You can even build your own exception-handling classes based on this exception class.) Notice that you can use the Message property of the exception class to get the exception that was thrown to give you a description of itself.

Get Code __finally *Sorted*

Another way of preventing your code from ever bringing the computer to its knees is by using try . . . __finally. With a try . . . __finally, you can make sure that a certain set of code statements runs whether there has been a major problem or not. Use these steps to check this out:

1. **Choose File⇨New Application from the main menu, and place one Edit component and a Button component (from the Standard page of the Component Palette) on the form.**

2. **Double-click the Button component to go into the Button component's** `OnClick` **event handler in the Code Editor, where you can type the following lines of code:**

```
try
  {
  StrToInt(Edit1->Text) ;
  }
__finally
  {
  ShowMessage(
    "The finally code block always executes") ;
  }
```

3. **Press F9 to run the application.**

When you press the application's button, the code that you typed in Step 2 attempts to convert the `Edit1` into a number. If the conversion is not successful (because the Edit component contains letters, not just numbers), an exception is raised. In any case, the `The finally code block always executes` message is displayed.

Throwing an Exception

This exception stuff looks as though it can be pretty handy. Wouldn't it be great if you could create exceptions of your very own to kick out of functions? Well, you can.

Suppose that the user types something truly dumb (imagine that!). You can throw your own exceptions. Here's an example of how you can handle that situation by using an exception:

```
if (Edit1->Text == "")
  throw "Nothing Entered In Edit1" ;
```

You use the `throw` keyword to throw an exception of your own. In this case, you're actually throwing a message string (refer to Chapters 15 and 16 for more on data types) out with the exception. The bigger code picture looks like this:

```
try
  {
  if (Edit1->Text == "")
```

```
      throw "Nothing Entered In Edit1" ;
      .
      .
      .
      }
catch (char *Message)
    {
    ShowMessage(Message) ;
    }
```

Notice that the catch picks up a char* data type. That means the specific throw error message is displayed. You can use this technique to check user entries on controls on a form as part of the validation.

Don't think that you can throw only simple data types; you can also fit classes or objects into your exception-handler catapult. You can then pass over much more information and even provide the event handler built-in functionality.

Building an Exception-Handling Class

An *exception-handling class* is the program's reaction or the information provided to warn the user that some error has occurred or that the function's result does not match the program criteria.

Time to flex those fingers and put some of this theory into action by building your own exception-handling class. Just follow the steps in this example:

1. **Choose File⇨New Application from the main menu, and place two Edit components and a Button component (from the Standard page of the Component Palette) in the form.**

   Three controls — Button1, Edit1, and Edit2 — are now on the form.

2. **Click the Code Editor (press F12 to get the Code Editor), and then press Ctrl+F6 to go to the new form's header file.**

3. **Enter the following lines in the header file directly after the list of #include lines near the top of the file:**

```
class UserError {
public:
    int Code ;
    AnsiString Message ;
    void LogError(void)
        { ShowMessage(Message) ; }
} ;
```

That's the error-handling class.

4. Press F12 to go back to the form itself.

5. Double-click the Button component that you placed on the form in Step 1.

You then end up in the Code Editor in the `OnClick` event handler, where you enter the following lines:

```
try
  {
  if (Edit1->Text == "")
    throw "Nothing Entered In Edit1" ;
  if (Edit2->Text == "")
    {
    UserError UErr ;
    UErr.Code = -1 ;
    UErr.Message = "Please Complete Edit2" ;
    throw UErr;
    }
  }
catch(char *Message)
  {
  ShowMessage(Message) ;
  }
catch(UserError Err)
  {
  Err.LogError() ;
  }
```

6. Press F9 to run the program.

With the program running, if you clear out either of the Edit controls before pressing the button, you get a message informing you that the Edit control on the form has caused an exception. Notice that each exception type finds its own exception-handling statement according to the data type that was thrown with the exception.

One of the benefits of using exception handling is that all locally declared variables (the variables that you declared within the function that the exception occurred in) are freed when an exception is raised.

Identifying Exceptions Candidates

So what about some real examples of how exceptions can change your coding life? Exception handling makes a real difference in three cases:

- Data conversion
- Code savers
- Database handling

Now I cover what I consider to be the most important of the three situations — data conversion. Converting data from one format to another, especially where the data has been provided by the user or any other nonvalidated source, can be fraught with danger. You can protect code lines that perform these operations as follows:

```
try
  {
  int i = StrToInt(Edit1->Text) ;
  }
catch (const EConvertError &convertE)
  {
  ShowMessage(" Bong!") ;
  }
```

Don't assume that the user will enter what you expect. Using the steps in the previous section, if a user enters letters in the Edit1 box instead of entering numbers, the conversion is going to go bust on you. But you don't need to worry because by placing the code within the braces of the try and handling rogue entries in the catch section, you protect the code from bad user entries that "blow up" your program.

C++Builder 3 Exception Class Types

C++Builder 3 provides you with some ready-made classes that were derived from the exception class. It's worth becoming familiar with these classes because they provide information pertinent to their type of exceptions. Use the following reference syntax to catch these exception types:

```
catch (const exception_class_type &exception_variable_name)
```

In the previous line of code, you specify the class type of the exception that you want to catch and provide a variable name that you want to use to refer to the exception within the `catch` section of code. A real-world example looks like the following code:

```
catch(const EDBEngineError &dbErr)
```

This statement catches all exceptions that were caused by a Borland Database Engine error using the `EDBEngineError` class. (For more on the Borland Database Engine, refer to Chapter 10.) References to this exception are made through the variable `dbErr`, although you can use any name that you like.

Table 18-1 gives you an introduction to the ready-made exception classes that C++Builder 3 provides for you.

Table 18-1	Exception Classes and How They Are Used
Exception Class	*Use*
EAbort	Throw this exception when you want to stop a sequence of events that has been triggered, but don't necessarily want a whole "song-and-dance" routine performed to announce the fact.
EAccessViolation	Use this exception class if you need to check for invalid memory access errors.
EBitsError	Throw an exception object of this type if you use an invalid index on a Boolean array.
EClassNotFound	If you manually remove component references from your form's header file, you may see this exception.
EComponentError	If C++Builder 3 cannot register or rename a component, this is the exception type that it raises.
EConvertError	If you try to convert a string to an integer and the attempt fails, this is the exception class. Code such as `int i = StrToInt(iABCi);` is a prime contender for this exception.
EDatabaseError	This exception class covers a multitude of sins where database access is concerned. Always check out the `Message` property contents for a clue when you get this exception!
EDBEditError	If you set a `Mask` property (Chapter 6 explains `Mask` properties) that does not fit the type of data that a data-aware edit box is placing below it, this is the exception class you get.

Exception Class	Use
EExternalException	This is the class of exception generated for any exceptions that cannot be identified.
EDBEngineError	This exception class is derived from EDatabaseError and provides some extra properties.

Integrating Exception Handling into Your Applications

So much for using exceptions within the C++ language itself. It's a powerful enough technique using solely what you've seen already. In true C++Builder 3 style, though, you're provided with more features that allow you to *fully* integrate exception handling into your applications. You have the Application object to thank for these features.

For an Application object, you can create your own handler and hook it in, as with any other event handler that you create. You first need to define an exception-handler function with the same signature as the Application object's. The function should take two arguments: one of TObject type and the other of Exception type. Here's an example of the first line of the function that you can use to start defining your own exception handler:

```
void __fastcall TForm1::myHandleException(
            TObject *Sender, Exception *E)
```

TECHNICAL STUFF

Count on loop control with the ErrorCount **exception**

You can interrogate an array of Error objects by using the ErrorCount exception class as a loop control.

The following example shows how a catch statement can be written to provide you with information from a database error array.

```
catch (
  const EDBEngineError &dbErr)
  {
```

```
for (int i=0;
    i < dbErr.ErrorCount; i++)
    ShowMessage(
      dbErr.Errors[i]->Message
    + " " +
    IntToStr(dbErr.ErrorCount)
      ) ;
}
```

Any member functions that you add to a form also need to be declared in the form's header file.

Enough talk — the best way to understand this is to just work with it, so now you see how to add an application-level exception log table to a program. You need to first create the table that's going to hold the log of program exceptions that are not handled directly by `catch` statements throughout your program. Here goes:

1. **Choose Tools⇨Database Desktop from the C++Builder 3 main menu.**

   This starts the database maintenance utility called Database Desktop.

2. **Choose File⇨New⇨Table from the main menu of Database Desktop.**

   You are presented with the Create Table dialog box.

3. **Click OK to create a Paradox 7-type table.**

4. **Add the following fields to the table by entering** TimeStamp **and then pressing the Tab key, entering @ and then pressing the Tab key twice, entering** Description **and then pressing the Tab key, entering** A **and then pressing the Tab key, and finally, entering** 255.

5. **Click Save As.**

6. **Select** BCDEMOS **from the Alias drop-down menu.**

7. **Enter** LogFile.DB **into the File name edit box that appears after Step 5.**

8. **Click Save.**

9. **Close the Database Desktop utility by selecting File⇨Exit from the utility's main menu.**

   Now the Database Desktop has performed its duty. A table has been saved in the BCDEMOS database, which gets installed when you install C++Builder 3.

10. **Go back to C++Builder 3 by clicking the main form of the program.**

11. **Drop a Table component and DataSource component from the Data Access page of the Component Palette onto the program's main form.**

12. **Set the** DatabaseName **property of the Table component to** BCDEMOS **using the property's drop-down menu in the Object Inspector.**

13. **Select** LogFile.DB **from the Table component's** TableName **property drop-down menu.**

14. **Set the** Active **property of the Table component to** true.

15. **Set the** DataSet **property of the DataSource component to** Table1.

16. **Press F12 to get into the Code Editor.**

17. **Press Ctrl+End.**

    This command moves you to the bottom of the source file of the form.

18. **Enter the following function in its entirety into the Code Editor:**

```
void __fastcall TForm1::myHandleException(TObject
     *Sender, Exception *E)
  {
  ShowMessage(" AppXHandler: " + E->Message) ;

  Table1->Append() ;
  Table1->FieldByName(
    "TimeStamp")->AsDateTime = Now() ;
  Table1->FieldByName(
    "Description")->AsString = E->Message ;
  Table1->Post() ;
  }
```

19. **Click the main form for this example, and then select the Events tab on the Object Inspector.**

20. **While still in the Object Inspector, double-click the empty field next to the `OnCreate` event handler name for the form, and enter the following line:**

```
Application->OnException = myHandleException ;
```

    This step substitutes the `myHandleException` function for the default application exception handler.

21. **Go to the header file by pressing Ctrl+F6 to declare the `myHandleException` in the form class.**

22. **Add the following line in the public section of the form's class:**

```
void __fastcall myHandleException(
     TObject *Sender, Exception *E) ;
```

23. **Drop a Button component button onto the form. Double-click the button to take you into the Code Editor, where you can type the following lines of code:**

```
throw EExternalException(
      "Generate Exceptions As U Like!") ;
```

    This last step provides unhandled exceptions for the example.

24. **Press F9 to run the program so that you can see the fruits of your labor.**

Now, every time you click your new button, you are creating an unhandled exception, which causes the myHandleException function to be called. The code that you placed in the myHandleException function displays a message and then adds a record to the table noting that an exception has occurred.

When you get bored watching the message, turn your attention to the Database Explorer (choose Database⇨Explorer from the main menu), and look at the log table entries. Not only has the exception message been added, but you can also see exactly when the exception occurred, thanks to the date and time entries.

Part V
The Part of Tens

The 5th Wave   By Rich Tennant

" RUMOR HAS IT THAT TOM'S COMPANY IS BEING BOUGHT OUT BY A
MULTI-NATIONAL."

In this part . . .

By now, you're probably feeling like a C++Builder 3 master architect and programming guru, constructing nifty (and dependable) applications in record time. But even the pros can benefit from a few tricks of the trade and, indeed, are always open to new ideas.

In this part, you find lists of do's and don'ts (ten in each chapter, give or take a couple) that you want to commit to memory. The material here is brief and easy to digest, so I wouldn't be surprised if you read this part first!

Chapter 19

Ten Ways to Get the Most Out of C++Builder 3

• •

In This Chapter

▶ Understanding string conversions

▶ Using components

▶ Placing comments

▶ Naming objects

▶ Providing program user interface tips

▶ Borrowing from Delphi

▶ Building reusable code segments by using components and classes

▶ Keeping application functional "rules" separate

• •

*U*nderneath the Borland C++Builder 3 modest exterior beats the heart of an industrial-strength C++ compiler. As you get more serious about building applications — and the applications that you build become more complicated — you'll probably want to let C++Builder 3 expose more of its application development muscle. In this chapter, I mix direct coding tips with hints on coding practice, the intention being to prevent you from stubbing your toe on some of the hazards around your construction site.

Performing String Conversions

C++Builder 3 provides more than one method of storing *strings,* the fancy name for a set of contiguous characters. Consider the difference between these two types of strings:

> ✔ **AnsiString class:** The Edit component, for example, has a Text property for holding users' entries that employs the AnsiString type. This AnsiString C++ class is used to implement strings throughout C++Builder 3 components. A native C++ string doesn't play ball like AnsiString because it's nowhere near as sophisticated. A native C++

string is simply an *array* of characters (a data type that essentially acts like a bunch of cells to store information). It holds no information that refers to the string's size or any other string property.

- **Native C++ character array strings:** In native C++ character array strings, the first data element begins at 0 (zero). The character data for the string then continues until a special character acts as a "stop sign." This stop character has a value of 0 — the so-called *null character* or *terminating null*.

At some point, you may have to introduce these two types of strings to each other in one of your applications, especially if you want to hook in some existing C++ code. Because the two data types go about holding their data differently, you may have to do some converting between the AnsiString and null-terminated string before you can copy a string from one type into the other.

To convert from a C++ character array to an AnsiString type is easy. Because AnsiStrings are smarter than C++ character array string types, you don't have to do a great deal to them; just assign the value of the character array straight to the AnsiString variable. The following lines of code give you an example:

```
char WhistleWhileYouWork[] =
      "Hi Ho, Hi Ho, it's off to work we go..." ;
Button1->Caption = WhistleWhileYouWork ;
```

The process for converting from an AnsiString type to a C++ character array string type is a little less obvious. Fortunately, the AnsiString type has a built-in member function called c_str(). Use the c_str() function as it returns the contents of the AnsiString in a null-terminated string format. When you need to, copy the result from this function to a waiting character array. The following snippet of code gets the user input from an edit box and places it in a null-terminated string:

```
strcpy( cTemp, Edit1->Text.c_str() ) ;
```

Using Third-Party Components

In addition to the components that come already installed on the C++Builder 3 component palette, a whole industry has sprung up to provide extra components that you can buy and install. You can then use these additional components as you would all others. C++Builder 3 components can be based on either C++ or Object Pascal (the language of Delphi — another Borland development tool), so you can also use any of the thousands of tried-and-tested Delphi components.

Most companies that offer third-party components offer the source code as well, often for an extra fee, so that you can see how the component is constructed (*source code* refers to the actual .cpp or .pas files that you write, edit, and compile). If possible, you should always buy this source code, too. Here's why:

✔ A company that makes its source code available obviously has nothing to hide about the way the product is built, so chances are good that the component is well written.

✔ You can unearth massive amounts of useful information by looking through the source code written by experienced developers.

✔ If the company that supplies the component runs into trouble, you can always support your application if you have the source code.

How can you find out what sort of components are out there? Try trade shows, conferences, magazines, and other developers. For many people, one-stop shopping on the Internet provides the needed component. Thousands of components are available in cyberspace as freeware, shareware, and pay-and-download programs. A selection of third-party components for you to try is included on the CD in the back of this book.

Obtaining components over the Internet has potential dangers. Don't assume that just because you download a component from an advertiser on the Web that it's well-written, thoroughly tested, and does what the developer claims. I'm not doubting the integrity of the many excellent developers who vend their wares over the Net, but don't forget that your end user must rely on whatever it is *you* choose to provide. Try out the downloaded component demo first and e-mail any questions you have about how you intend to use the component to the developer.

After considering the preceding words of warning, don't be disheartened. Using other people's components is a great way to leap-frog hours or maybe days of work.

Inserting Comments into Your Code

Suppose that you're asked to add some features and fix some problems in an application that you and a colleague wrote months ago. You have all but forgotten the project, but you vaguely remember the bits that you did write. The problem is that your partner has left the company, and you never got to see the code that she wrote.

Sound familiar? These kinds of situations do arise from time to time, and access to some answers (or even just a clue!) in the code can certainly make your job easier.

Intelligent and consistent use of commenting saves you and your colleagues a great deal of wasted time trying to remember what you were thinking about on that Friday afternoon a year ago when you wrote the program!

If you aren't sure how to actually place comments in C++ code, the following table shows the syntax for C++ comment lines and blocks.

Syntax	Description
//	Comments out the rest of the line.
/*	Starts a comment block.
*/	Ends a comment block.

Here's an example of how a comment block can look in your code:

```
nAdjust =
    nValue - nFactor ; // This part of the line's a comment
/*
Here you can
 write a whole paragraph
       if you need to. . .
*/
```

One of the primary places you should religiously place comments is at the top of each C++ source file. The following is an example of a code file header comment block. At the very least, you know who to call to find out what's going into the code (unless, of course, you're the person who wrote it!).

```
//---------------------------------------------------
// Unit Name:  Unit1.cpp
// Author:     Your Name
// Date Created:  Christmas Day
//
// Purpose
// =======
// Explain here the job this unit does...
//
// Modifications:
//
// Date        Done By       Details
// ====        =======       =======
// 05-Apr-98   Your Name     Added a new widget
//
// Copyright (c) A.Company 1998
//---------------------------------------------------
```

Function header comments not only help separate functions within the source code file, but also provide an opportunity to state what you're setting out to do in a function and how you're actually going to do it. Think about how these comments could save you time if you haven't seen a particular function before and need to determine what the code is supposed to do. Here's a suggested starting point for a function header:

```
//
// Function: myFunction
// Purpose: Brief explanation of what function does and
//          how it does it.
//
//
void myFunction()
  .
  .
  .
```

Naming Objects and Variables

In the line of application development duty, you create objects and variables of all types (as you know by now, *objects* contain data and the routines that process the data; *variables* are names used to represent a piece of information). C++Builder 3 provides default names (Edit1, Edit2, and so on) for the objects that you create using the Form Designer (the C++Builder 3 tool that allows you to place and manipulate components, among other things), but these names are far from ideal for all but the simplest applications. Imagine having a form with ten edit boxes. You would soon be in trouble, wondering whether Edit7 holds the phone number or fax number.

A good habit to develop is to rename controls as you place them in forms. Indicate the type of variable by using an abbreviation as a prefix. All form names can begin with frm, all buttons with btn, and so on, as you can see from the table that follows. Follow the prefix with a meaningful name that refers to the control's task, such as btnClose and edName.

Components renamed in this way also show up in an orderly fashion in the Object Inspector (you use the Object Inspector to modify a component's properties and events). The following table shows some common prefixes that can be used for basic C++Builder 3 component types.

Prefix	Component Type
btn	TButton
cb	TComboBox
ds	TDataSource
ed	TEdit
frm	TForm
n	Integer
lbl	TLabel
pnl	TPanel
qry	TQuery
str	String
tbl	TTable
tim	TTimer
w	Word

Supplying User Interface Tips

If you're new to developing Windows applications, the choices you have available for what to include in the user interface may seem overwhelming. Keep in mind that your interface should be reasonably intuitive and user-friendly. With that in mind, I offer the following suggestions:

✔ If you've built list boxes or combo boxes that allow the user to make selections within selections, think about providing a *TreeView* component for the user to navigate (see Figure 19-1). This type of component offers the user a way to not only view but also manage multiple-level data. (Chapter 8 has more information on TreeViews.)

✔ Most computer users are accustomed to Windows applications looking and behaving in a certain way. If you stick to these conventions, you make life easier for your users. If you ignore these conventions, you increase the frequency of users swearing at their computer screens while trying to work with something you built. The File⇨Exit command, for example, should always be assigned the shortcut keys Alt+F, Alt+X, respectively; and F1 should always be the key to press for help.

✔ Provide your users instant access to menu options with *speed buttons* (that's the name for the buttons that are lined up under the main menu in a window within an area called a *speed bar*). The great thing is that you don't have to duplicate the code from menu command code; just hook the speed button's OnClick event to the appropriate menu event handler.

Figure 19-1:
TreeView
components,
such as the
one in this
figure, help
the user
organize file
hierarchies.

 Don't be tempted to use oversized buttons and spread your application around numerous forms. This is a trap that snares many developers who are new to Windows. You can offer the same functionality using more varied control types.

Using Delphi Code

C++Builder 3 is capable of something clever that adds greatly to its flexibility. You can incorporate Delphi code and forms straight into your C++Builder 3 applications. (Delphi is Borland's Pascal-based rapid application development tool.) There may be Delphi code that's just right for part of your current application. Ideally, you won't need to go through the rigmarole of rewriting the code in C++ or even having to make any changes in it.

If you want to include a complete form by using Delphi, choose Project➪ Add to Project (or press Shift+F11) to display the Add to Project dialog box. Select Pascal Unit (*.pas) from the Files of type drop-down list. Then select your Delphi code unit, and click the Open button. The form is now part of your project.

You can find out whether the Delphi form has been added to your project by choosing View➪Project Manager.

Now that the form is part of the project, how do you go about using it? Just include it in the calling unit by choosing File➪Include Unit Hdr. C++Builder 3 automatically creates a C++ header file for you. Then show the form by using code such as the following:

```
frmDelphiForm->ShowModal() ;
```

Avoiding Code Déjà Vu

What can be more frustrating than knowing you've already coded a task or function in another project, but you can't find the code that you wrote? Even worse, you find the code that you wrote, but you end up rewriting it anyway because extracting the pieces that you need would take just as much time. Obviously, the more code you can reuse, the less code you have to write, and the faster you get the job done. Also, if you are using proven functions, classes, and components, your programs take less time to test and debug.

Building components is an obvious way of writing code that you can plug into your programs, but even when you don't package code this way, you can still benefit from a code-reuse strategy:

- **Always try to solve a problem in the most general terms.** When you come across a similar situation in the future, you may well have some code that goes at least part way toward providing a solution. Try to build functionality into classes that perform specific tasks. (See Chapter 16 for more information on classes.)

- **While cutting your code, always express your ideas in small, simple code functions and source code files.** You're more likely to reuse a small file that performs a single straightforward task than to reuse a large, application-specific source code file that performs several operations.

- **Make sure each source code file does only one job.** If you need to write a function that performs a task on two strings, for example, pass in the two strings as parameters rather than use globally accessible variables. In this way, you make the function more self-contained and easier to add to your list of the top 1,001 useful functions.

- **Start thinking about accumulating useful code right now.** Make sure that you add at least one entry to your useful-code library from every decent-size program you write; that way you are always working toward your aim of maximum code reuse.

- **Don't try to do anything too fancy.** Your library addition can consist of just a folder in which you collect your own set of useful code units. Don't forget that you can include the location of your library folder in the Include path of your project's options.

Understanding Business Objects

Spot the workplace object in the following list:

- Fax machine
- Photocopier
- *Star Trek* desk clock
- Bill-processing rules class

I suppose that all these items are business objects in one way or another. But only the fourth item fits the bill as far as C++Builder 3 is concerned.

You can create a business object as a class or (ideally) as a nonvisual component. Then you can just drop the object onto a form and reference the object's properties and methods to apply calculations and verification for the form.

Suppose that you are writing an order-processing system. You can write a class to verify that all of the conditions have been met to allow the order to proceed, as well as to provide functionality such as automatic discounting according to specific rules. The following code segment shows how you can organize these rules in a self-contained class. Other parts of the application gain access to these rules via the class member functions and do not perform these tasks directly:

```
class TOrderValidation
{
private:    // User declarations
        int nOrderNo ;
public:     // User declarations
        TOrderValidation(void);
        int GetOrderNo(void) ;
        bool InStock(int PartNo) ;
        void ApplyDiscount(void) ;
};
```

No code outside the class has anything to do with *how* the validation process operates. Implementing a change means making a single visit to just the OrderValidation class. You still need to recompile the applications that rely on this object to implement the changes across the board, but you don't have to make any code changes in them.

Chapter 20

Ten Common Mistakes You Won't Make Again

I rounded up a bunch of common pitfalls that nearly all C++Builder 3 programmers stumble into sooner or later. So don't be disheartened if you commit one of the goofs listed in this chapter when building an application. And if you haven't encountered problems like these before, you can't say you weren't warned.

Don't Leave Off Ending Comments

The symptom: Your program won't compile and the Message Window says `Unexpected end of file in comment started on line XX` (XX being the number of the line in question).

This compiler error message is telling you that you started a comment section using /* and forgot to end the comment with */. After you press F9 to compile, link, and run your program, C++Builder 3 runs through your code, hits the end of the file without finding an end comment, and you get the error message.

To fix this problem, return to the line of code cited in the error message, and look carefully to see where you need to add `*/` to end the comment section.

Don't Skip the Next Statement in a Loop

The symptom: The program "hangs up" your machine.

When you need to perform a section of code more than once, but you're not sure of the exact number of times you need to repeat it, use a `while` loop to test your code prior to executing it. When the `while` statement becomes `false`, the program execution moves on to the line of code following the closing brace (`}`) of the `while` statement. (See Chapter 15 for more on `while` statements.)

The catch is that you may inadvertently write some code in which the `while` loop tests a condition that will never change to `false`. The program winds up in a never-ending loop, which makes the program appear to stop.

An example of how a program can get hung up because of a never-ending `while` loop occurs when the program is stepping through the rows of a data table in your code. The following code shows you an example of how the `while` loop *should* be constructed:

```
Table1->First() ;
while (!Table1->Eof)
   {
   // perform data processing tasks here

   Table1->Next() ;
   }
```

In this code sample, the program sets the table to the first record, and then the `while` statement checks to see whether this is the last record in the table. If it isn't, the code inside the { and } (the starting and closing braces) is executed to move the table on to its next record.

It's easy to inadvertently miss the `Table1->Next() ;` line of code. This oversight effectively stalls the program on the first record of the table forever, or at least until you stop the action by forcing the program to end. The best way to avoid this problem is to place the `Table1->Next() ;` line into the `while` loop *before* you type the rest of the body of the loop. Then you can rest assured that the loop will eventually end!

Don't Use = (Instead of ==) in an if Statement

The symptom: The code section associated with an if statement is either always executed or never executed.

The if statement is used to test the condition of variables inside your program to allow program decisions to be made. Basically, you're telling the computer to execute a particular statement *if* a certain condition holds true.

Along with comparing values higher or lower than one another, if statements are also often used to check two values for equality. The syntax for that comparison looks something like the following:

```
if (a == b)
```

In the preceding line of code, two = (equal) signs are entered next to each other. If, by mistake, you happen to use a single = character, like this

```
if (a = b)
```

you are going to get a different, and often unexpected, result. The preceding line of code says the value of variable a is equal to b, but does not test the two variables for equality.

Because the second if statement is syntactically correct, when you compile and run your program by pressing F9, C++Builder 3 won't stop with a compile error. Instead, the warning message Possibly incorrect assignment appears with a reference to the line number that contains the if statement in question. That's your cue to check that line's syntax.

Don't Forget to Place break Statements in switch Statements

The symptom: A switch statement calls more lines of code than anticipated.

You can use the switch statement to help organize complex decision-making inside your code. If you're new to C++ development, one potential stumbling block that may trip you up with the switch statement happens when you place a break statement inside each case branch. The problem lies in not having a break for each case, which causes the program execution to march on to the next case and execute it without jumping out of the switch. The following code shows a typical switch statement construct:

```
switch(j)
  {
  case 0:
    Function0() ;
    break ;
  case 1:
    Function1() ;
    break ;
  case 2:
    Function2() ;
    break ;
  default :
    DefaultFunc() ;
  }
```

When the program is running, the code in this example checks the value of the variable j and then compares the value of j to each of the values next to the case statements in turn. When the program finds a match, the function following the case statement is called. Each function call is followed by a break statement.

The break statements are placed after each function call to make the program immediately move to the next line following the closing } (brace) after each function is called. In other words, only one case section is executed every time the program passes through the switch statement.

If the break statements had not been included in the previous section of code, when the program finds a matching value for variable j in a case statement, all the functions for the case statements that follow will also be called. This can produce unexpected program behavior (to say the least).

So, if you have trouble with your switch statements, one of the first items on your troubleshooting checklist should be to make sure that break statements are where you need them.

Don't Forget that Array Indexes Start at Zero

The symptom: Array contents appear to be corrupted.

Computers consider zero to be as significant as the number one, so the first element in a C++ array has an index of 0, and the last item in an array has an index equivalent to the number of items in an array -1. (An *index* is the number assigned to each element in an array.)

If you create an array that holds ten integers, it may look like this:

```
int Numbers[10] ;
```

If you want to load these integers with numbers, you may decide to use a for loop. If you mistakenly code the for loop like this

```
for (i=1; i<11; i++ )
  Numbers[i] = i*2 ;
```

the for loop loads numbers into the array beginning from the second item in the array. It will skip the first array item altogether (the first array item being the integer with an array index of 0). This can cause some unpredictable results in your program because the first array item may hold absolutely any value left over from the last time that part of the system's memory was used. The correct code for this loop is

```
for (i=0; i<10; i++ )
  Numbers[i] = i*2 ;
```

This loads array items 0 through 9 with the results of the calculation i* 2 ;.

Don't Overlap Components

The symptom: Components on a form don't show up where and when you want them to.

Assume that you're placing a number of *Panel* components onto a form in your application with the intention of showing and hiding them in turn (to save on some window "real estate"). You may end up placing one Panel on top of another one by accidentally clicking the first one when placing the second one. The first Panel ends up being the "parent" of the second Panel. Then when the first Panel is hidden, so is the second one.

As you can see in Figure 20-1, Panel2 is contained within Panel1. If you are constructing a form that needs to show and hide overlaying Panels, you can avoid this situation by always leaving an area of the *form background* visible (the form background is the area marked with a grid pattern). Click the form background area when you introduce new Panels into a form. When the Panel is on the form, click and drag the Panel to where you need it.

Figure 20-1:
Be careful
when
placing
Panels; you
may end up
with a
strange
configuration
(like this
one).

Don't Goof Up FieldByName *References*

The symptom: You get an error while accessing a data field only when your program is running.

The *Table* component has a member called FieldByName that you can use to reference individual fields within a data table. The FieldByName method takes one argument of a string type. That argument should hold the name of the field you want to reference. Here's how it may look as code:

```
Table1->FieldByName("Name").AsString = Edit1->Text ;
```

This code line loads the field called "Name" with the contents of the Text property of the Component called Edit1. C++Builder 3 can compile and link this line whether or not the actual data table has a "Name" field. If you place an incorrect string as the argument here, you get an error message that says Field 'Name' not found only when the program is running.

You need to first make sure that the arguments that you pass in these calls are correct because C++Builder 3 cannot check these references for you as it compiles your program.

Don't Get Your TabStops *Out of Order*

The symptom: Pressing the Tab key when the program is running causes the cursor to jump out of sequence from control to control all over the form.

In Windows programs, users can move around the controls that you place on a form by using the Tab key. The order in which the application visits each control is called the *tab order*. Each control has a TabOrder property that enables you to determine the sequence that the Tab key follows when navigating the controls on a form at runtime.

C++Builder 3 goes a long way in helping you with tab orders by providing each new component with sequential TabOrder property values. The C++Builder 3 automatic ordering works fine as long as you add components in the order and location on the form in which they will finally reside in the finished program.

Imagine that you've placed five EditBox components, one above the other, to form a column. C++Builder 3 sees to it that the TabStop property for each EditBox holds a value one higher than that held by the TabStop property of the previous EditBox (you can access the TabStop property through the Object Inspector). When you compile and run the program, the user is able to use the Tab key to move down the EditBox components in an orderly fashion.

If you need to move these EditBoxes around or change their order for any reason, you must first adjust the TabStop properties for each EditBox to reflect their new positions. Otherwise, when the user presses the Tab key, the program jumps from EditBox to EditBox up and down the form in no particular order.

The unordered navigation of the form can be easily cured by first right-clicking the form to bring up the speed menu. Then select the Tab Order option from the menu to access the Edit Tab Order dialog box. You can then raise or lower the TabStop value of each control in the form by using the buttons on the Edit Tab Order dialog box, or by clicking and dragging each control listed into the desired tab order.

Don't forget to check your program prior to releasing your software by trying out the tab ordering of the controls on your form. Just press F9 to run the program, and then use the Tab key to navigate around your form before you pass the program on to others.

Don't Omit the { and } When Grouping Lines of Code

The symptom: The program does not compile and gives you a Declaration syntax error message.

Many code constructs within C++ require braces ({ }) to indicate the beginning and end of sections of code. Examples of code constructs that rely on these braces are functions, if statements, while statements, for loops, and others.

So what happens if you forget to provide a pair of start and end braces for a code section? The compiler picks up the fact that something is wrong in your program, but not at the place that you may suspect. The message you'll most likely get is `Declaration syntax error`, and the line where the opening brace for the next function resides is highlighted. Even though this isn't the most informative error message in computerdom, you can at least deduce that something is missing from the function that immediately precedes the error message. You can then go in and add your braces.

Don't Overwrite Memory with Oversized Variables

The symptom: Strange values appear in program variables or unpredictable results occur when operating your program.

C++Builder 3 does not prevent you from overwriting memory that you have not specifically allocated to a variable. For example, the following line of code shows a character array that has been declared with the capacity to hold ten characters:

```
char strTemp [10] ;
```

C++Builder 3 won't give you a warning if you place a string longer than ten characters into the `strTemp` variable in this line. In fact, C++Builder 3 would actually allow you to include the following line of code in your program:

```
sprintf(strTemp, "12345678912345678912345567") ;
```

If you do include this line of code in your program, you are effectively overwriting areas of memory that do not belong to this variable and could overwrite the values of other program variables as well. This results in data loss, and there's no predicting how the program will react to these values overwriting the contents of other variables.

Make sure that you stick to the size capacities of the variables you declare. The symptoms of memory-overwriting problems can be very inconsistent and difficult to diagnose — so be especially careful with the size of your variables.

Appendix

About the CD

• •

*W*elcome to the companion CD-ROM that provides you with source code for the program examples in *Borland C++Builder 3 For Dummies.* Here are some of the other items that you can find on the CD:

- ✔ JBuilder Professional (90-day trial)
- ✔ IB*DOC v1.1 (freeware)
- ✔ RxLib Components (freeware)
- ✔ Orpheus 2.1 (trial version)
- ✔ InfoPower++ for C++Builder (trial version)

System Requirements

Make sure your computer meets the minimum system requirements listed below. If your computer doesn't match up to most of these requirements, you may have problems using the contents of the CD:

- ✔ A PC with a 486 or faster processor
- ✔ Microsoft Windows 95 or Windows NT
- ✔ At least 32MB total RAM installed on your computer
- ✔ At least 50MB hard drive space available to install all the software from this CD
- ✔ A CD-ROM drive — double-speed (2x) or faster.

If you need more information on the basics, check out *PCs For Dummies,* 5th Edition, by Dan Gookin; or *Windows 95 For Dummies,* 2nd Edition, by Andy Rathbone (all published by IDG Books Worldwide, Inc.).

How to Use the CD

You can just follow the steps in this section to use the contents included on the *Borland C++Builder 3 For Dummies* CD.

1. **Insert the CD into your computer's CD-ROM drive.**

   Give your computer a moment to take a look at the CD.

2. **When the light on your CD-ROM drive goes out, double-click the My Computer icon (located in the upper-left corner of your desktop).**

   This action opens the My Computer window, which shows you all the drives attached to your computer, the Control Panel, and a couple of other handy things.

3. **Double-click the icon for your CD-ROM drive.**

   Another window opens, showing you all the folders and files on the CD.

4. **Double click the file called License.txt.**

   This file contains the end-user license that you agree to by using the CD. When you finish reading the license, close the program (most likely NotePad) that displayed the file.

5. **Double click the file called Readme.txt.**

   This file contains instructions about installing the software from this CD. It might be helpful to leave this text file open while you are using the CD.

6. **Double click the folder for the software you are interested in.**

   Be sure to read the descriptions of the programs in the next section of this appendix (much of this information also shows up in the Readme file). These descriptions will give you more precise information about the programs' folder names and about finding and running the installer program.

7. **Find the file called Setup.exe (or Install.exe, or something similar), and double-click that file.**

   The program's installer will walk you through the process of setting up your new software.

What You'll Find

Here's a summary of the software on this CD.

C++Builder 3 For Dummies Example Projects

Within the *Source* folder, you will find folders named after the chapters of the book that they refer to. You can browse the source code here on the CD, but if you want to make changes or experiment with the code, you will need to have these files on your hard drive. To make it easy, we have included a self-extractor called Cbuilder.exe at the root of the CD.

To install all of the source code examples for this book onto your computer, double-click the Cbuilder.exe file to bring up the WinZip Self-Extractor dialog box, type the full pathname of the folder C:\C++Builder For Dummies, and then click the Unzip button. You will see a WinZip Self-Extractor message box informing you that 216 files have been successfully unzipped to your hard disk. You are now ready to access any of the example projects using C++Builder 3.

Borland JBuilder Professional Publisher's Edition (90-day trial)

JBuilder is the rapid application development tool from Borland that allows you to build applications using the industry's fastest growing language, *Java*. If you would like to learn more about the language that is taking the industry by storm, you have a prime opportunity by installing this trial version. To learn more, check out Borland's Web site at www.borland.com. To install JBuilder, run the file D:\Jbuilder\jbuilder\setup.exe.

IB*Doc v1.1 (freeware)

If you want to use InterBase in your client/server C++Builder 3 development projects (the local version of InterBase comes with the client/server version of C++Builder), you will want to know about *IB*Doc*. It's a tool that enables you to report on all of the details of your InterBase database, including tables, fields, stored procedures, and so much more. IB*Doc was developed by Matt Hopkins of Dunstan Thomas (UK) Ltd, one of the world's leading InterBase experts, and is made freely available for all InterBase developers. For more information, check out the InterBase Web site at www.interbase. dthomas.co.uk. To run IB*Doc from the CD, run the file D:\Ibdoc\Ibdoc.exe. To install IB*Doc, copy the Ibdoc.exe file to your hard drive.

RxLib Components (freeware)

RxLib Components are respected throughout the world as being in the upper-echelon of C++Builder 3 and Delphi components, and they come to you *free*. Once they're installed to your Component Palette, marvel at how you can extend the functionality of C++Builder 3 using its component-based architecture. To learn more, check out the Epsylon Technologies Web site at rx.demo.ru. To install the RxLib components, run the file D:\Rxlib240\Rxinst.exe.

Orpheus 2.1 (trial version)

Orpheus Trail Run for C++Builder 3 provides yet more components with which to extend your C++Builder development boundaries. Take a test drive of this trial version by installing the components to your Component Palette. For more information about Orpheus, check out the TurboPower Software Web site at www.turbopower.com. To install Orpheus, run the file D:\Orpheus\ortrc.exe.

InfoPower++ for C++Builder (trial version)

InfoPower, from Woll2Woll Software, has led the field in component technology since the earliest rapid application tools emerged. Install this trial version of its *InfoPower++ for C++Builder* components, and see your development productivity and user interface standards soar. To learn more, go to the Web site at www.woll2woll.com. To install, run the file D:\Infopower\ipt++.exe.

If You've Got Problems (Of the CD Kind)

I tried my best to compile programs that work on most computers with the minimum system requirements. Alas, your computer may differ, and some programs may not work properly for some reason.

The two likeliest problems are that you don't have enough memory (RAM) for the programs you want to use or you have other programs running that are affecting installation or running of a program. If you get error messages like Not enough memory or Setup cannot continue, try one or more of these methods, and then try using the software again:

✔ **Turn off any antivirus software that you have on your computer.**
Installers sometimes mimic virus activity and may make your computer
incorrectly believe that it is being infected by a virus.

✔ **Close all running programs.** The more programs you're running, the
less memory is available to other programs. Installers also typically
update files and programs. So, if you keep other programs running,
installation may not work properly.

✔ **Have your local computer store add more RAM to your computer.**
This is, admittedly, a drastic and somewhat expensive step. However, if
you have a Windows 95 PC, adding more memory can really help the
speed of your computer and allow more programs to run at the same
time. This may include closing the CD interface and running a product's
installation program from Windows Explorer.

If you still have trouble installing the items from the CD, please call the IDG
Books Worldwide Customer Service phone number: 800-762-2974 (outside
the U.S.: 317-596-5430).

Index

(continued)

IDG Books Worldwide, Inc., End-User License Agreement

READ THIS. You should carefully read these terms and conditions before opening the software packet(s) included with this book ("Book"). This is a license agreement ("Agreement") between you and IDG Books Worldwide, Inc. ("IDGB"). By opening the accompanying software packet(s), you acknowledge that you have read and accept the following terms and conditions. If you do not agree and do not want to be bound by such terms and conditions, promptly return the Book and the unopened software packet(s) to the place you obtained them for a full refund.

1. **License Grant.** IDGB grants to you (either an individual or entity) a nonexclusive license to use one copy of the enclosed software program(s) (collectively, the "Software") solely for your own personal or business purposes on a single computer (whether a standard computer or a workstation component of a multiuser network). The Software is in use on a computer when it is loaded into temporary memory (RAM) or installed into permanent memory (hard disk, CD-ROM, or other storage device). IDGB reserves all rights not expressly granted herein.

2. **Ownership.** IDGB is the owner of all right, title, and interest, including copyright, in and to the compilation of the Software recorded on the disk(s) or CD-ROM ("Software Media"). Copyright to the individual programs recorded on the Software Media is owned by the author or other authorized copyright owner of each program. Ownership of the Software and all proprietary rights relating thereto remain with IDGB and its licensers.

3. **Restrictions on Use and Transfer.**

   (a) You may only (i) make one copy of the Software for backup or archival purposes, or (ii) transfer the Software to a single hard disk, provided that you keep the original for backup or archival purposes. You may not (i) rent or lease the Software, (ii) copy or reproduce the Software through a LAN or other network system or through any computer subscriber system or bulletin-board system, or (iii) modify, adapt, or create derivative works based on the Software.

   (b) You may not reverse engineer, decompile, or disassemble the Software. You may transfer the Software and user documentation on a permanent basis, provided that the transferee agrees to accept the terms and conditions of this Agreement and you retain no copies. If the Software is an update or has been updated, any transfer must include the most recent update and all prior versions.

4. **Restrictions on Use of Individual Programs.** You must follow the individual requirements and restrictions detailed for each individual program in the "About the CD" appendix in this Book. These limitations are also contained in the individual license agreements recorded on the Software Media. These limitations may include a requirement that after using the program for a specified period of time, the user must pay a registration fee or discontinue use. By opening the Software packet(s), you will be agreeing to abide by the licenses and restrictions for these individual programs that are detailed in the "About the CD" appendix and on the Software Media. None of the material on this Software Media or listed in this Book may ever be redistributed, in original or modified form, for commercial purposes.

5. **Limited Warranty.**

   (a) IDGB warrants that the Software and Software Media are free from defects in materials and workmanship under normal use for a period of sixty (60) days from the date of purchase of this Book. If IDGB receives notification within the warranty period of defects in materials or workmanship, IDGB will replace the defective Software Media.

   (b) **IDGB AND THE AUTHOR OF THE BOOK DISCLAIM ALL OTHER WARRANTIES, EXPRESS OR IMPLIED, INCLUDING WITHOUT LIMITATION IMPLIED WARRANTIES OF MERCHANTABILITY AND FITNESS FOR A PARTICULAR PURPOSE, WITH RESPECT TO THE SOFTWARE, THE PROGRAMS, THE SOURCE CODE CONTAINED THEREIN, AND/OR THE TECHNIQUES DESCRIBED IN THIS BOOK. IDGB DOES NOT WARRANT THAT THE FUNCTIONS CONTAINED IN THE SOFTWARE WILL MEET YOUR REQUIREMENTS OR THAT THE OPERATION OF THE SOFTWARE WILL BE ERROR FREE.**

   (c) This limited warranty gives you specific legal rights, and you may have other rights that vary from jurisdiction to jurisdiction.

6. **Remedies.**

   (a) IDGB's entire liability and your exclusive remedy for defects in materials and workmanship shall be limited to replacement of the Software Media, which may be returned to IDGB with a copy of your receipt at the following address: Software Media Fulfillment Department, Attn.: *Borland C++Builder 3 For Dummies,* IDG Books Worldwide, Inc., 7260 Shadeland Station, Ste. 100, Indianapolis, IN 46256, or call 800-762-2974. Please allow three to four weeks for delivery. This Limited Warranty is void if failure of the Software Media has resulted from accident, abuse, or misapplication. Any replacement Software Media will be warranted for the remainder of the original warranty period or thirty (30) days, whichever is longer.

   (b) In no event shall IDGB or the author be liable for any damages whatsoever (including without limitation damages for loss of business profits, business interruption, loss of business information, or any other pecuniary loss) arising from the use of or inability to use the Book or the Software, even if IDGB has been advised of the possibility of such damages.

   (c) Because some jurisdictions do not allow the exclusion or limitation of liability for consequential or incidental damages, the above limitation or exclusion may not apply to you.

7. **U.S. Government Restricted Rights.** Use, duplication, or disclosure of the Software by the U.S. Government is subject to restrictions stated in paragraph (c)(1)(ii) of the Rights in Technical Data and Computer Software clause of DFARS 252.227-7013, and in subparagraphs (a) through (d) of the Commercial Computer–Restricted Rights clause at FAR 52.227-19, and in similar clauses in the NASA FAR supplement, when applicable.

8. **General.** This Agreement constitutes the entire understanding of the parties and revokes and supersedes all prior agreements, oral or written, between them and may not be modified or amended except in a writing signed by both parties hereto that specifically refers to this Agreement. This Agreement shall take precedence over any other documents that may be in conflict herewith. If any one or more provisions contained in this Agreement are held by any court or tribunal to be invalid, illegal, or otherwise unenforceable, each and every other provision shall remain in full force and effect.

Installation Instructions

• •

*J*ust follow these steps to install the *Borland C++Builder 3 For Dummies* CD and use its contents.

1. **Insert the CD into your computer's CD-ROM drive.**

   Give your computer a moment to take a look at the CD.

2. **When the light on your CD-ROM drive goes out, double-click the My Computer icon (probably located in the upper-left corner of your desktop).**

   This action opens the My Computer window, which shows you all the drives attached to your computer, the Control Panel, and a couple of other handy things.

3. **Double-click the icon for your CD-ROM drive.**

   Another window opens, showing you all the folders and files on the CD.

4. **Double click the file called License.txt.**

   This file contains the end-user license that you agree to by using the CD. When you finish reading the license, close the program (most likely NotePad) that displayed the file.

5. **Double click the file called Readme.txt.**

   This file contains instructions about installing the software from this CD. It might be helpful to leave this text file open while you are using the CD.

6. **Double click the folder for the software you are interested in.**

7. **Find the file called Setup.exe (or Install.exe, or something similar), and double-click that file.**

   The program's installer will walk you through the process of setting up your new software.

For more information about the CD, please see the Appendix.

Discover Dummies Online!

The Dummies Web Site is your fun and friendly online resource for the latest information about ...*For Dummies*® books and your favorite topics. The Web site is the place to communicate with us, exchange ideas with other ...*For Dummies* readers, chat with authors, and have fun!

Ten Fun and Useful Things You Can Do at www.dummies.com

1. Win free ...*For Dummies* books and more!
2. Register your book and be entered in a prize drawing.
3. Meet your favorite authors through the IDG Books Author Chat Series.
4. Exchange helpful information with other ...*For Dummies* readers.
5. Discover other great ...*For Dummies* books you must have!
6. Purchase Dummieswear™ exclusively from our Web site.
7. Buy ...*For Dummies* books online.
8. Talk to us. Make comments, ask questions, get answers!
9. Download free software.
10. Find additional useful resources from authors.

Link directly to these ten fun and useful things at **http://www.dummies.com/10useful**

For other technology titles from IDG Books Worldwide, go to **www.idgbooks.com**

Not on the Web yet? It's easy to get started with *Dummies 101*®: *The Internet For Windows*® *95* or *The Internet For Dummies*®, 5th Edition, at local retailers everywhere.

Find other ...*For Dummies* books on these topics:
Business • Career • Databases • Food & Beverage • Games • Gardening • Graphics • Hardware
Health & Fitness • Internet and the World Wide Web • Networking • Office Suites
Operating Systems • Personal Finance • Pets • Programming • Recreation • Sports
Spreadsheets • Teacher Resources • Test Prep • Word Processing

IDG BOOKS WORLDWIDE BOOK REGISTRATION

Register This Book and Win!

We want to hear from you!

Visit **http://my2cents.dummies.com** to register this book and tell us how you liked it!

- ✔ Get entered in our monthly prize giveaway.
- ✔ Give us feedback about this book — tell us what you like best, what you like least, or maybe what you'd like to ask the author and us to change!
- ✔ Let us know any other ...*For Dummies*® topics that interest you.

Your feedback helps us determine what books to publish, tells us what coverage to add as we revise our books, and lets us know whether we're meeting your needs as a ...*For Dummies* reader. You're our most valuable resource, and what you have to say is important to us!

Not on the Web yet? It's easy to get started with *Dummies 101*®: *The Internet For Windows*® *95* or *The Internet For Dummies*,® 5th Edition, at local retailers everywhere.

Or let us know what you think by sending us a letter at the following address:

...*For Dummies* Book Registration
Dummies Press
7260 Shadeland Station, Suite 100
Indianapolis, IN 46256-3945
Fax 317-596-5498

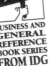

BUSINESS AND
GENERAL
REFERENCE
BOOK SERIES
FROM IDG

COMPUTER
BOOK SERIES
FROM IDG